Study Guide for use with

Principles of
Macroeconomics

second canadian edition

ROBERT H. FRANK, Cornell University

BEN S. BERNANKE, Princeton University

LARS OSBERG, Dalhousie University

MELVIN L. CROSS, Dalhousie University

BRIAN K. MacLEAN, Laurentian University

PREPARED BY

JACK MOGAB, Southwest Texas State University

BRUCE McCLUNG, Southwest Texas State University

LINDA MULLER NIELSEN, Mount Royal University College and St. Mary's University College

Toronto   Montréal   Boston   Burr Ridge, IL   Dubuque, IA   Madison, WI   New York   San Francisco   St. Louis
Bangkok   Bogotá   Caracas   Kuala Lumpur   Lisbon   London   Madrid   Mexico City   Milan   New Delhi
Santiago   Seoul   Singapore   Sydney   Taipei

The McGraw·Hill Companies

McGraw-Hill Ryerson

Study Guide for use with
Principles of Macroeconomics
Second Canadian Edition

ISBN: 0-07-095106-3

1 2 3 4 5 6 7 8 9 10 CP 0 9 8 7 6 5

Printed and bound in Canada

Publisher: Lynn Fisher
Senior Marketing Manager: Kelly Smyth
Developmental Editor: Daphne Scriabin
Senior Supervising Editor: Margaret Henderson
Production Coordinator: Paula Brown
Copy Editor: Rohini Herbert
Composition: Jay Tee Graphics
Cover Design: Sharon Lucas
Printer: Canadian Printco

Contents

To the Student

Welcome to the study of macroeconomics. We believe you will find the subject thoroughly intriguing as you gain a clearer understanding of many important issues that may now seem perplexing. For example, why does the economy experience booms and busts? What causes inflation? Why is unemployment persistently high in some countries? How can it be that there is more money in the "money supply" than the total amount of coins and paper currency? Why does a country import certain goods that can be produced domestically? How can governments get away with spending more money than what they take in, and what are the consequences?

These and many other topics are addressed in *Principles of Macroeconomics*, 2nd Canadian Edition, by Robert Frank, Ben Bernanke, Lars Osberg, Melvin Cross, and Brian MacLean, for which this Study Guide has been written. The Study Guide chapters parallel the chapters in the textbook, and each contains the following seven sections designed to assist your learning and to enhance your understanding of economics:

1. **Chapter Overview.** This initial brief paragraph summarizes the chapter's main ideas and provides a link to both past and future material.
2. **Chapter Review**. These reviews are organized by the headings at the beginning of each chapter and subdivided into learning objectives (LO). These are the important concepts to master. **Hints and Notes** are embedded within some of the chapter reviews and are designed to alert you to "tricks, clues, and short-cuts."
3. **Quick Quiz.** These are multiple-choice questions at the end of each chapter review subsection, testing your knowledge of the material.
4. **Self-Test: Key Terms**. All new terms are listed. Check your understanding by completing the sentences using key terms from the provided list.
5. **Self-Test: Multiple-Choice Questions.** Strengthen your grasp of the chapter material by choosing the correct answer from the alternatives for each question. Your ability to answer multiple-choice questions should serve as a good indicator of success in exams. You may wish to study for exams by reviewing these questions.
6. **Self-Test: Short-Answer Problems.** Here you will discover how the tools of economics can be used to explore and clarify important issues. Problems are developed step by step. You are asked to analyze graphs and tables, to perform basic computations, and to provide the best answers for a variety of fill-in statements.
7. **Solutions**. Solutions—with explanations for the more difficult questions—are provided for the quick quiz, key-term, and multiple-choice questions, as well as for the short-answer/problems.

In addition, there is a sample mid-term examination and a sample final examination. Both examinations contain two parts: multiple-choice questions and short-answer problems. The multiple-choice questions are selected from this study guide while the short-answer questions are new questions intended to challenge students' comprehension of the economic theory discussed in the text. As always, time allocation is critical when writing exams. Most instructors will typically expect students to answer (on average) 1 multiple choice question per minute—budget your time accordingly. The sample mid-term examination covers material in Chapters 1 through 5 inclusively. It was designed to be completed in 50 minutes for the "A" students (20 minutes for the multiple-choice / 30 minutes for the short-answer questions) and completed by all students in 75 minutes. The sample final examination—covering all chapters but heavier on the second half of the text—follows a similar pattern: 80 minutes for the "A" student and approximately 105 minutes for all students. When you tackle these exams, note both your score and your time; combined they will give you a good indication of how well you will perform on your instructor's exams.

Here are some suggestions to help make your study of economics successful:

Class Preparation: How to Get the Most out of Your Class
It is essential that you prepare BEFORE attending class so that you can understand the lecture and ask questions. The instructor typically does not present all the materials in the text, but concentrates on explaining the more complex ideas and applications.

In preparing for class, first read the complete chapter identifying areas that you do not understand. Return to the chapter when you feel you have *at least* one hour of uninterrupted study and slowly go through the material sequentially pausing to reflect on the difficult areas. After you have completed reading a topic, take a few minutes to read the Recap box. Verify that (1) you know (i.e., remember) the topic and important terms; (2) you understand (i.e., comprehend) that material; (3) you can relate the terms to one another when appropriate; and (4) you can relate the topic to the other topics in the chapter. On occasion, you may need a third pass at the chapter material before you feel comfortable with testing your knowledge. At this stage you are prepared to tackle the study guide. With your text in hand, read and study each Chapter Review, one at a time. Start by reading the text until you reach the "Recap box." Go to the Study Guide, read the Chapter Review and the associated learning objectives and answer the Quick Quiz questions. Complete all the assigned topics in the above manner and write down any questions you have for the instructor. Once you have completed all the chapter reviews, you are prepared to complete all the Self-Test questions. Rather than mark your answers directly on the Study Guide, it is often better to write the answers on a clean sheet of paper—verify your answers and discard the sheet. In this manner, when you return to the Study Guide to prepare for exams, you will not be tempted to gloss over questions that already have the correct answers pencilled in. You will undoubtedly find that you make the same mistake twice—a good method to identify problem material!

Class Attendance: Get Your Money's Worth, and Do Not Miss Key Information
Frankly, economics is such a demanding course that you will need all the resources you can get. A key resource comes from your instructor's lectures. The instructor's style and presentation will show you not only what the instructor considers to be important but also how s/he approaches this subject. Getting notes from a friend will not give you this information. If you have followed the above suggestions in preparing for class, you will have some knowledge and understanding of the assigned topics. In class, the trick is to carefully combine four classroom skills—listening, taking notes, asking questions, and responding to questions. Listen with your mind. Be selective in what you write down. If you try to write everything that the instructor says, you will not have time to learn anything. For example, do not write a definition that has been given in the text. Listen for examples that differ from those in the text, special emphasis on a relationship between topics, and frequently repeated principles. Asking questions is the responsibility of the student. If you do not know enough to ask questions, you have not done your job. If you have difficulty formulating questions during class, you should spend some time before class developing a list of

questions you need to have answered. On the other side of the coin, you should also respond to the instructor's questions. You should not be shy about answering questions in class. An incorrect answer given in class is a free shot, while the same wrong answer on the test is very costly. The most effective way to use class time is to develop your ability to comprehend and apply economics concepts.

Reinforcing Your Learning after Class

Even if you have meticulously prepared for class and utilized those four classroom skills, you still have a couple of things to do before you will be at the mastery level of the material. First, your class notes would be sketchy. You need to rewrite these notes in a more complete way before they get cold. Next, return to the Study Guide. Randomly select a couple of questions from the first Quick Quiz. Answer those questions without referring to the text, and check your answers with the Solutions at the end of the Study Guide chapter. If your answers are correct, go on to the next Quick Quiz, continuing in this manner until you have covered the assigned topics. If your answers to the questions on a learning objective are incorrect, go back and study the text and your class notes. Then attempt several more questions (there are additional problems at the end of the text chapters) on the learning objective. If your answers are still incorrect, either ask questions in the next class, or go see your instructor for help.

If You Want to Learn It, Teach It

Before going on to the next chapter in the text and Study Guide, go to the end of the text chapter and read the "Review Questions." If you can answer those questions, you have learned what the authors of the text and Study Guide hoped you would learn. To further test your comprehension of a topic, try explaining it in your own words to a classmate. Illustrate the idea with an example. If you can explain it clearly and give a good example, you have mastered the concept and it is time to move on to the next chapter.

A Final Word

If the strategy outlined above seems like a lot of work, it is. You cannot achieve success in economics without hard work. As a bench mark, students can expect to spend 3 hours of uninterrupted study time for every hour spent in class. For the typical 3-hour lecture week, this implies finding *9 hours each week*, throughout the semester, to study the material. Consequently, you will find that all your instructors, regardless of their discipline, identify time management as the most critical skill for students to develop during the first years of post-secondary study.

Acknowledgments

It is a pleasure to acknowledge the assistance and support of McGraw-Hill Ryerson in the preparation of this Study Guide. Particular thanks go to Ron Doleman and Daphne Scriabin. Thanks for the support of Gita, Sarah, and Erling.

Linda Muller Nielsen

June 2005

1 Thinking Like an Economist

OVERVIEW

This chapter introduces the concept of scarcity as the fundamental economic problem. With limited resources available to satisfy limitless needs and wants, scarcity implies recognizing trade-offs and selecting the best alternative. From this perspective, economics is the study of how individuals, firms, and/or governments (i.e., decision makers) make choices under conditions of scarcity and how the results of those choices affect society. The cost-benefit principle presented in this chapter illustrates the use of an abstract economic model as a means to capture an individual's decision-making process. Applying the cost-benefit principle may lead to poor choices if an individual does not properly define the relevant alternatives, benefits, and costs. To this extent, some common pitfalls to decision making under the cost-benefit principle are discussed. Throughout the text, students will be exposed to a few "core" principles of the discipline. In an effort to promote the understanding of these concepts, they will be viewed from many different contexts, and their relevance will be illustrated with examples from our daily lives.

Chapter Review

1.1 Economics: Studying Choice in a World of Scarcity

Scarcity implies choice. Selecting the best choice requires the ability to identify all alternatives and recognize the benefits and costs associated with each alternative.

▶ **LO 1. Explain scarcity problem.**

The scarcity problem derives from the fact that although we have boundless needs and wants, the resources available to us are limited: having more of one thing often means having less of another. These choices, or trade-offs, are central to the discipline of economics.

▶ **LO 2. Define cost-benefit principle.**

Under the cost-benefit principle, an individual (or a firm or a society) will be better off taking an action if, and only if, the extra benefits from taking the action are greater than the extra costs.

Quick Quiz

1. The concept of scarcity applies equally to the Prime Minister and a homeless person because
   A. both have the same legal rights protected by the Canadian Charter of Rights.
   B. they have the same access to the markets for goods and services.
   C. there are only 24 hours in the day for both of them.
   D. both must pay sales tax on their purchases.
   E. both must breathe air in order to live.

2. The cost-benefit principle
   A. is not one of the authors' core ideas in economics.
   B. implies that the cost of all alternatives should be included when choosing among alternatives.
   C. states that an action will make an individual better off only if the extra benefit is at least as great as the extra cost.
   D. states that an action will make an individual better off only if the extra benefit is greater than the extra cost.
   E. states that an action will make an individual better off only if the extra benefit is less than the extra cost.

1.2   Applying the Cost-Benefit Principle

When applying the cost-benefit principle, decision makers are assumed to have some fundamental objective—firms, for example, might want to select an alternative which maximizes their profits. With well-defined objectives in mind, measures for the relevant costs and benefits are created. In a number of instances, dollar values or relevant market data are not available. For these cases, there will not be any tangible numerical values to compare. Nevertheless, the cost-benefit approach can conceptually provide a credible framework for valuable analysis.

▶ **LO 3.   Define rationality and explain relevance to cost-benefit principle.**

A rational individual is someone with well-defined goals and who tries to fulfill those goals as best as he or she can. Rational people will typically employ some form of the cost-benefit analysis to achieve their objectives, even if it occurs through an intuitive or approximate way rather than though explicit and precise calculations.

▶ **LO 4.   Define economic surplus and opportunity cost.**

Economic surplus is simply the benefit from taking an action less its cost. A rational person would engage in *any* activity which generates positive economic surplus. If a number of available choices all generate positive economic surpluses, a decision maker typically selects the alternative providing the greatest amount of economic surplus. When determining the total value of the extra cost of taking an action, we not only include the costs unique to this action

BUT also include the opportunity cost. The opportunity cost of any activity is the value of the next-best alternative that must be forgone to undertake the activity.

NOTE:

The true cost of a semester's worth of postsecondary education, for example, is not only the cost of tuition, textbooks, and other costs unique to studying but also the value of the next-best alternative (i.e., not attending college or university). For many students, this may be the dollar value associated with being in the workforce. For others, it may be benefit forgone by not taking a three-month trip to South East Asia. In either case, the students would factor in the value of their next-best alternative as part of the cost side in the cost-benefit analysis.

▶ LO 5.   Understand role of abstract economic models.

An abstract model represents a simplification of a more complex phenomenon. It captures essential elements of a situation and permits us to analyze them in a logical manner. Since the decision-making process is indeed a complex phenomenon, economists rely on numerous abstract models to provide a framework for the behaviour we observe in everyday life.

HINT:

In order to successfully understand economics and perform well on exams, you must think in terms of the ideas presented in the textbook and lectures. Do not give in to the temptation to create your own model. In a physics class, it is unlikely you would question the existence or behaviour of gravity. Even though you have made many economic decisions already, it does not mean you fully understand all the underlying concepts any more than being held down to the planet means you fully understand the physicist's model of gravity.

▶ LO 6.   Identify difference between positive and normative economics.

Positive economics offers cause-and-effect explanations of economic relationships. The propositions, or hypotheses, which emerge from these explanations can either be confirmed or refuted by data. The data can also provide some estimate of the magnitude of the relationship. Economic models are examples of positive economics. Normative economics, on the other hand, are statements that reflect subjective value judgments and are based on ethical positions. As such, data cannot be used to confirm or refute these statements.

Quick Quiz

3. If the benefit you receive for a precooked meal is $15 and your opportunity cost of the precooked meal is $12, the economic surplus of having a precooked meal equals
   A. $27.
   B. $3.
   C. –$3.
   D. $12/$15.
   E. $15/$12.

4. Which of the following statements is consistent with the concept of positive economics?
   A. mandatory retirement for university professors should be extended until the age of 70.
   B. minimum wage rates should be raised by 5 percent to help the working poor.
   C. Canada should always balance the annual federal budget.
   D. the federal government should give more money to the Department of National Defence, since much of their capital equipment is outdated.
   E. a decrease in the Goods and Services Tax (GST) should raise government's tax revenues.

5. Joe has decided to purchase his textbooks for the semester. His options are to purchase the books via the Internet with next-day delivery to his home at a cost of $250, or to drive to campus tomorrow to buy the books at the university bookstore at a cost of $245. Last week he drove to campus to buy a concert ticket because they offered 20 percent off the regular price of $20.
   A. it would not be rational for Joe to drive to campus to purchase the books because the $5 saving is only 2 percent of the cost of the books, and that is much less than the 20 percent he saved on the concert ticket.
   B. it would be rational for Joe to drive to campus because it costs less to buy the books there than via the Internet.
   C. it would be rational for Joe to drive to campus because the $5 saving is more than he saved by driving there to buy the concert ticket.
   D. it would not be rational for Joe to drive to campus to purchase the books because the cost of gas and his time must certainly be more than the $5 he would save.
   E. there is insufficient information to determine whether it would be rational or not for Joe to purchase the books via the Internet or on campus.

6. Economists use _____ to simplify complex behaviour.
   A. positive economics.
   B. normative economics.
   C. opportunity costs.
   D. economic models.
   E. economic surplus.

1.3 – 1.6 Three Common Pitfalls

It is important to avoid the errors associated with implementation of the cost-benefit principle. There is a tendency to ignore certain relevant costs and/or include irrelevant costs in the decision-making process.

▶ **LO 7.   Explain relevance of opportunity costs and importance of time value of money.**

The first pitfall is ignoring opportunity costs. When considering the costs of an activity, it is necessary to take into account not only the outlays required but also the value of forgone opportunities. The key to using the concept of opportunity cost is in recognizing precisely what a given action prevents one from doing. In addition, the timing of the action that one is prevented from doing must be taken into account. The value of an action in the future is less than the value of that same action today. This is referred to as the time value of money: a given dollar amount today is equivalent to a larger dollar amount in the future because the money can be invested in an interest-bearing account in the meantime. Future values should be discounted by an appropriate discount (interest) rate to determine the present value of the future action.

▶ LO 8.   Explain relevance of sunk costs.

Another common pitfall is the failure to ignore sunk costs. A sunk cost is a cost that is beyond recovery at the moment a decision must be made. Because sunk costs must be borne whether or not an action is taken, they are irrelevant to the decision of whether to take the action. Failure to ignore sunk costs will result in overstating the costs of an action and may result in a less than optimal decision.

NOTE:

A sunk cost is irrelevant only if it has already occurred. A firm deciding whether or not to build an overseas plant will assume that over the long run revenues will be greater than costs, including sunk costs—otherwise it would not be in their interest to build the plant. Once the plant is constructed and the firm commits to an overseas operation, any sunk cost associated with the decision becomes irrelevant.

▶ LO 9.   Define and explain relevance of average-marginal distinction.

The third pitfall is the failure to distinguish between average and marginal costs and benefits. Marginal cost is the *increase* in total cost that results from carrying out *one additional unit* of the activity. Similarly, marginal benefit is the *increase* in the total benefit that results from carrying out *one additional unit* of the activity. The average cost of undertaking n units of an activity is the total cost of the activity divided by n. The average benefit of undertaking n units of an activity is the total benefit divided by n.

HINT:

Marginal analysis is critical in understanding decision making in the discipline of economics. Whenever confronted with a problem, start by examining the marginal implications for the decision maker.

▶ LO 10.   Define fixed and variable costs.

Sometimes the failure to distinguish between average and marginal costs arises from a failure to distinguish fixed costs and variable costs. A fixed cost is a cost that does not vary with the level of an activity, while a variable cost is a cost that varies with the level of an activity.

► **LO 11.   Define principle of relevant costs.**

The principle of relevant costs states that only opportunity costs matter. Some costs (e.g., variable costs, marginal costs) matter in making decisions: other costs (e.g., sunk costs and average costs) do not matter.

Quick Quiz

7. Mark recently switched his long-distance telephone service from Rogers to Telus and had to pay his local telephone company a $10 fee to make the change. As an incentive to try its long-distance services, Telus promised to reimburse him for the switching fee if he chooses to switch to another carrier after trying their service. From Mark's perspective, the switching fee is a
    A. fixed cost and a sunk cost.
    B. fixed cost but not a sunk cost.
    C. variable cost and a sunk cost.
    D. variable cost, but not a sunk cost.
    E. neither a fixed cost nor a sunk cost.

8. At the University of Toronto, tuition is $50 per credit hour up to a maximum of 12 credit hours, student fees are $150 per student per semester, room and board cost $1,500 per student each semester, and books cost an average of $60 per course. For a student taking 12 or fewer credit hours, fixed costs would include
    A. tuition, students' fees, and room and board, while variable costs would include only the cost of books.
    B. students' fees and room and board, while variable costs would include tuition and the cost of books.
    C. tuition, students' fees, room and board, and the cost of books but no variable costs.
    D. tuition and room and board, while variable costs would include students' fees and the cost of books.
    E. tuition and students fees, while variable costs would include room and board and the cost of books.

9. One of the pitfalls of implementing the cost-benefit analysis is
    A. assuming that decision-makers are rational.
    B. selecting an incorrect ethical statement.
    C. the failure to distinguish between fixed and sunk costs.
    D. the failure to distinguish between average and marginal costs and benefits.
    E. the failure to include sunk costs.

10. Which of the following costs should be included when analyzing choices within a cost-benefit framework?
    A. fixed costs.
    B. sunk costs.
    C. marginal costs and variable costs.
    D. sunk costs and marginal costs.
    E. fixed costs and variable costs.

11. Sonja is the sole owner of Words.com, providing translation services via the Internet, where she earns an annual salary of $50,000 plus the potential for future profits. She is considering an offer for a top management position with another Internet firm at a salary of $75,000 per year, but without profit sharing.

    A. she should accept the management position because she would earn more income with the other firm.

    B. she should refuse the management position because, despite the higher salary, the future profits from her current business will be greater.

    C. a cost-benefit analysis of her decision to retain her current position should include an opportunity cost of $75,000.

    D. a cost-benefit analysis of her decision to retain her current position should not include an opportunity cost of $75,000 because her current salary plus future profits could be greater than the salary offered by the other firm.

    E. a cost-benefit analysis of her decision to retain her current position should include an average cost of $75,000.

1.7 Economics: Micro and Macro

▶ **LO 12.**   **Define microeconomics and macroeconomics.**

Microeconomics is the study of individual choice under scarcity and its implications for the behaviour of prices and quantities in individual markets. Macroeconomics is the study of the performance of national economies and the policies governments use to try to improve that performance.

Quick Quiz

12. Macroeconomics differs from microeconomics in that

    A. the concept of scarcity applies to microeconomics but does not apply to macroeconomics.

    B. microeconomics studies individual markets, while macroeconomics studies groups of markets, including the whole economy.

    C. rational decisions are relevant to macroeconomics but not microeconomics.

    D. macroeconomics is the study of how people make choices under conditions of scarcity, while microeconomics is concerned with the results of those choices for society.

    E. macroeconomics explains such concepts as how prices are determined in markets, while microeconomics explains the overall price level.

1.8   The Philosophy of This Text

▶ **LO 13.   Recognize importance of core ideas.**

The strategy of this text is to concentrate on a few core ideas developed in the discipline of economics and to promote the understanding of these ideas by returning to each of them repeatedly, in many different contexts. When new material is presented, students should anticipate that one (or more) of the core principles will provide a guide to understanding the observed behaviour.

1.9   Economic Naturalism

▶ **LO 14.   Apply economic principles to understand observations in everyday life.**

In an effort to promote the understanding of these core principles, the authors use insights from economics to make sense of observations in everyday life.

Self Test: Key Terms

Use the terms below to complete the following sentences. (Answers are given at the end of the chapter.)

average benefit	microeconomics
average cost	normative economics
economics	opportunity cost
economic surplus	positive economics
fixed cost	rational person
macroeconomics	sunk cost
marginal benefit	time value of money
marginal cost	variable cost

1. A person who has well-defined goals and tries to fulfill those goals as best he/she can is a

    _____.

2. If the benefit of taking an action equals $15 and the cost is $10, there is a(n)

    _____ of $5.

3. An action will make and individual better off if the _____ is greater

    than the _____.

4. A cost that is beyond recovery at the moment a decision must be made is a(n)

    _____.

5. To describe the study of individual choices and group behaviour in individual markets, economists conventionally use the term _____.

6. Because it varies with the level of activity, a(n) _____ should be taken into account when making a decision.

7. Concepts such as the national unemployment rate, the overall price level, and the total value of national output are explained in _____ .

8. If you choose to attend your economics class tomorrow rather than going to a movie, the movie is the _____ of going to class.

9. How people make choices under conditions of scarcity and the results of those choices for society is the definition of _____.

10. The opportunity cost of resources that are expended in the future will be lower than the opportunity cost of resources expended today because of the _____.

11. The total cost of an activity divided by n equals the _____ of undertaking n units of the activity.

12. In deciding whether or not to drive your car to Whistler during winter break, the monthly payment on your car loan is considered a(n) _____ and, therefore, would not be included in your cost-benefit analysis.

13. _____ economics is based on cause-and-effect explanations that can be confirmed or refuted by data.

14. The total benefit of an activity divided by n equals the _____ of undertaking n units of the activity.

15. _____ economics reflects subjective value judgments and is based on ethical positions.

Self Test: Multiple-Choice Questions

Circle the letter than corresponds to the best answer. (Answers are given at the end of the chapter.)

1. Economics is conventionally divided into two subjects called
   A. marginal benefit and marginal cost.
   B. reservation price and opportunity cost.
   C. microeconomics and macroeconomics.
   D. rational economics and irrational economics.
   E. economic surplus and economic deficit.

2. In deciding the number of students to allow to enroll in the economics classes, the Chairperson of the Economics Department is making a(n) _____ decision.
    A. microeconomic.
    B. macroeconomic.
    C. economic surplus.
    D. marginal choice.
    E. imperfect.

3. Suppose the most you would be willing to pay to have your driveway shovelled after a major snowstorm is $25. This dollar value represents
    A. opportunity cost.
    B. economic surplus.
    C. reservation price.
    D. ethical position.
    E. conditional position.

4. The time value of money implies that the value of a dollar earned
    A. today is worth less than a dollar spent tomorrow.
    B. in the future decreases as the interest rate that can be earned on interest-bearing money market accounts increases.
    C. in the future decreases as the interest rate that can be earned on interest-bearing money market accounts decreases.
    D. in the future increases as the interest rate that can be earned on interest-bearing money market accounts increases.
    E. in the future is unrelated to the interest rate that can be earned on interest-bearing money market accounts.

5. Ian paid $475 for an airline ticket to fly to Acapulco, Mexico, for a spring break vacation. Unfortunately, he fell ill and could not go to Acapulco. When he called the airline to cancel the ticket, he was reminded that the ticket was nonrefundable but that he could exchange it for another ticket within one year if he pays a $75 fee at the time of the exchange. Several months later, he is deciding whether to exchange the ticket for a ticket of the same price to Acapulco. The opportunity cost of going to Acapulco would equal the
    A. ticket price of $475 plus the $75 exchange fee, if he has no other trip that he will take within the year.
    B. ticket price of $475 plus the $75 exchange fee, if he has another trip that he will take within the year.
    C. $75 exchange fee, if he has no other trip that he will take within the year.
    D. $75 exchange fee, if he has another trip that he will take within the year.
    E. $0, if he has no other trip that he will take within the year.

6. When economists say there is no such thing as a free lunch, they mean that
    A. we must pay money for everything we get.
    B. it is against the law to accept goods or services without paying for them.
    C. the more lunch a person eats, the more weight the person will gain.
    D. each day we decide to eat lunch is another day we must pay out money.
    E. every choice we make involves a tradeoff.

7. Jackson just paid $1,000 cash for a 1979 Corvette, and he needs to travel to Vancouver this summer. He can either drive his car or take a bus. In order to make a rational decision, he decides to calculate the costs of driving the car on the trip. He knows the cost of the car was $1,000, he estimates the cost of gas at 10 cents per kilometre, the car repair shop estimates maintenance at 3 cents per kilometre, his car insurance premium is $600 for 6 months, and from a Web site he determines that depreciation is about $1 per kilometre. Which of the above costs are sunk costs and, therefore, should not be included in his analysis?
   A. maintenance, depreciation, insurance premium, and loan payment costs are sunk costs and, therefore, should not be included in his analysis.
   B. maintenance, depreciation, and insurance premium costs are sunk costs and, therefore, should not be included in his analysis.
   C. depreciation, insurance premium, and the cost of the car are sunk costs and, therefore, should not be included in his analysis.
   D. the insurance premium and the cost of the car are sunk costs and, therefore, should not be included in his analysis.
   E. only the cost of the car is a sunk costs and, therefore, should not be included in his analysis.

8. Which of the following statements is consistent with the concept of normative economics?
   A. a sudden frost in the wine-growing regions of British Columbia should lead to an increase in the price of wine from these regions.
   B. a sudden frost in the wine-growing regions of British Columbia should lead to a decrease in the price of wine from these regions.
   C. a decrease in the Alberta business tax rates should attract new firms to Calgary.
   D. pensioners on fixed income should receive subsidies when inflation is greater than 5 percent per year.
   E. on average, economics majors should receive better starting salaries than business majors.

9. In applying the cost-benefit principle, one should calculate the
   A. total cost and total benefit and choose an activity where they are equal.
   B. marginal cost and marginal benefit and choose an activity where the marginal benefit exceeds the marginal cost.
   C. total cost and total benefit and choose that quantity of an activity where the total cost exceeds the total benefit by the greatest amount.
   D. average cost and average benefit and choose an activity where the average benefit exceeds the average cost.
   E. marginal cost, total cost, marginal benefit, and marginal cost and choose an activity where the marginal cost equals the total cost and the marginal benefit equals the total benefit.

10. The Third Wave Computer Company employs Sally to assemble personal computers. Sally can assemble 1 computer if she works 1 hour, 4 computers in 2 hours, 7 computers in 3 hours, 9 computers in 4 hours, and 10 computers in 5 hours. Each computer consists of a motherboard that costs $250, a hard drive that costs $150, a case that costs $25, a monitor that costs $200, a keyboard that costs $50, and a mouse that costs $25. The cost of employing

Sally is $50 per hour. What is the marginal cost of producing the computers Sally assembles during her second hour of work?
A. $2,150.
B. $2,850.
C. $2,800.
D. $700.
E. $750.

11. Jim, a student at the University of Calgary, is enrolled in 15 credit hours this semester. His grade in the Calculus class is a passing grade, but below his expectations. Fearing that his grade may slip into the failing range, he is considering withdrawing from the course. He tells a friend, "I would drop the course, but I don't want to waste the $500 I paid in tuition for the course." His friend replies, "The $500 tuition you paid for the course is irrelevant to your decision. Your grade in the course is the only thing that is important now." The friend is
A. incorrect because the tuition will have to be paid again when Jim retakes the course.
B. correct because the tuition is a fixed cost and fixed costs should never be considered when making decisions.
C. incorrect because the tuition is a variable cost and variable costs should always be considered when making decisions.
D. correct because the tuition is a sunk cost and sunk costs should not be considered when making decisions.
E. incorrect and obviously he or she is so rich that money means nothing to him/her.

12. Monica has purchased a $25 ticket to attend a Back Street Boys concert on Friday evening. Subsequently, she is asked to go to dinner and dancing at no expense to her. If she uses cost-benefit analysis to choose between going to the concert and going on the date, she should
A. include only the entertainment value of the concert in the opportunity cost of going on the date.
B. include the cost of the ticket plus the entertainment value of the concert in the opportunity cost of going on the date.
C. include only the cost of concert ticket in the opportunity cost of going on the date.
D. include neither the cost of the ticket nor the entertainment value of the concert in the opportunity cost of going on the date.
E. have a psychiatric evaluation because dates cannot be evaluated using cost-benefit analysis.

13. Rajiv has estimated that the additional benefit of writing 100 more lines of computer programming code is $10 and the additional cost is $6. He should
A. not write the code because it would not be a rational choice.
B. write the code because it would be a rational choice.
C. write the code because it would be a rational choice and an optimal quantity.
D. not write the code because it would not be a rational choice, even though it would be an optimal quantity.
E. not write the code because it would not be a rational choice, nor would it be an optimal quantity.

14. Samantha has estimated that with a university degree she will be able to earn an additional $40,000 of income annually. The cost of attending a local university is $25,000, while an out-of-province university costs $35,000 (all estimates are calculated in current dollars). Samantha would make a rational decision if she chooses to attend
  A. the out-of-province university, but not the local university.
  B. the local university, but not the out-of-province university.
  C. neither the local nor the out-of-province university.
  D. either the local or the out-of-province university.
  E. any university regardless of cost and income.

15. The Web site for this textbook can be viewed simultaneously by thousands of students around the world without paying money to view it. Does this suggest that the concept of scarcity does not apply to Web sites?
  A. no, because each of the students incurs an opportunity cost measured by the next best alternative to viewing the Web site.
  B. yes, because an additional student viewing the Web site does not prevent another student from viewing it.
  C. yes, because the students do not have to pay money to view the Web site, and thus they do not have to forgo something else to view it.
  D. no, because the more students view it, the slower will be the transmission of the information to each of the students.
  E. yes, because the technology of the Internet and the World Wide Web has made the principles of economics outdated.

16. Keyshawn Smith, a professional football player, has been offered two different compensation packages by his team from which he must choose one. Package A will pay him a signing bonus of $2 million when he signs his contract at the beginning of the year and a monthly salary during the season of $500,000. Package B will pay him a monthly salary during the season of $500,000 and a $2.1 million bonus at the end of the year. The minimum interest rate on a one-year certificate of deposit that would make Package A at least as valuable a benefit as Package B is
  A. 1 percent.
  B. 2.5 percent.
  C. 5 percent.
  D. 10 percent.
  E. 15 percent.

17. If Sally works for 10 hours, she can sell 15 insurance contracts, and if she works for 11 hours, she can sell 18 insurance contracts. The marginal benefit of the 11th hour of Sally's work equals
  A. 18 insurance contracts.
  B. 15 insurance contracts.
  C. 33 insurance contracts.
  D. 1 insurance contract.
  E. 3 insurance contracts.

18. Using the information in multiple-choice question 9 and assuming Jackson decides to drive his car to Vancouver and back on a two-month trip, which of the listed costs would be fixed costs, and which would be variable costs?

   A. The cost of the car would be a fixed cost, and the cost of gas, insurance, maintenance, and depreciation would variable costs.

   B. The costs of the car and insurance would be a fixed cost, and the cost of gas, maintenance, and depreciation would variable costs.

   C. The costs of the car, depreciation, and insurance would be fixed costs, and the cost of gas and maintenance would variable costs.

   D. All of the costs would be variable costs.

   E. All of the costs would be fixed costs.

19. Shelia is a volleyball player who wears out 10 pairs of shoes each volleyball season. Before the season, she purchases all 10 pairs because she can get a volume discount from the manufacturer's representatives. She gets a price quote from two representatives from whom she has previously purchased shoes. Representative A will sell her 10 pairs for $495 plus a shipping fee of $11. Representative B will sell her the same 10 pairs for $509. The average cost of buying the shoes from Representative A is _____ and from Representative B is

   _____.

   A. $50.60; $50.90.

   B. $506; $509.

   C. $56; $59.

   D. $49.50; $50.90.

   E. $495; $509.

20. Sonya's is employed at a stock brokerage firm where she earns $25 per hour. The office she works at is located downtown. To get to work each day, she must either ride a series of buses, which takes one-and-a-half hours at a cost of $2, or take a cab, which takes 30 minutes and costs $20. The opportunity cost of riding the bus is _____ and taking the cab is _____.

   A. $2; $20.

   B. $37.50; $12.50.

   C. $35.50; -$5.

   D. $39.50; $32.50.

   E. $27; $20.

Self-Test: Short-Answer Problems

(Answers and solutions are given at the end of the chapter.)

1. Time Value of Money and Cost-Benefit Analysis

Tom put $10,000 in a two-year certificate of deposit (CD) at his bank. One year later, Tom finds out that his CD is currently valued at $11,000. During the same time period, his friend Shirley invested the same amount of money in a stock market mutual fund, and it increased in value to $12,500. She suggests to Tom that he should withdraw his money from the CD and invest it in the mutual fund. Tom is hesitant to do so because he knows that there is an early withdrawal penalty of $500 if he takes the money out of the CD before the two-year period expires.

A. Calculate the interest rate that Tom is earning on his CD. _____

B. Assume the interest rate on the CD in the second year is 8 percent. What would be the value of the CD at the end of the second year? $ _____

C. What would be the opportunity cost if Tom removes the money from the CD at the end of the first year? $ _____

D. Assuming the same rate of return on the mutual fund in the second year as Shirley earned during the first year, what would be the marginal benefit to Tom of investing in the mutual fund? _____

E. Based on the assumptions in the questions above, would it be rational for Tom to shift his money from the CD to the mutual fund? _____ Why? _____
_____.

2. Resource Allocation

Seth owns a company that employs homeless people to sell flowers each Saturday evening between 10 p.m. and midnight on the downtown street corners of Centreville and Outerville. The following table shows their total revenues earned in each town when Seth employs 1–4 sellers. Answer the questions below based on the information in the table.

Number of sellers	Total Revenue in Centreville	Average Revenue	Marginal Revenue	Total Revenue in Outerville	Average Revenue	Marginal Revenue
0	$ 0	XXXX	XXXX	$ 0	XXXX	XXXX
1	30	$30	$30	50	$50	
2	55	$27.5	–	65	$32.5	
3	75	$25		75	$25	
4	90	$22.5		80	$20	
5	100	$20		80	$16	

A. In columns 3 and 6, calculate the average revenue for sellers 1–5 in Centreville and in Outerville, respectively.

B. In columns 4 and 7, calculate the marginal revenue for sellers 1–5 in Centreville and in Outerville, respectively.

C. If Seth has three sellers working in Centreville and three sellers working in Outerville, are his resources efficiently allocated? _____ If not, what combination of the six sellers would give him the most efficient allocation of sellers? _____ sellers in Centreville and _____ sellers in Outerville.

D. If Seth efficiently allocates a total of four sellers, he should deploy _____ in Centreville and _____ in Outerville.

3. An Economic Naturalist's Study Choices

Ben has two tests this week, one in biology and one in mathematics. As an economic naturalist, he has estimated in the table below the expected benefits, measured in terms of his test scores, of studying for each test.

Hours of Study	Mathematics Test Score	Marginal Benefit of Studying Math	Biology Test Score	Marginal Benefit of Studying Biology
0	37	XXXX	58	XXXX
1	53		70	
2	67		80	
3	79		88	
4	89		94	
5	96		98	
6	100		100	

A. In column 3 of the above table, calculate the marginal benefit of studying mathematics for 1–6 hours.

B. In column 5 of the above table, calculate the marginal benefit of studying biology for 1–6 hours.

C. If Ben has allocated a total of six hours of studying for these two tests, each additional hour of studying for the mathematics test means that he will forgo an additional hour of studying for biology. Within this context, an additional hour of studying for mathematics will result in an increase in his _____ test score (the marginal benefit), but there will be a tradeoff that can be measured as a reduction in his _____ test score (the marginal cost).

D. Assuming that Ben has allocated a total of six hours of studying for the two tests, complete the table below by calculating the total score on the two tests combined for the different combinations of studying time.

Hours Studying for the Math Test	Hours Studying for the Biology Test	Combined Test Scores
6	0	
5	1	
4	2	
3	3	
2	4	
1	5	
0	6	

E. The maximum combined test scores are achieved if Ben studies _____ hours of mathematics and _____ hours of biology.

SOLUTIONS

Quick Quiz

1. C. Scarcity applies to anyone that faces limited resources. The Prime Minister and a homeless person both have a finite amount of time in a given day.
2. D.
3. B. The benefit ($15) minus the opportunity cost ($12).
4. E. Conditional statements do not necessarily have to be true. The data will either confirm or refute the statement.
5. C. It is rational for Joe to purchase the books on campus because his willingness to drive there to save $4 on the concert ticket implies that the minimum he would accept for driving to campus is less than the $5 he would save by buying the books there.
6. D.
7. B. The fee does not change with the number of long-distance phone calls Mark makes and is, therefore, a fixed cost. If he decides to change his long-distance carrier, he will be reimbursed the amount of the switching fee. The switching is redeemable and, thus, is not a sunk cost.
8. B. The student fees and the room and board costs do not change with the number of credit hours and are, therefore, fixed costs. All other costs change with the number of credit hours and are variable costs.
9. D.
10. C.
11. C. There is insufficient information to determine which choice she should make, but an optimal choice should include the opportunity cost of the $75,000 salary offer if the management position is the best alternative to her current position.
12. B.

Self-Test: Key Terms

1. rational person.
2. economic surplus.
3. marginal benefit, marginal cost.
4. sunk cost.
5. microeconomics.
6. variable cost.
7. macroeconomics.
8. opportunity cost.
9. economics.
10. time value of money.

11. average cost.
12. fixed cost.
13. positive.
14. average benefit.
15. normative.

Self Test: Multiple-Choice Questions

1. C.
2. A. It is a microeconomic decision because affects the supply in an individual market.
3. C.
4. B. As interest rates rise, it takes fewer dollars today to reach a given value at some specified time in the future.
5. C. If he has no other trip to take within the year, the unused ticket will be unredeemable (and, thus, represents a sunk cost) and should not be considered an opportunity cost. Thus, the opportunity cost is only the cost of the exchange fee. If he has another trip to take within the year, the opportunity cost of going to Acapulco would depend, in part, upon the price of the ticket to the new location.
6. E.
7. D. Because the cost of the car and the insurance and are not redeemable, they should not be included in the opportunity cost of the trip.
8. D. This is the only statement that reflects a subjective value judgment and cannot be confirmed or refuted by data.
9. B. Only marginal costs and benefits are relevant under the cost-benefit analysis, not average costs and benefits—see Pitfall #3.
10. A. Sally produces an additional 3 computers during the second hour of employment. The components of each costing $700 (3 × $700 = $2,100). In addition you must add the $50 cost of employing Sally for the hour. Therefore, the marginal cost of producing the computers during Sally's second hour of work = $2,100 + $50 = $2,150.
11. D.
12. A. The entertainment value of the concert will be forgone is she goes to dinner and dancing and, thus, is an opportunity cost. The cost of the concert ticket, however, is a sunk cost and should not be considered an opportunity cost of going to dinner and dancing.
13. B. It is a rational choice because the additional benefit is greater than the additional cost, but it may or may not be an optimal amount. We would require information on the benefits and costs of additional lines of computer code beyond the current 100 lines being considered.
14. D. Since the marginal benefit ($40,000 of additional income) is greater than the marginal cost of both schools, it would be rational to go to either school.
15. A.
16. C.
17. E. The marginal benefit equals the 18 contracts she could sell in 11 hours minus the 15 contracts she could sell in 10 hours.
18. B. The cost of the car and the insurance do not change with mileage and, thus, are fixed costs. All other costs vary with mileage and, therefore, are variable costs.

19. A.

20. E. Because Sonya has only the two options to get to work before she can begin earning her salary, taking a cab is the quickest means of getting there and requires that she forgo the $20 cab fare. By taking the bus she forgoes $2 in bus fare, but because it takes an hour longer, she forgoes $25 in income as well.

Self-Test: Short-Answer Problems

1. A. 10 percent ($11,000 − $10,000 divided by $10,000)

   B. $11,880 ($11,000 × 1.08)

   C. $1,380 ($11,000 × 0.08 = $880 in forgone interest income plus the $500 early withdrawal penalty.)

   D $2,625 (The value of the CD minus the early withdrawal fee would give Tom $10,500 to invest. The mutual fund would earn 25 percent a year. Thus, $10,500 times 0.25).

   E. Yes, because the marginal benefit ($2,625) is greater than the marginal cost ($1,380).

2. A.; B.

Number of Sellers	Total Revenue in Centreville	Average Revenue	Marginal Revenue	Total Revenue in Outerville	Average Revenue	Marginal Revenue
0	$ 0	XXXX	XXXX	$ 0	XXXX	XXXX
1	30	$30	$30	50	$ 50	$50
2	55	27.50	25	65	32.50	15
3	75	25	20	75	25	10
4	90	22.50	15	80	20	5
5	100	20	10	80	16	0

   C. No; 4; 2.

   By shifting one seller from Outerville to Centreville, Seth will decrease his revenue in Outerville by $10 but will increase his revenue in Centreville by $15, resulting in a net benefit of $5. At this allocation, the marginal benefit of the last seller employed in each town is equal to $15, and thus, his resources are allocated efficiently.

   D. 3; 1.

   His first seller would be deployed in Centreville where the marginal revenue (benefit) of the first seller is highest, and the next three would be deployed in Centreville because the marginal benefit of sellers 1, 2, and 3 is greater than that of the second seller in Outerville. The sellers are imperfectly divisible, and thus, this is the most efficient allocation possible with four sellers.

3. A., B.

Hours of Study	Mathematics Test Score	Marginal Benefit of Studying Math	Biology Test Score	Marginal Benefit of Studying Biology
0	37	XXXX	58	XXXX
1	53	16	70	12
2	67	14	80	10
3	79	12	88	8
4	89	10	94	6
5	96	7	98	4
6	100	4	100	2

C. mathematics; biology.

D.

Hours Studying for the Math Test	Hours Studying for the Biology Test	Combined Test Scores
6	0	158
5	1	166
4	2	169
3	3	167
2	4	161
1	5	151
0	6	137

E. 4, 2.

2 Comparative Advantage: The Basis for Exchange

OVERVIEW

Economies can be based on specialization and the exchange of goods and services or on generalization and self-sufficiency in the production of goods and services. This chapter uses the concept of opportunity cost to illustrate how economic systems based on specialization and exchange are considerably more productive than those lacking specialization. When each individual specializes in a task at which he or she is relatively more efficient (i.e., has a lower opportunity cost), the total amount of goods and services is maximized. Using this comparative advantage approach to production ensures that a nation has the maximum amount of goods for consumption. The principle of comparative advantage can also be extended to exchange between nations; each nation will specialize in goods and/or services for which it is relatively more efficient in production than its trading partners. The greater the difference in opportunity costs, the greater are the benefits to exchange and trade.

Chapter Review

2.1 Exchange and Opportunity Cost

For any level of activity, scarcity implies choices; each choice will subsequently have an associated opportunity cost. Society will be better off, in the sense that it can maximize output, if its productive activity is based on using resources with the lowest opportunity cost. This implies that individual specialization and exchange of goods and services will create more output than individual self-sufficiency.

▶ **LO 1.   Define absolute advantage, comparative advantage, and productivity.**

A person has an absolute advantage over another if he or she takes fewer hours to perform a task than the other person. A person has a comparative advantage over another if that person's *opportunity cost* of performing a task is lower than another person's opportunity cost. An individual's labour productivity (output per hour of labour time), for example, is frequently calculated to compare the opportunity costs of one good in terms of another. In general terms, productivity is the number of units of output/hour divided by the units of input/hour.

NOTE:

It cannot be emphasized strongly enough that the principle of comparative advantage is a relative concept—one that makes sense only when the productivities of two or more producers (or countries) are being compared.

▶ **LO 2.   Understand implication of comparative advantage.**

The principle of comparative advantage asserts that total output is largest when each person (or each country) concentrates on the activities for which his or her opportunity cost is lowest.

▶ **LO 3.   Identify sources of comparative advantage.**

On an individual level, the sources of comparative advantage come from inborn talent, education, training, and experience. On a national level, comparative advantage occurs from differences in natural resources and/or from differences in society, culture, institutions, and public policy.

Quick Quiz

1. When each individual concentrates on performing the tasks and producing the goods for which he or she has the lowest opportunity cost, they are producing in accordance with the principle of
    A. increasing opportunity cost.
    B. decreasing opportunity cost.
    C. comparative advantage.
    D. scarcity.
    E. absolute advantage.

2. At the individual level, comparative advantage results from
    A. differences in natural resources.
    B. cultural differences.
    C. language differences.
    D. amount of resources available.
    E. differences in education or training.

3. Jane can produce 50 pizzas or 100 hamburgers per day, while Sam can produce 30 pizzas or 90 hamburgers per day. Jane has an absolute advantage in the production of
    A. pizzas only and has a comparative advantage in the production of pizzas.
    B. hamburgers only and has a comparative advantage in the production of hamburgers.
    C. hamburgers and pizzas, as well as a comparative advantage in the production of hamburgers.
    D. hamburgers and pizzas, as well as a comparative advantage in the production of pizzas.
    E. hamburgers and pizzas, as well as a comparative advantage in the production of hamburgers and pizzas.

2.2   Comparative Advantage and Production Possibilities

▶ **LO 4.   Define production possibilities curve (PPC) in a one-person economy.**

The production possibilities curve (PPC) is a *graph* illustrating the maximum amount of one good that can be produced for every possible level of production of the other good. Combining the assumption of scarcity (more of one good implies less of another) and constant opportunity costs (same opportunity cost regardless of how much is produced), the PPC will be a negatively sloped straight line for a one-person economy.

NOTE:

When interpreting the slope of the PPC, its absolute value is the opportunity cost of producing an additional unit of the good on the x-axis measured in terms of the amount of production of the good on the y-axis. A slope of |6|, for example, means that the resources necessary to produce six units of good y must be given up in order to produce one additional unit of x.

▶ **LO 5.   Identify attainable, unattainable, efficient, and inefficient points on a PPC.**

Points that lie outside the PPC represent combinations of goods that cannot be produced using the currently available resources and are called unattainable points. Points that lie on or below the curve are attainable points. Any combination of goods for which currently available resources enable an increase in the production of one good without a reduction in the production of the other good represent inefficient points. Similarly, any combination of goods for which currently available resources do not allow an increase in the production of one good without a reduction in the production of the other good represent efficient points. Therefore, points that lie on the PPC are both efficient and attainable points.

▶ **LO 6.   Identify factors influencing the PPC.**

For an individual (one-person economy), the slope and position of the PPC with respect to the origin are influenced by the level of inborn talent, education, training, and experience.

▶ **LO 7.   Compare one-person PPC with a two-person and multi-person PPC.**

For a two-person economy where individuals have constant but *different opportunity costs* of production, the graph contains two distinct linear portions with a "kink" at the level of production of the good on the x-axis where the lower opportunity cost person is replaced by the individual with the higher opportunity cost. This leads to a PPC which is bent outward (concave to the origin). For a multi-person PPC where there are many constant, but different, opportunity costs, each individual's contribution is extremely small. Consequently, the linearity of the PPC tends to fade into a much smoother curve.

▶ **LO 8.   Define principle of increasing opportunity costs.**

The principle of increasing opportunity cost states that in expanding the production of any good, those resources with the lowest opportunity cost should be employed first. Only when all of the lowest cost resources are employed does it make economic sense to use resources that have higher opportunity costs.

▶ **LO 9.   Understand benefits and costs of specialization.**

The benefits of specialization derive from the increase in total output and, consequently, total consumption that occurs when producing according to the principle of comparative advantage. Productivity of individual workers can increase substantially with specialization and can lead to significant improvements in living standards. On the other hand, some have argued that this fragmentation of workplace tasks and the subsequent (and often mundane) repetitive tasks can impose psychological costs.

NOTE:

Theoretically, excessive specialization can be detrimental. We can provide for our material needs in the shortest time, however, if we concentrate a significant portion of our efforts on those tasks for which we have a competitive advantage. The result will be more free time to do whatever other activities we may desire.

Quick Quiz

4. One of the major factors contributing to Canada achieving a global comparative advantage in producing agricultural products is that Canada has
    A. more capital used in the production of agricultural products than other nations.
    B. more farmers than other nations.
    C. a better educational system than other nations.
    D. one of the highest per capita endowments of farmland.
    E. more farmers with an innate superiority over farmers in other nations.

5. When expanding the production of any good, the principle of increasing opportunity costs implies that we use resources with higher opportunity costs
    A. all the time.
    B. before we use resources with lower opportunity costs.
    C. after we use all resources with lower opportunity costs.
    D. when we have a comparative advantage.
    E. when trading with other nations.

6. The slope of an individual's production possibilities curve
    A. decreases as more units of a particular good are produced.
    B. is negative and constant along the entire curve.
    C. is positive and constant along the entire curve.
    D. varies as the amount of output changes.
    E. is the same for all individuals.

7. Specialization of labour enables an economy to produce a larger amount of goods due to the innate differences in people's skills and due to the
   A. rigidly segment work.
   B. switching back and forth among numerous tasks.
   C. breaking a task down into mind-numbing repetitive tasks.
   D. deepening skills through practice and experience.
   E. eliminating the need to train and educate the workers to perform different tasks.

8. A point on Joseph's production possibilities curve represents 6 music CDs and 2 videos produced in a week. A combination of 4 music CDs and 2 videos is an
   A. efficient and attainable point.
   B. efficient but not attainable point.
   C. attainable and inefficient point.
   D. unattainable point.
   E. unattainable and inefficient point.

9. In a two-person economy, the slope of the PPC is
   A. negative and constant along the entire curve.
   B. negative and bends outward (concave to the origin).
   C. negative and bends inward (convex to the origin).
   D. positive and constant along the entire curve.
   E. positive and bends inward (convex to the origin).

2.3   Comparative Advantage and International Trade

► **LO 10.   Understand benefits and costs of trade.**

Similar to individuals gaining from specialization and exchange, nations can also gain from specialization (in goods and services with a comparative advantage) and trade. As long as trading nations have different opportunity costs of production, there can be gains from trade. The greater the difference in opportunity costs, the greater are the potential benefits from trade. Note that nations can benefit from trade even if one country has an absolute advantage in all goods.

NOTE:

While trade will lead to overall benefits for a nation (i.e., ability to consume outside their PPC), this does not necessarily mean that all individual citizens will be better off. It takes time for resources to move from the industry with the comparative disadvantage to the industry with the comparative advantage. During the transition period, individuals will be unemployed and other resources underemployed.

Quick Quiz

10. Despite the benefits of specialization and exchange indicated in the theory of comparative advantage, some groups have opposed free trade agreements because
    A. wealthier economies gain, but poor nations lose from free trade.
    B. in order for one nation to gain from trade, another nation must lose.
    C. absolute advantage provides greater gains than does comparative advantage.
    D. every individual does not gain from trade.
    E. contrary to the theory of comparative advantage, evidence suggests that there are few benefits from free trade.

Self-Test: Key Terms

Use the terms below to complete the following sentences. (Answers are given at the end of the chapter.)

absolute advantage	inefficient point
attainable point	production possibilities curve
comparative advantage	productivity
efficient point	unattainable point

1. A combination of goods represented by a point on a production possibilities curve is an efficient point and a(n) _____ .
2. Jean's opportunity cost of cooking gourmet dinners is lower than Bill's opportunity cost. Jean, therefore, has a _____ vis-à-vis Bill in cooking gourmet dinners.
3. If a movement from combination A to combination B requires a reduction in the production of one good in order to increase the production of the other good, the point representing combination A is a(n) _____ .
4. A graph that describes the maximum amount of one good that can be produced for every possible level of production of the other good is a _____.
5. Any combination of goods that cannot be produced using the currently available resources is a(n) _____ .
6. Juan takes fewer hours to create a Web page than does Simon. Juan, therefore, has a _____ vis-à-vis Simon in the creation of Web pages.
7. If a movement from combination A to combination B does not requires a reduction in the production of one good in order to increase the production of the other good, the point representing combination A is a(n) _____.
8. An individual's _____ is his output per hour of labour time.

Self-Test: Multiple-Choice Questions

Circle the letter that corresponds to the best answer. (Answers are given at the end of the chapter.)

1. Production possibilities curves are downward sloping, reflecting the principle of
   A. scarcity.
   B. comparative advantage.
   C. increasing opportunity cost.
   D. absolute advantage.
   E. decreasing opportunity cost.

2. Maria can produce 100 kilograms of tomatoes or 25 kilograms of squash in her garden each summer, while Tonya can produce 50 kilograms of tomatoes or 25 kilograms of squash. If we place squash on the x-axis and tomatoes on the y-axis, the absolute values of the slope of Maria's and Tonya's production possibility curves, respectively, are
   A. 1/4 and 1/2.
   B. 1/2 and 1/4.
   C. 4 and 2.
   D. 2 and 4.
   E. 100 and 50.

3. A country's production possibilities curve is concave to the origin (i.e., bowed outward) because
   A. of the principle of scarcity.
   B. the production of a good is expanded by first employing those resources with an absolute advantage.
   C. the production of a good is expanded by first employing those resources with the lowest opportunity cost.
   D. there is a tradeoff that requires a decrease in the production of one good in order to increase the production of another good.
   E. of the principle of absolute advantage.

4. The gains from specialization and exchange are greatest when individuals or nations
   A. have comparative and absolute advantage in the goods they produce, and the differences in opportunity costs are minimal.
   B. have comparative and absolute advantage in the goods they produce, and the differences in opportunity costs are large.
   C. have only a comparative advantage in the goods they produce, and the differences in opportunity costs are minimal.
   D. have only an absolute advantage in the goods they produce, and the differences in opportunity costs are large.
   E. have neither comparative nor absolute advantage in the goods they produce, but the differences in opportunity costs are large.

5. Professor N. Gregory Mankiw has a comparative advantage in the production of economics textbooks and a neighbour's child has a comparative advantage in mowing the lawn. Professor Mankiw
   A. will never mow his own lawn.
   B. will only write economics textbooks.
   C. may be better off mowing his lawn if he felt like taking a break from writing textbooks.
   D. will always be better off hiring the neighbour's child to mow his lawn.
   E. may be better off hiring the neighbour's child to write his economics textbook if his lawn needs mowing.

6. Despite the benefits of specialization and exchange indicated in the theory of comparative advantage, some groups have opposed free trade agreements because
   A. wealthier economies gain but poor nations lose from free trade.
   B. in order for one nation to gain from trade, another nation must lose.
   C. they do not understand the theory of comparative advantage.
   D. every individual does not gain from trade.
   E. contrary to the theory of comparative advantage, evidence suggests that there are few benefits from free trade.

7. Yolanda can produce 2 dresses or 4 shirts in 8 hours of work, while Sandra can produce 3 dresses or 7 shirts in the same amount of time. Yolanda has a(n)
   A. absolute advantage in producing dresses and shirts and a comparative advantage in producing dresses, while Sandra has a comparative advantage in producing shirts.
   B. comparative advantage in producing shirts, while Sandra has an absolute advantage in producing dresses and shirts and a comparative advantage in producing dresses.
   C. comparative advantage in producing dresses, while Sandra has an absolute advantage in producing dresses and shirts and a comparative advantage in producing shirts.
   D. absolute advantage in producing dresses and shirts and a comparative advantage in producing shirts, while Sandra has a comparative advantage in producing dresses.
   E. absolute advantage and a comparative advantage in producing dresses and shirts.

8. Point A on a production possibilities curve represents a combination of 10 bicycles (y-axis) and 4 tricycles (x-axis), and point B represents 6 bicycles and 6 tricycles. The absolute value of the slope of the production possibilities curve between points A and B equals
   A. 2.
   B. 4.
   C. 1/2.
   D. 1/4.
   E. 6.

9. In a two-person economy, Little Joe can trap a maximum of 6 rabbits or catch 10 fish a week, while his father can trap 12 rabbits or catch 15 fish per week. If their family wants to consume 20 fish per week, while maximizing their joint production
   A. the father should specialize in producing only fish, and Little Joe should produce both fish and rabbits.
   B. Little Joe should specialize in producing only fish, and his father should produce both fish and rabbits.

C. Little Joe should specialize in producing fish, and his father should produce rabbits.

D. Little Joe should specialize in producing only rabbits, and his father should produce fish.

E. each should produce both fish and rabbits.

10. When individuals or groups specialize in producing those goods for which they have a comparative advantage and exchange those goods with one another
   A. those with an absolute advantage will gain the most, while those without an absolute advantage will lose.
   B. those with a comparative advantage will gain the most, while those without a comparative advantage will lose.
   C. total production will be greater than it will be without specialization but will be the greatest if they produce those goods in which they only have an absolute advantage.
   D. total production will be less than it will be without specialization.
   E. total production will be the greatest that they can achieve given the available resources.

11. Increased specialization in the production of goods
   A. always increases net benefits.
   B. never increases net benefits.
   C. has benefits but no costs.
   D. has costs but no benefits.
   E. has costs and benefits.

12. The opportunity for a small nation to trade with an economic superpower will increase the consumption possibilities for the
   A. small nation and the economic superpower.
   B. small nation only.
   C. economic superpower only.
   D. economic superpower but will decrease the consumption possibilities for the small nation.
   E. small nation but will decrease the consumption possibilities for the economic superpower.

13. Over the years, small annual productivity gains due to specialization
   A. are outweighed by the increases in costs such that livings standards remain constant.
   B. can cumulate to large differences in livings standards compared with countries that do not encounter productivity gains.
   C. are typically matched by all countries, leaving relative living standards constant.
   D. only occur in developed nations.
   E. have no effect on a country's living standards.

14. If a high-wage country opens up trade with a low-wage country.
   A. all labour in both countries will benefit.
   B. unskilled workers in both countries will benefit.
   C. unskilled workers in both countries may be hurt.
   D. unskilled workers may be hurt in the high-wage country.
   E. unskilled workers may be hurt in the low-wage country.

15. Consider a two-person nation that produces nuts and sugar cane and each person has a different opportunity cost for producing these goods. If this two-person nation opens up trade with the rest of the world and the trading price lies *between* the opportunity costs of the two individuals, the two-person nation can maximize its consumption opportunities by moving production to
   A. completely specialize in nuts.
   B. completely specialize in sugar cane.
   C. the "kink" on the PPC.
   D. a point inside the PPC.
   E. a point outside the PPC.

Self-Test: Short-Answer Problems

(Answers and solutions are given at the end of the chapter.)

1. Production Possibilities Curve for an Individual
   A. If Ian allocates all of his resources, he can write 4 short stories in a month, or he can allocate all of his resources to crafting 20 leather belts. Draw his production possibilities curve, measuring the production of leather belts on the vertical axis, and short stories on the horizontal axis, on the graph below (be sure to label the axes!).

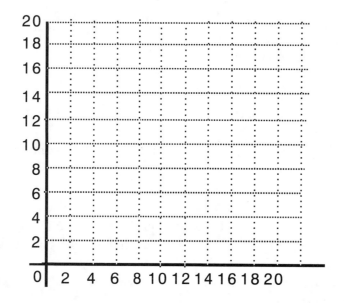

   B. Ian is currently allocating all of his resources to producing leather belts. If he decides to reallocate his resources so as to produce 1 short story, he will incur an opportunity cost of
       _____.

   C. Based on your answer to question 1B, the absolute value of the slope of Ian's production possibilities curve equals _____ .

   D. On the graph above, draw a point representing the combination of 12 leather belts and 4 short stories (label it A). Point A is a(n) _____ point.

E. On the graph, draw a point representing the combination of 5 leather belts and 3 short stories (label it B). Point B is a(n) _____ and _____ point.

F. On the graph, draw a point representing the combination of 2 leather belts and 2 short stories (label it C). Point C is a(n) _____ and _____ point.

2. Production Possibilities and Comparative Advantage

Sean and Shirley are proprietors of small fabrication plants that design and manufacture integrated chips (ICs) for specialized electronic products. The table below shows their respective productivity for ICs used in cellular phones and video-game machines.

	Time to Design and Manufacture ICs for Cellular Phone	*Time to Design and Manufacture ICs for Video-Game Machines*
Sean's plant	4 days	4 days
Shirley's plant	1 day	2 days

A. Draw the production possibilities curves for Sean's and Shirley's fabrication plants on the graph below showing their respective production of ICs for cellular phones and video-game machines in 40 days.

ICs for
Game
Machines

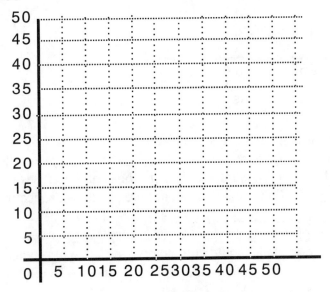

ICs for Cellular Phones

B. Sean's plant has an opportunity cost of producing ICs for cellular phones of _____ and for producing ICs for video-game machines of _____ . Shirley's plant has an opportunity cost of producing ICs for cellular phones of _____ and for producing ICs for video-game machines of _____ .

C. _____ has an absolute advantage in producing ICs for cellular phones and video-game machines.

D. _____ has a comparative advantage in producing ICs for cellular phones and _____ has a comparative advantage in producing ICs for video-game machines.

E. In order to maximize the total production of ICs for cellular phones and video-game machines, Sean should specialize in the production of ICs for _____ and Shirley should specialize in the production of ICs for _____.

F. As the demand for its ICs for cellular phones increased to 45 per month, Shirley buys Sean's fabrication plant. Draw the production possibilities curve showing the combined maximum production of the two fabrication plants.

ICs for
Game
Machines

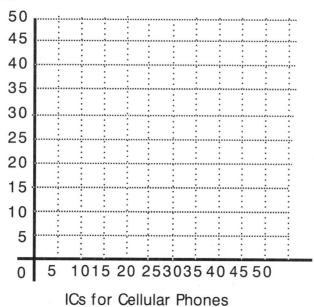

ICs for Cellular Phones

G. Prior to the merger of the fabrication plants and specialization, the slopes of Shirley's and Sean's PPCs were (constant/decreasing/increasing) _____. After the merger and specialization, the slope of the combined plants PPC (is constant/ decreases/increases) _____ after _____ ICs for cellular phones are produced, reflecting the principle of _____.

H. In order to maximize production of ICs and produce 45 ICs for cellular phones per month, _____ fabrication plant should completely specialize in producing ICs for cellular phones and _____ fabrication plant should produce ICs for cellular phones and video-game machines.

I. Your answers to questions 2G and 2H imply that in order to maximize production of ICs while producing 45 ICs for cellular phones, they must allocate 3/4 of the combined production time of the two plants (i.e., 40 days of production in Shirley's fabrication plant plus 20 days of production in Sean's fabrication plant = 60 days divided by 80 of combined production days). The remaining 1/4 of the combined time would be allocated to producing ICs for video-game machines. If prior to the buyout, each fabrication plant had allocated 3/4 of its time (i.e., 30 days) to producing ICs for cellular phones, Shirley's fabrication plant would have produced _____ ICs and Sean's fabrication plant would have produced _____ ICs. Similarly, if each fabrication plant had allocated 1/4 (i.e., 10 days) of its time producing ICs for video-game machines, Shirley's fabrication plant would have produced _____ ICs and Sean's fabrication plant would have produced _____ ICs.

J. Based on your answer to question 2I, the total combined number of ICs that would have been produced prior to the merger and specialization would have equaled _____ ICs, but after the merger and specialization the two fabrication plants would produce _____ ICs.

K. Based on your answers to question 2J, the gains from specialization would equal _____ ICs.

3. Gains from Trade
The following table shows the combinations of strawberries and personal computers (PCs) that can be produced by Centralamericana.

Strawberries (millions of tonnes)	Personal Computers (thousands of PCs)
8	0
6	8
0	12

A. On the graph below, plot Centralamericana's production possibilities curve.

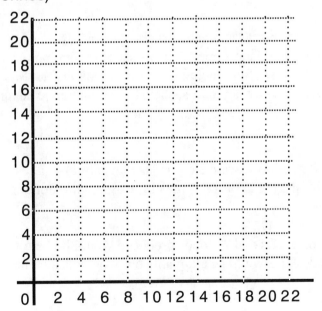

Strawberries (mil. tonnes)

Personal Computers (1,000s)

B. The economy of Centralamericana is closed (i.e., no trade is allowed) and it has chosen to produce a combination of 6 million tonnes of strawberries and 8,000 PCs. Identify this combination on the above graph by labelling it point A.

C. By means of an international treaty, the economy of Centralamericana is opened to international trade. The prevailing exchange rate is 1 million tonnes of strawberries for 1,000 PCs. On the graph, draw Centralamericana's new PPC after its economy opening to international trade, assuming it is producing at point A and could exchange as much of its strawberry and PC production as it chooses to at the prevailing exchange rate.

D. If Centralamericana started at Point A and chose to sell 4,000 PCs (at the prevailing exchange rate), it would then be able to consume _____ million tonnes of strawberries and _____ thousand PCs. Label this point B. As a result of trade, it would have increased its consumption of strawberries by _____ millions tonnes compared with what it would have been able to produce without trade.

E. If Centralamericana started at point A and chose to sell 3 million tonnes of strawberries at the prevailing exchange rate), it would then be able to consume _____ million tonnes of strawberries and _____ PCs. Label this point C. As a result of trade, it would have increased its consumption of PCs by _____ millions tonnes compared with what it would have been able to produce without trade.

SOLUTIONS

Quick Quiz

1. C.
2. E.
3. D. Jane can produce more pizzas and hamburgers than can Sam and, thus, has an absolute advantage in producing both. Jane's opportunity cost of producing pizzas is 2 hamburgers, while Sam's opportunity cost of producing pizzas is 3 hamburgers. Since Jane's opportunity cost of producing pizzas is less than Sam's, she has a comparative advantage in producing pizzas.
4. D.
5. C.
6. B. The individual's PPC is downward sloping (i.e., negative) as a result of the scarcity problem and a straight line (i.e., constant) under the assumption of constant opportunity costs.
7. D.
8. C. The combination of 4 CDs and 2 videos produced would lie below Joseph's production possibilities curve and, thus, would be attainable but would also be inefficient.
9. B.
10. D.

Self-Test: Key Terms

1. attainable point.
2. comparative advantage.
3. efficient point.
4. production possibilities curve.
5. unattainable point.
6. absolute advantage.
7. inefficient point.
8. productivity.

Self Test: Multiple-Choice Questions

1. A.
2. C. The slope of Maria's PPC equals $100 \div 25 = 4$, and Tonya's equals $50 \div 25 = 2$.
3. C. By exploiting the lowest cost production first, the opportunity cost of producing additional units of a good increases and, thus, the slope of PPC increases (i.e., it is bowed outward).
4. B.
5. C. We can only be certain that Professor Mankiw will be better off writing his textbook rather than mowing his lawn if he is equally happy doing either. But if he was tired of working on his book and felt like getting a little exercise, mowing his lawn would be preferable to writing his text.
6. D.
7. C. Yolanda's opportunity cost of producing dresses is 2 shirts, while Sandra's opportunity cost of producing dresses is 2 1/3 ($7 \div 3$) shirts. Since Yolanda's opportunity cost of producing dresses is less than Sandra's, she has a comparative advantage in producing dresses. Sandra can produce more dresses and shirts than Yolanda and, thus, has an absolute advantage in producing both. Sandra's opportunity cost of producing a shirt is 3/7 of a dress; while Yolanda's is 1/2 dress. Thus, Sandra has a comparative advantage in producing shirts.
8. A. The slope equals the absolute value of $(10 - 6)$ divided by $(4 - 6)$, or $4 \div 2$ which equals 2.
9. B. Little Joe's opportunity cost of catching a fish is 3/5 rabbit, while his father's is 4/5 rabbit. Little Joe has a comparative advantage in catching fish and, thus, should specialize in fishing to catch his 10 fish. The father should catch the additional 10 fish and his remaining time (1/3 of a week) spent trapping rabbits.
10. E.
11. E.
12. A.
13. B. Small gains in productivity enable countries to invest more resources in education, research and development, and technological improvements. In turn, each of these enables a nation to continue to increase productivity. Over the years, these small advantages can cumulate to a point of significant differences in living standards among countries.
14. D.
15. C. Moving production to a point inside the PPC is, by definition, inefficient, and moving production to a point outside the PPC is impossible, given a country's current resources. If the trading price lies between the two opportunity costs, moving production to the "kink" shifts the trade and consumptions possibility curve the farthest away from the PPC. Any other production point along the PPC will lead to smaller consumption gains through trade.

Self-Test: Short-Answer Problems

1.

A

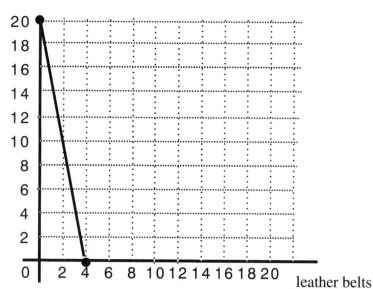

Leather
Belts

B. 5

C. 5

D.

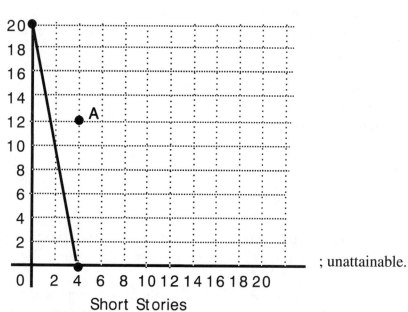

; unattainable.

E.

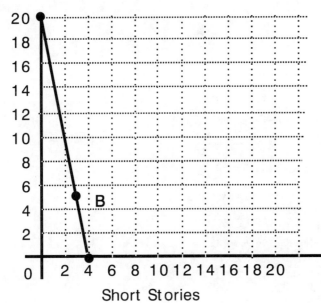

; attainable; efficient.

F.

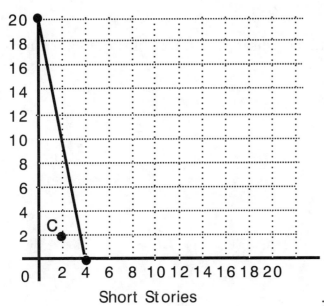

; attainable; inefficient.

2.
A.

ICs for
Game
Machines

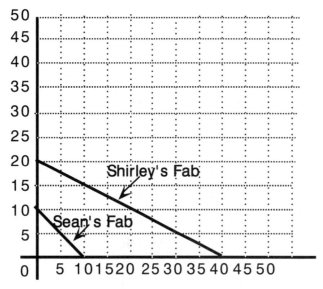

ICs for Cellular Phones

B. 1 IC for video-game machines; 1 IC for cellular phones; 1/2 IC for video-game machines; 2
    ICs for cellular phones.
C. Shirley.
D. Shirley; Sean.
E. video-game machines; cellular phones.

F.

ICs for
Game
Machines

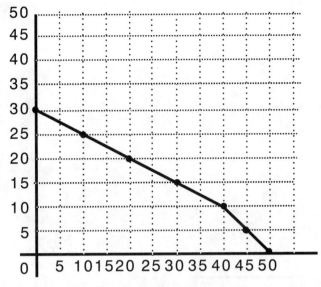

ICs for Cellular Phones

G. Constant; increases; 40; increasing opportunity cost.
H. Shirley's; Sean's.
I. 30; 7 1/2; 5; 2 1/2.
J. 45 (add the values calculated in I.); 50 (all of Shirley's days on cellular phones = 40 ICs + half of Sean's days (20 days) on cellular phones = 5 ICs + other half of Sean's days (20 days) on video-game = 5 ICs).
K. 5.

3.

A.

Strawberries

(mil. tonnes)

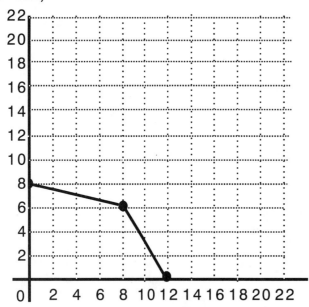

Personal Computers (1,000s)

B.

Strawberries

(mil. tonnes)

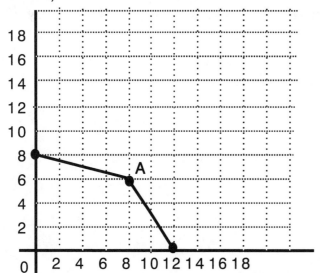

Personal Computers (1,000s)

C.
Strawberries
(mil. tonnes)

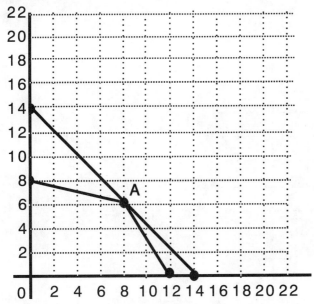

Personal Computers (1,000s)

E. 10; 4; 3 (without trade, only produce 7 million tonnes of strawberries when they produce 4,000 PCs).

Strawberries
(mil. tonnes)

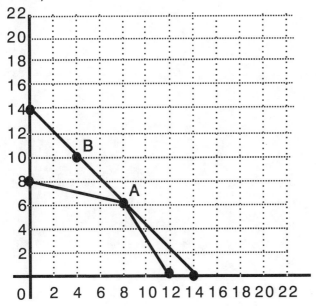

Personal Computers (1,000s)

F. 3; 11; 1(without trade, only produce 10,000 PCs when they produce 3 million tonnes of
    strawberries).

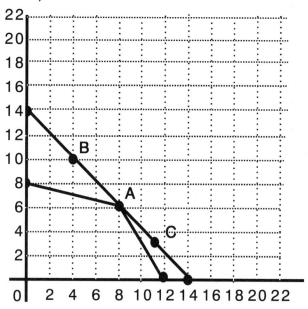

Strawberries
(mil. tonnes)

Personal Computers (1,000s)

3 Supply and Demand: An Introduction

OVERVIEW

All societies, regardless of their cultural, social, political, or institutional framework must answer certain basic economic questions. How are resources to be allocated? What combination of goods should be produced? What production techniques should be used? How will the goods and services be distributed among the people? This chapter explores how *markets* can answer these questions. The price and quantity of a good or service exchanged in a market depends on the costs incurred by suppliers as well as the value placed by those who wish to purchase the good. The ensuing demand and supply analysis helps us to understand how the desires and actions of millions of people can effectively be coordinated to create a stable economic environment. In addition, it has powerful predictive abilities with respect to the direction of prices and quantities when we observe fundamental changes in markets. It is important to note that markets are not a panacea for all economic ills. If the central assumptions of the model do not hold, markets do not efficiently allocate resources and we need to revise our economic analysis.

Chapter Review

3.1 Markets and Prices

Markets consist of many buyers and sellers, and the interaction between the two groups will provide a stable equilibrium in terms of prices and quantities. If, at any given price, the interests of buyers and sellers differ, there is an inherent tendency for markets to move toward this stable equilibrium.

▶ **LO 1.** **Define market.**

A market consists of all potential buyers and sellers of a particular good or service at a specific location and time. For example, we might be interested in the market for peaches-and-cream corn in Ottawa during the month of August.

► **LO 2.   Define supply curve.**

The supply curve illustrates the total quantity of a good or service that sellers are willing to sell at each price. It is based on the assumption that (1) producers will be willing to sell the good as long as the price they receive is sufficient to cover their opportunity costs, and (2) different people have different opportunity costs. At lower prices, those individuals with low opportunity costs will be willing to sell a good. Only with a higher price will the higher-opportunity-cost individuals find it beneficial to become producers. Therefore, the principle of increasing opportunity costs ensures that the supply curve is upward sloping.

► **LO 3.   Define demand curve.**

The demand curve illustrates the total quantity of a good or service that buyers are willing (and able) to purchase at each price. The nature of the relationship between the price of a good and the quantity buyers wish to purchase is well known to all of us from practical experience. At lower prices, buyers generally want to purchase more than at higher prices, and therefore the demand curve is downward sloping.

► **LO 4.   Understand market equilibrium.**

In a market, the term equilibrium denotes a "state of rest" where there is no incentive for either the buyer or the seller to alter their behaviour. The equilibrium price and equilibrium quantity of a good are determined at the point where the demand curve intersects the supply curve. This market equilibrium occurs when all buyers and sellers are satisfied with their respective quantities at the market price.

NOTE:

"Satisfied" does not mean that buyers would not like a lower price or that sellers would be displeased with a higher price. It simply means those buyers willing to pay the equilibrium price can acquire exactly the amount they wish. Likewise, sellers who are willing to accept the equilibrium price can sell the exact amount they wish.

► **LO 5.   Define excess supply (surplus).**

At prices above the equilibrium price, buyers wish to purchase a relatively small amount of a good, but many suppliers can cover their opportunity costs, and so a large amount of the good is produced. When quantity supplied exceeds quantity demanded, the market experiences excess supply or a surplus.

► **LO 6.   Define excess demand (shortage).**

At prices below the equilibrium price, buyers wish to purchase a relatively large amount of the good, but few suppliers can cover their opportunity costs, and so only a small amount of the good is produced. When quantity demanded exceeds quantity supplied, the market experiences excess demand or a shortage.

▶ **LO 7.**   **Explain how market returns to equilibrium under surpluses and shortages.**

In the case of a surplus, suppliers are unable to sell all they have produced and consequently are dissatisfied with the current market situation. Lowering the price induces some consumers to make purchases that were passed over at the higher price. Similarly, the lower price means some firms no longer cover their opportunity costs and leave the market. The net result is for price to be lower and the difference between quantity supplied and quantity demanded to narrow. Firms continue to reduce price until excess supply is zero. At this point, firms reach the equilibrium price and are satisfied with the market situation. For excess demand, a similar process is at work. Consumers are dissatisfied; some are unable to acquire the good at the going price. These unfulfilled consumers have an incentive to offer a higher price in order to increase the chance they will receive some of the product. The higher price drives some of the consumers out of the market while encouraging new suppliers to join the market. The net result is for price to be higher and the difference between quantity demanded and quantity supplied to shrink. Consumers continue to offer higher prices until excess demand is zero. Therefore, the market has a tendency to move toward the equilibrium prices and quantities, regardless of whether the price is initially above or below the equilibrium value.

▶ **LO 8.**   **Understand demand and supply in market for foreign exchange.**

The foreign exchange rate is the price of one unit of a country's currency in terms of units of another country's currency and is determined in foreign exchange markets. If we consider the euro–Canadian dollar exchange rate, we can express the exchange rate as the amount of euros per $1 Canadian. The demand for dollars comes from Europeans who wish to purchase Canadian goods, services, financial assets, and real assets (e.g., condos in Whistler). Conversely, if Canadians wish to purchase European goods, services, financial assets, and real assets, they must supply Canadian dollars in order to purchase the euros required for the transactions. Demand and supply analysis can be used to determine the equilibrium exchange rate and the quantity of a currency exchanged as well as the mechanism that brings us back to equilibrium if any surpluses or shortages exist.

Quick Quiz

1. The demand curve illustrates the relationship between the quantity demanded of a good and
   A. consumers' incomes.
   B. consumers' expectations .
   C. consumers' preferences.
   D. prices of other goods.
   E. its own price.

2. A market in equilibrium would feature
   A. excess supply.
   B. unexploited opportunities.
   C. excess demand.
   D. wild variation in price.
   E. no tendency to change.

3. As the price of $1 Canadian falls in terms of British pounds (£), Canadians will _____ more _____ in the British pound / Canadian dollar foreign exchange market.
   A. demand; euros.
   B. demand; dollars.
   C. supply; pounds.
   D. supply; dollars.
   E. supply; euros.

4. If the price of good is currently below its equilibrium price, we observe excess _____. As a result, prices will _____, and the quantity of the good exchanged will _____.
   A. supply; decrease; decrease.
   B. supply; decrease; increase.
   C. demand; increase; increase.
   D. demand; increase; decrease.
   E. demand; decrease; increase.

5. The supply curve illustrates the relationship between the quantity supplied of a good and
   A. producers' costs of production.
   B. producers' expectations.
   C. producers' choice of technology.
   D. its own price.
   E. prices of other goods.

6. By definition, the market for a particular good consists of
   A. all citizens of a nation.
   B. all potential buyers and sellers.
   C. all buyers and sellers.
   D. sellers only.
   E. buyers only.

7. Suppose that at a price of $5, quantity demanded is 300 units and quantity supplied is 700 units. This market will experience a(n) _____ of _____ units.
   A. excess demand, 400 units.
   B. excess supply, – 400 units.
   C. excess demand, – 400 units.
   D. excess supply, 400 units.
   E. shortage, 400 units.

8. If the price of a good is above the equilibrium price, then
    A. suppliers, dissatisfied with growing inventories, will lower the price.
    B. suppliers, dissatisfied with growing inventories, will raise the price.
    C. suppliers, satisfied with the higher price, will raise the price higher.
    D. demanders, wanting to ensure they acquire the good, will bid the price lower.
    E. demanders, wanting to ensure they acquire the good, will bid the price higher.

3.2 Markets and Social Welfare

▶ **LO 9.   Define efficient quantity and economic efficiency.**

When markets are not in equilibrium, there exist mutually beneficial exchanges that result in increases in total economic surplus. The efficient quantity of a good is the quantity that results in the maximum possible economic surplus from producing and consuming the good. If, and only if, the market fully reflects the costs and benefits associated with the production and consumption of the good, this quantity occurs at the equilibrium price and quantity. Economic efficiency occurs when *all* goods and services are produced and consumed at levels that produce the maximum economic surplus for society.

▶ **LO 10.   Explain difference between equilibrium principle and efficiency principle.**

The efficiency principle states that economic efficiency occurs when total economic surplus is maximized—all benefits and costs are captured with the production and consumption of the good. The equilibrium principle states that a market in equilibrium leaves no unexploited opportunities for individuals (i.e., all potential buyers and sellers) but may not exploit all gains achievable through collective action. This is known as the "smart for one, dumb for all" behaviour. In essence, the market is in equilibrium, but it does not reflect all the costs and benefits to society.

Quick Quiz

9. If your next-door neighbour spends $10,000 on landscaping her front lawn, in equilibrium, the market for landscaping services in your city will
    A. reflect the equilibrium principle only.
    B. reflect the efficiency principle only.
    C. reflect both the equilibrium and efficiency principles.
    D. contain no unexploited opportunities.
    E. be provided by one firm only.

10. Economic efficiency occurs when
   A. a market's marginal benefit equal a market's marginal cost.
   B. marginal benefit equals marginal cost for each and every market.
   C. all goods and services are produced and consumed at their respective socially optimal levels.
   D. a good or service is produced and consumed at its socially optimal level.
   E. whenever demand equals supply.

3.3   Explaining Changes in Prices and Quantities

► **LO 11.   Explain difference between change in quantity demanded and change in demand.**

A change in quantity demanded represents a *movement* along the demand curve that occurs in response to a change in price. A change in demand represents a complete *shift* in the demand curve that occurs in response to a change in any factor, other than price, influencing the demand for a good or service.

NOTE:

*Understanding the difference between a "change in quantity demanded" and a "change in demand" is critical to understanding the manner in which markets operate—particularly when we explain the graphical implications. Whenever we talk about the relationship only between the two variables on the axes (price and quantity), we are looking at a **movement along the curve** (change in quantity demanded). Whenever we talk about the relationship between one of the variables not on the axes, we are looking at a **shift in the curve** (change in demand). A similar analysis holds for changes in quantity supplied and change in supply.*

► **LO 12.   Explain difference between change in quantity supplied and change in supply.**

A change in quantity supplied represents a *movement* along the supply curve that occurs in response to a change in price. A change in supply represents a complete *shift* in the supply curve that occurs in response to a change in any factor, other than price, influencing the supply of a good or service.

► **LO 13.   Identify factors which shift supply curve.**

Changes in the following factors have a tendency to shift the supply curve to the right (i.e., an increase in supply): (1) decreases in the cost of factors of production (labour, materials, and so on); (2) technological improvements (reduces production costs); (3) increases in government subsidies; and (4) increases in the number of firms. When these factors move in the opposite direction, supply decreases. Note that expectations on behalf of suppliers may also shift the supply curve.

► **LO 14.   Identify factors which shift demand curve.**

Changes in the following factors have a tendency to shift the demand curve to the right (i.e., an increase in demand): (1) decrease in the price of complements; (2) increase in the price of substitutes; (3) increase in income (for normal goods); (4) increase in preference by demanders of the good or service; and (5) increase in population of potential buyers. When these factors move in the opposite direction, demand decreases. Note that expectations on behalf of demanders may also shift the demand curve.

► **LO 15.   Explain how shifts in demand _or_ supply affect equilibrium price and quantity.**

The following four simple rules illustrate how a shift in either curve will change equilibrium values: (1) an increase in demand leads to an increase in both equilibrium price and quantity; (2) a decrease in demand leads to a decrease in both equilibrium price and quantity; (3) an increase in supply leads to a decrease in equilibrium price and an increase in equilibrium quantity; and (4) a decrease in supply leads to an increase in equilibrium price and a decrease in equilibrium quantity.

► **LO 16.   Explain how shifts in demand _and_ supply affect equilibrium price and quantity.**

When both demand and supply shift simultaneously, one of the equilibrium variables (either price or quantity) definitely moves in a specific direction, whereas the value of the remaining variable may increase, decrease, or remain constant. In these cases, the demand curve has a tendency to move this "indeterminate" variable in one direction, while the supply curve has a tendency to move it in the opposite direction. The final direction is determined by the relative magnitudes of the shifts. There are four combinations of demand and supply shifts leading to the following changes in equilibrium: (1) increase in both demand and supply—equilibrium quantity increases, price is indeterminate; (2) decrease in both demand and supply—equilibrium quantity decreases, price is indeterminate; (3) increase in demand and decrease in supply—equilibrium price increases, quantity is indeterminate; and (4) decrease in demand and increase in supply—equilibrium price decreases, quantity is indeterminate.

NOTE:

There are no "short cuts" to understanding the simultaneous shifts in demand and supply—you need to methodically go through each example. Some students find it helpful to (1) take each shift separately and identify its effect on equilibrium price and quantity, and (2) combine the two effects to identify the indeterminate variable and determine the direction of the other variable.

Quick Quiz

11. The following factor will lead to an increase in demand for barbequed chickens:
   A. an outbreak of bird flu virus.
   B. a medical report indicating that consumption of chicken lowers cholesterol levels.

    C. a decrease in the price of chicken feed.
    D. a decrease in government subsidies to chicken producers.
    E. an increase in government subsidies to chicken producers.

12. An increase in the demand for coal with no concurrent change in the supply of coal will result in a(n) _____ equilibrium price and a(n) _____ equilibrium quantity.
    A. higher; lower.
    B. lower; lower.
    C. higher; unchanged.
    D. higher; higher.
    E. lower; higher.

13. As the price of cookies increases, firms that produce cookies will
    A. increase the supply of cookies.
    B. increase the quantity of cookies supplied.
    C. decrease the supply of cookies.
    D. decrease the quantity of cookies supplied.
    E. leave their production unchanged.

14. Which of the following would not shift the supply curve for Pentium 4 processors?
    A. a decrease in the price of silicon wafers.
    B. an increase in the demand for Pentium 4 processors.
    C. an improvement in the technology used to make processors.
    D. an increase in the wage rate paid to "clean room" workers.
    E. an earthquake centred in Silicon Valley.

15. If the demand and supply of MP3 players simultaneously increased, the new equilibrium quantity exchanged in the market
    A. will increase.
    B. will decrease.
    C. will remain constant.
    D. may either increase or decrease.
    E. may increase, decrease, or remain constant.

16. Suppose the price of gasoline increases. We would expect the
    A. demand for gasoline to decrease.
    B. demand for sport utility vehicles (SUVs) to decrease.
    C. demand for SUVs to increase.
    D. quantity of gasoline demanded to increase.
    E. quantity of SUVs demanded to decrease.

Self-Test: Key Terms

Use the terms below to complete the following sentences. (Answers are given at the end of the chapter.)

change in demand
change in quantity demanded
change in quantity supplied
change in supply
complements
demand curve
economic efficiency
efficient quantity
equilibrium
equilibrium price
equilibrium quantity

excess demand
excess supply
foreign exchange rate
inferior good
market
market equilibrium
normal good
shortage
substitutes
supply curve
surplus

1. The _____ is the amount of a good or service that will be exchanged when quantity demanded equals quantity supplied.

2. When consumers are willing and able to purchase more of a good or service at each price, then a(n) _____ has occurred.

3. If an increase in income causes consumers to purchase more of a particular good, then that good is classified as a(n) _____.

4. The total quantity consumers are willing and able to purchase of a good or a service at each price is illustrated by a(n) _____.

5. When the price of a good or service changes, a firm reacts to this through a(n) _____.

6. _____ occurs when the price of a good or service is below the equilibrium price.

7. The set of all buyers and sellers of toothpaste constitutes the _____ for toothpaste.

8. When all of the forces that influence a system are cancelled by each other, resulting in a stable situation, the system is said to be in a state of _____.

9. The _____ shows the total quantity of a good or service that sellers are willing to make available at each price.

10. When the price of a good is above the equilibrium price, _____ results.

11. As incomes grow, consumers purchase fewer used cars at each price. Used cars are therefore a(n) _____.

12. When consumers alter their purchases of a good or service because the price of the good or service has changed, this is termed a(n) _____.

13. When the price of good X increases, consumers purchase less of service Y. Good X and service Y must therefore be _____.

14. A change in the price of labour will cause a(n) _____.

15. A _____ is achieved when all buyers and sellers of a good or service are satisfied with their respective quantities at the market price.

16. Goods A and B are classified as _____ if, as the price of good A rises, demand for good B increases.

17. The price that results from the intersection of the supply and demand curves is referred to as the _____.

18. A(n) _____ occurs when the price of a good or service is below the equilibrium price.

19. The _____ measures the price of one unit of a country's currency in terms of another country's currency.

20. When all goods and services are produced and consumed at their respective socially optimal levels, a society has attained _____.

21. A(n) _____ develops when quantity supplied exceeds quantity demanded.

22. The quantity of a good that results in the maximum possible economic surplus from producing and consuming the good is called the_____.

Self-Test: Multiple-Choice Questions

Circle the letter that corresponds to the best answer. (Answers are given at the end of the chapter.)

1. If the price of tea increases and the demand for sugar decreases, then
    A. tea and sugar are complements.
    B. tea is a normal good and sugar is inferior.
    C. tea and sugar are substitutes.
    D. tea is an inferior good and sugar is normal.
    E. tea and sugar are unrelated to each other.

2. If the demand for a good increases as consumer's incomes rise, the good is termed a(n)
    A. inferior good.
    B. complement good.
    C. normal good.
    D. substitute good.
    E. typical good.

3. Which of the following is not a characteristic of a market in equilibrium?
    A. quantity demanded equals quantity supplied.
    B. excess supply is zero.
    C. all consumers are able to purchase as much as they wish.

  D. excess demand is zero.

  E. The equilibrium price is stable, that is, there is no pressure for it to change.

4. The equilibrium price and quantity of any good or service is established by
  A. only demanders.
  B. only suppliers.
  C. government regulations.
  D. both demanders and suppliers.
  E. custom and tradition.

5. If when the price of X increases, the demand for Y increases, we can conclude that
  A. X and Y are complements.
  B. X and Y are substitutes.
  C. X and Y are normal.
  D. X and Y are inferior.
  E. X and Y are superior.

6. At the beginning of the fall semester, college towns experience large increases in their populations, causing a(n)
  A. increase in the quantity of apartments demanded.
  B. increase in the supply of apartments.
  C. increase in the demand for apartments.
  D. decrease in the quantity of apartments supplied.
  E. decrease in the supply of apartments.

7. An increase in the price of Tomko toothpaste, a substitute for Durrell toothpaste, causes the
  A. quantity of Durrell toothpaste demanded to increase.
  B. quantity of Tomko toothpaste demanded to increase.
  C. demand for Tomko toothpaste to decrease.
  D. demand for Tomko toothpaste to increase.
  E. demand for Durrell toothpaste to increase.

8. In a free market, if the price of a good is below the equilibrium price, then
  A. government needs to set a higher price.
  B. suppliers, dissatisfied with growing inventories, will raise the price.
  C. demanders, wanting to ensure they acquire the good, will bid the price higher.
  D. government needs to set a lower price.
  E. suppliers, dissatisfied with growing inventories, will lower the price.

9. A decrease in supply, holding demand constant, will always result in a(n)
  A. higher equilibrium price.
  B. lower equilibrium price.
  C. larger equilibrium quantity.
  D. larger quantity demanded
  E. indeterminate change in the equilibrium quantity.

10. Increases in the prices firms pay for inputs causes a(n)
    A. decrease in quantity supplied.
    B. increase in supply.
    C. increase in quantity supplied.
    D. decrease in supply.
    E. output prices to fall.

11. When a market is not in equilibrium, then
    A. it is always possible to identify unexploited opportunities.
    B. demanders are dissatisfied with the market.
    C. suppliers are dissatisfied with the market.
    D. government intervention is necessary.
    E. it will have a tendency to remain in disequilibrium.

12. If a market is at point of equilibrium and then demand increases while supply decreases, the change in the equilibrium price is _____ and the change in the equilibrium quantity is _____.
    A. positive; positive.
    B. positive; negative.
    C. positive; indeterminate.
    D. indeterminate; positive.
    E. negative; negative.

13. If the full marginal costs of producing a certain good are greater than the seller's marginal costs, then
    A. the market will produce the socially optimal outcome.
    B. the equilibrium price will reflect the true cost of production.
    C. too little of the good will be produced.
    D. too much of the good will be produced.
    E. the total economic surplus will be maximized.

14. When the demand for a good increases, firms respond by
    A. increasing their supply.
    B. decreasing their costs.
    C. increasing their price.
    D. increasing their quantity supplied.
    E. decreasing their supply.

15. Suppose that at a price of $5, quantity demanded is 700 units and quantity supplied is 300 units. This market will experience a(n) _____ of _____ units.
    A. excess demand, 400 units.
    B. excess supply, –400 units.
    C. excess demand, –400 units.
    D. excess supply, 400 units.
    E. shortage, 400 units.

16. We observe that the equilibrium price of coffee falls and the equilibrium quantity falls. Which of the following best fits the observed data?
   A. an increase in demand with supply constant.
   B. an increase in demand coupled with a decrease in supply.
   C. an increase in demand coupled with an increase in supply.
   D. a decrease in demand with supply constant.
   E. constant demand and an increase in supply.

17. Suppose that the equilibrium price of pickles falls while the equilibrium quantity rises. The most consistent explanation for these observations is a(n)
   A. decrease in demand for pickles with no change in supply.
   B. increase in demand for pickles with no change in supply.
   C. decrease in the supply of pickles and an increase in the demand for pickles.
   D. decrease in the supply of pickles with no change in demand.
   E. increase in the supply of pickles with no change in demand.

18. If a shoe manufacturer discharges toxic liquids into a nearby river without compensating the costs incurred by individuals downstream, the shoe market will
   A. never reach an equilibrium.
   B. reach an equilibrium with the efficient quantity.
   C. reach an equilibrium but not an efficient quantity.
   D. have a lower than socially optimal quantity of shoes.
   E. have a higher than socially optimal price.

19. If the price of good is currently above its equilibrium price, we observe excess _____. As a result, prices will _____ and the quantity of the good exchanged will _____.
   A. supply; decrease; decrease.
   B. supply; decrease; increase.
   C. demand; increase; increase.
   D. demand; increase; decrease.
   E. demand; decrease; increase.

20. If Canada experiences a cold, wet summer followed by a long cold winter, we would expect that the price of $1 Canadian in terms of the Jamaican dollar to
   A. decrease due to an increase in demand for Canadian dollars.
   B. decrease due to an increase in supply of Canadian dollars.
   C. increase due to an increase in demand for Canadian dollars.
   D. increase due to an increase in supply of Canadian dollars.
   E. remain constant.

Self-Test: Short-Answer Problems

(Answers and solutions are given at the end of the chapter.)

1. Demand, Supply, and Market Equilibrium

The following question tests your understanding of quantity demanded, quantity supplied, and market equilibrium applied to the market for memory chips used in personal computers.

Price of a 512 MB SDRAM Memory Chip	Quantity of 512 MB SDRAM Demanded (in millions)	Quantity of 512 MB SDRAM Supplied (in millions)
$ 75	45	6
100	21	11
150	15	15
200	7	23
225	4	36

A. As the price of 512 MB memory chips rises, quantity demanded (rises/falls) _____. When the price of memory chips falls, quantity supplied (increases/decreases) _____.

B. In this market, an equilibrium occurs at a price of _____. At this price, (quantity demanded/demand) _____ equals (quantity supplied/supply) _____ with _____ million units exchanged.

C. At a price of $225, (supply/quantity supplied) _____ exceeds (demand/quantity demanded) _____ by an amount equal to _____ units. The market is, thus, experiencing (excess supply/excess demand) _____. As a result, (producers/consumers) _____ will (lower/raise) _____ the price of memory chips.

D. At a price of $100, (demand/quantity demanded) _____ exceeds (supply/quantity supplied) _____ by an amount equal to _____ units. The market is, thus, experiencing (excess supply/excess demand) _____. As a result, (producers/consumers) _____ will (lower/raise) _____ the price of memory chips.

2. Graphical Analysis of Demand and Supply Curve Shifts

Understanding which variables cause shifts in the demand curve or the supply curve and how these shifts are illustrated in a graph is a major objective of the chapter. The following question helps assess your comprehension of demand and supply shifts.

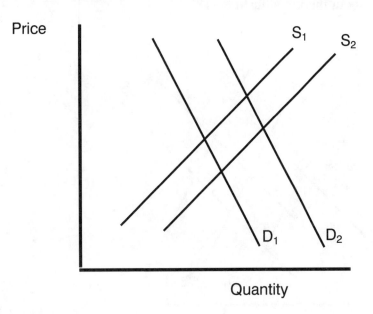

A. A shift from demand curve D_1 to D_2 indicates that (demand/quantity demanded) _____ has (increased/decreased) _____. This shift could be caused by an increase in the price of a (substitute/complement) _____.

B. A shift from supply curve S_2 to S_1 indicates that (supply/quantity supplied) _____ has (increased/decreased) _____. This shift could be caused by an increase in the (price of an input/quality of technology) _____.

3. Changes in Demand/Supply versus Changes in Quantity Demanded/Supplied

To fully understand how markets function, the difference between "changes in demand" and "changes in quantity demanded" must be clear in your mind. A similar distinction applies to supply and must be clear as well. A graph of a market shows the difference most plainly and also allows predictions to be made about market adjustments.

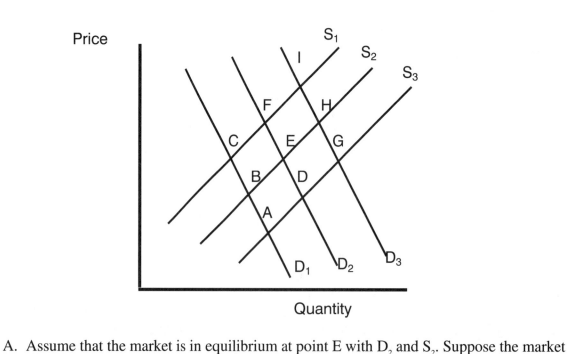

A. Assume that the market is in equilibrium at point E with D_2 and S_2. Suppose the market equilibrium changes to point B. This change reflects a (decrease in demand/decrease in quantity demanded) _____ coupled with a (decrease in supply/decrease in quantity supplied) _____.

B. Assume that the market is in equilibrium at point E with D_2 and S_2. Suppose the market equilibrium changes to point D. This changes stems from an (increase in demand/increase in quantity demanded) _____ combined with an (increase in supply/increase in quantity supplied) _____.

C. Assume that the market is in equilibrium at point H with D_3 and S_2. If demand remains constant and supply decreases, the new equilibrium price will (higher/lower) _____ and the new equilibrium quantity will be (smaller/larger) _____.

D. Assume that the market is in equilibrium at point E with D_2 and S_2. A simultaneous decrease in supply and an increase in demand would move the market to a new equilibrium at point (F/H/I) _____. The equilibrium price (falls/rises) _____ and the equilibrium quantity (falls/rises) _____. Without the aid of the above graph, only the (price/quantity) _____ change is certain to occur.

SOLUTIONS

Quick Quiz

1. E.
2. E.
3. D.
4. C. Whenever there is an excess demand, the actual quantity exchanged in the market will be equal to the amount suppliers are willing to supply at that price. That is, they cannot be forced to sell the amount currently demanded. Therefore, as prices increase, suppliers move up their supply curve, and the amount exchanged in the market increases.
5. D.
6. B.
7. D. Excess supply = (quantity supplied – quantity demanded) = (700 – 300) = 400.
8. A.
9. A. Since you have also received some benefits of your neighbour's landscaping expenses without paying your neighbour (e.g., improved neighbourhood appearance, potentially higher price for your house), the market for landscaping does not capture all the benefits.
10. C.
11. B. Medical report suggesting lower cholesterol levels will influence preferences. Answer E will shift the supply curve and there will be an increase *in quantity demanded* not an increase in demand.
12. D.
13. B.
14. B.
15. A. Individually, we know that increases in demand lead to higher prices and higher output while increases in supply lead to lower prices and higher output. Collectively, we see that equilibrium quantity will increase. In this case, price is indeterminate—we would need to observe the magnitudes of the shifts in order to say whether it has risen, fallen, or remained constant.
16. B. A change in the price of gasoline never causes a change in the *demand* for gasoline; only a change in the *quantity demanded*. However, since gasoline is a complement to SUVs, the higher price of gasoline will decrease demand for SUVs.

Self-Test: Key Terms

1. equilibrium quantity.
2. change in demand.
3. normal good.
4. demand curve.
5. change in quantity supplied.
6. excess demand.
7. market.
8. equilibrium.

9. supply curve.
10. excess supply.
11. inferior good.
12. change in quantity demanded.
13. complements.
14. change in supply.
15. market equilibrium.
16. substitutes.
17. equilibrium price.
18. shortage.
19. foreign exchange.
20. economic efficiency.
21. surplus.
22. efficient quantity.

Self-Test: Multiple-Choice Questions

1. A. As the price of tea increases, the quantity of tea demanded falls. Since sugar is frequently added to tea, the reduced consumption of tea means less sugar will be consumed, regardless of the current price of sugar.
2. C.
3. C. The proper statement is "all consumers *willing and able to pay the equilibrium price* are able to purchase as much as they wish."
4. D.
5. B.
6. C.
7. E.
8. C.
9. A.
10. D.
11. A. Answers D and E are never true. For answers B or C to be correct, one must know if the price is above equilibrium (suppliers are dissatisfied) or below (demanders are dissatisfied). However, when a market is in disequilibrium, one side will be dissatisfied and can identify unexploited opportunities.
12. C. When both supply and demand shift simultaneously, one can predict either the change in the equilibrium price or the equilibrium quantity but not both. In this question, the price change is positive, but the quantity change could be positive, negative, or zero. If you are still having difficulties with this topic, see Short-Answer Problems question 3 for further practice.
13. D. The supply curve, which includes all costs, will be to the left of the supply curve that includes only the seller's costs. As a result, the equilibrium price will be lower than the socially optimal price, and the equilibrium quantity will be larger than the socially optimal amount.
14. D.

15. A. Excess demand = (quantity demanded – quantity supplied) = (700 – 300) = 400.
16. D. If you are having trouble with this question, try drawing a graph.
17. E.   If you are having trouble with this question, try drawing a graph.
18. C.
19. B. Whenever there is an excess supply, the quantity exchanged in the market will be equal to the amount buyers are willing to purchase at that price. That is, they cannot be forced to buy the entire amount supplied. Therefore, as price decreases, buyers move down their demand curve, and the amount exchanged in the market increases.
20. B.

Self-Test: Short-Answer Problems

1. Demand, Supply, and Market Equilibrium.
    A. falls; decreases.
    B. $150; quantity demanded; quantity supplied; 15.
    C. quantity supplied; quantity demanded; (36 – 4) = 32; excess supply; producers; lower.
    D. quantity demanded; quantity supplied; (21 – 11) = 10; excess demand; consumers; raise.

2. Graphical Analysis of Demand and Supply Curve Shifts.
    A. demand; increased; substitute.
    B. supply; decreased; price of an input.

3. Changes in Demand/Supply versus Changes in Quantity Demanded/Supplied.
    A. decrease in demand; decrease in quantity supplied.
    B. increase in quantity demanded; increase in supply.
    C. higher; smaller.
    D. I; rises; rises; price (remember, when both curves shift, only one of the changes must occur—in this case, starting at point **E** and moving to point **I**, price must rise, but quantity could have increased, decreased, or remained constant).

4 Macroeconomics: The Bird's-Eye View of the Economy

OVERVIEW

This chapter introduces the subject matter of macroeconomics, including its central issues and basic analytical tools. Macroeconomics is the study of the performance of national economies and the policies governments use to try to improve that performance. Among the issues macroeconomists study are the sources of long-run economic growth, living standards, unemployment, and inflation. In addition to analyzing the factors that affect the performance of the national economies, macroeconomists also study macroeconomic decision-making, including monetary, fiscal, and structural policies. Finally, macroeconomists use "aggregation" to link individual behaviour to national economic performance.

Chapter Review

4.1 Major Macroeconomic Issues

Important questions which economists try to answer are: What causes economic growth to fluctuate over time, and why do economic growth and the standard of living vary among countries? Why does unemployment rise during periods of recession? Why are there always unemployed people, even when the economy is booming? Why do unemployment rates sometimes differ markedly from country to country? Why does the rate of inflation vary from one period to another, and what causes the rate of inflation to differ markedly among countries? What are the causes of trade surpluses and deficits?

▶ **LO 1.** **Explain economic growth and standard of living.**

Economic growth is a process of increasing the quantity and quality of goods and services that an economy can produce. By standard of living, economists mean the degree to which people have access to goods and services that make their lives easier, healthier, safer, and more enjoyable. People with a higher standard of living have more goods to consume, but even the wealthiest people are subject to the principle of scarcity. Standard of living is inextricably linked to economic growth because the more we produce, the more we can consume. The high standard of living that contemporary Canadians enjoy, for example, is the result of several centuries of economic growth.

▶ **LO 2.** **Calculate output per person and average labour productivity.**

One factor related to economic growth is the growth in population and hence the number of workers available to produce goods and services. Increases in population allow the total output of goods and services to increase. However, because the goods and services must be shared among a larger population, economic growth does not necessarily translate to a higher standard of living. Because of changes in population over time, *output per person* (output divided by the number of people in an economy) is a much better indicator of living standards than total output. Macroeconomists also study the relationship between *average labour productivity* (output divided by the number of employed workers) and living standards. Because of the connection between production and consumption, average labour productivity is closely related to output per person and living standards.

▶ **LO 3.** **Define recession, depression, expansion, and boom.**

Economies do not always grow steadily; they go through periods of unusual strength and weakness. Periods of rapid economic growth are called expansions, and when an expansion is particularly strong, it is called a boom. Pronounced slowdowns in economic growth are called recessions, and particularly severe slowdowns (for example, during the 1930s) are referred to as depressions.

▶ **LO 4.** **Define unemployment rate and explain its relationship to recessions and expansions.**

Fluctuations in the rate of economic growth cause changes in the unemployment rate, which comprises the fraction of the labour force which would like to be employed but cannot find work. Unemployment tends to rise during recessions and fall during expansions. But even during the "good times," some people are unemployed.

▶ **LO 5.** **Define inflation.**

Inflation is another important macroeconomic variable. Inflation explains the rate at which prices in general are increasing over time. Macroeconomists are interested in understanding the causes of inflation. Very high inflation will impose costs on the economy, as does negative inflation (know as deflation). When the inflation rate changes sharply, the distribution of income between borrowers and savers can change. We discuss in more detail the nature and costs of inflation in the chapter on "Measuring the Price Level and Inflation." Inflation and unemployment are often linked in policy discussions because some economists argue that unemployment can only be reduced if the inflation rate is allowed to rise.

► **LO 6.** **Define international trade deficit and trade surplus.**

The international flows of goods and services are both an economic issue and a political issue. Trade imbalances, which occur when the quantity of goods and services that a country sells abroad (its *exports*) differ significantly from the quantity of goods and services its citizens buy from abroad (its *imports*), often cause economic and political problems. When a nation exports more than it imports, it runs a trade surplus, while the reverse results in a trade deficit.

Quick Quiz

1. Economic growth is defined as a process of
    A. steady increase in the price of goods and services produced in the economy.
    B. steady increase in the quantity and quality of goods and services the economy can produce.
    C. constant increase in the quantity and quality of goods and services the economy can produce.
    D. constant decline in the quality of goods and services the economy can produce.
    E. constant increase in the number of jobs needed to produce the goods and service in the economy.

2. Microland has a population of 50 people and 40 of them worked last year, with a total output of $200,000. The average labour productivity of Microland equalled
    A. $200,000.
    B. $200.
    C. $4,000.
    D. $40,000.
    E. $5,000.

3. During the 1930s, economies around the world were in a(n)
    A. recession.
    B. depression.
    C. expansion.
    D. boom.
    E. aggregation.

4. The unemployment rate is the
    A. percentage of labour force that would like to be employed but cannot find work.
    B. number of people who would like to be employed but can find work.
    C. fraction of people who are not working.
    D. number of those in the population who are not working.
    E. number of unemployed people.

5. The inflation rate
   A. was higher in the 1990s than during the 1970s.
   B. increases the standard of living for people on fixed incomes.
   C. is the rate at which prices in general are increasing over time.
   D. is roughly equal in most countries.
   E. rises during recessions along with the unemployment rate.

6. If Macroland sells more goods to foreign buyers than it purchases from them, it will have a
   A. trade balance.
   B. trade deficit.
   C. trade surplus.
   D. budget deficit.
   E. budget surplus.

4.2   Macroeconomic Policies

▶ **LO 7.   Define macroeconomic policy.**

Macroeconomic policies are government actions designed to affect the performance of the economy as a whole. There are three major types of macroeconomic policy: monetary policy, fiscal policy, and structural policy.

▶ **LO 8.   Define monetary, fiscal and structural policy.**

Monetary policy refers to the changing of interest rates by the central bank to achieve macroeconomic objectives. In virtually all countries, monetary policy is controlled by the central bank. *Fiscal policy* refers to decisions that determine government's budget, including the amount and composition of government expenditures and government revenues. The term *structural policy* includes government policies aimed at changing the underlying structure, or institutions, of the nation's economy.

▶ **LO 9.   Explain budget deficit and budget surplus.**

When government expenditures are greater than government revenues, government runs a deficit, and when government revenues are greater than government expenditures, government runs a surplus.

Quick Quiz

7. Monetary policy
   A. refers to decisions that determine government's budget.
   B. is controlled by the Department of Finance only.
   C. is aimed at changing the underlying structure, or institutions, of the nation's economy.
   D. refers to the changes in interest rates by the central bank to achieve macroeconomic objectives.
   E. can result directly in a budget deficit or budget surplus.

8. The amount and composition of government expenditures and government revenues is determined by
   A. fiscal policy.
   B. monetary policy.
   C. structural policy.
   D. normative analysis.
   E. positive analysis.

9. When a government collects more in taxes than it spends, it runs a
   A. trade deficit.
   B. trade surplus.
   C. budget deficit.
   D. budget surplus.
   E. trade imbalance.

4.3 Aggregation

▶ **LO 10.   Define aggregation.**

Aggregation is the adding up of individual economic variables to obtain economywide totals.

▶ **LO 11.   Discuss the strengths and weaknesses of aggregation.**

While aggregation provides a "bird's-eye view" of the economy, it is necessary to suppress certain details one views on a microeconomic or individual level, in order to make sense of the collection of variables.

▶ **LO 12.   Explain how economists aggregate units of goods which are dissimilar.**

In order to assess the value of goods, services, and events which are dissimilar in character, economists have to choose certain common features that tie them together. In addition, it is necessary to avoid the "fallacy of composition," which is the error of assuming that what is true for an individual entity must be true for the whole.

Quick Quiz

10. When macroeconomists add together the purchases of houses, cars, food, clothing, entertainment, and other goods and services by households in an economy in a given year, they are using
    A. microeconomic policy.
    B. economic analysis.
    C. aggregation.
    D. macroeconomic policy.
    E. fiscal policy.

11. The strength of aggregation is that it helps reveal the "big picture," but its major weakness is that it
    A. is involved with the price of individual commodities.
    B. involves the values of the person doing the analysis.
    C. gives excessive importance to details.
    D. does not add together data on different individuals.
    E. may obscure important details.

12. The "fallacy of composition" refers to
    A. inaccurate data used in a study.
    B. falsely assuming that what is true for an individual is true for the whole.
    C. the difficulty in comparing different types of national indicators.
    D. problems arising in Canada when aggregating provincial data.
    E. uncertainty about what population groups to include in national data.

Self-Test: Key Terms

Use the terms below to complete the following sentences . (Answers are given at the end of the chapter.)

aggregation   macroeconomic policy
average labour productivity   monetary policy
fallacy of composition   structural policy
fiscal policy

1. Decisions related to the amount and composition of government expenditures and government revenues determine a nation's _fiscal policy_ .
2. Output divided by the number of employed workers equals _average labour productivity_
3. An important tool that macroeconomists use to link individual behaviour to national economic performance is _aggregation_ .

4. A nation's central bank can alter the amount of the economy's money supply through its control of *monetary policy* .

5. An important objective of macroeconomics is helping government officials develop better *macroeconomic policy* .

6. The move away from government control over the economy and toward a more market-oriented approach in such countries as Poland, the Czech Republic, and Hungary is a large-scale example of *structural policy*.

7. The error of assuming that what is true for the individual agent or firm is applicable to the whole economy is called *fallacy of composition* .

Self-Test: Multiple Choice Questions

Circle the letter that corresponds to the best answer. (Answers are given at the end of the chapter.)

1. Our standard of living is directly tied to economic growth because
   A. everyone in society shares equally in the fruits of economic growth.
   B. the two terms are synonymous.
   C. in most cases, economic growth brings an improvement in the average person's standard of living.
   D. government can only improve people's standard of living if the economy is growing.
   E. a higher standard of living causes an increase in economic growth.

2. The unemployment rate increases during
   A. expansions and booms.
   B. expansions and recessions.
   C. booms and recessions.
   D. recessions and depressions.
   E. booms and depressions.

3. If a country imports more than it exports, it has a(an)
   A. trade balance.
   B. trade deficit.
   C. trade surplus.
   D. budget deficit.
   E. inflation.

4. Government policies that affect the performance of the economy as a whole are called
   A. economic analysis.
   B. budgetary analysis.
   C. aggregation.
   D. microeconomic policy.
   E. macroeconomic policy.

5. Microland has a population of 50 people and 25 of them worked last year with a total output
    of $500,000. The output per person of Microland equalled
    A. $500,000.
    B. $200.
    C. $20,000.
    D. $10,000.
    E. $1,000.

    Out per person = total output / # of people in the economy

6. When a government's expenditures are greater than its revenues, it has a
    A. budget deficit.
    B. budget surplus.
    C. trade deficit.
    D. trade surplus.
    E. trade imbalance.

7. A government decides to convert from a system of government-controlled prices to a free
    market. This is an example of
    A. structural policy.
    B. fiscal policy.
    C. monetary policy.
    D. aggregation.
    E. inflation.

8. During the Great Depression, some officials decided that the federal government should
    decrease public spending, assuming that since it is prudent for individuals in financial trouble
    to decrease spending, it would be good for the nation as a whole. The decreased government
    spending only deepened the depression. This is an example of
    A. aggregation.
    B. deflation.
    C. recession.
    D. fallacy of composition.
    E. monetary policy.

9. The *decisive* factor behind the Great Depression, according to the textbook, was
    A. the 1929 crash of the US stock market.
    B. business cycles.
    C. poor economic policy making.
    D. World War I.
    E. capitalism.

10. The "scarcity problem" refers to
    A. a lack of government tax revenue.
    B. low population density.
    C. inadequate resources to meet all of peoples' needs and wants.
    D. a low rate of financial investments.
    E. a shortage of natural resources in small countries.

11. Output per worker in Canada is now about _____ as high as it was in 1926.
- A. twice.
- B. four times.
- C. five times.
- D. ten times.
- E. eleven times.

12. When labour productivity is measured in terms of output divided by number of workers (rather than by number of *hours* worked), the countries which have relatively higher productivity rates are those with
- A. more women in the labour force.
- B. stronger unions.
- C. a high percentage of agricultural workers.
- D. higher wage rates.
- E. longer working hours.

13. A period of *particularly* strong economic growth is called
- A. a recession.
- B. a recovery.
- C. an explosion.
- D. a boom.
- E. an expansion.

14. During the last 50 years, the highest unemployment rate in Canada was about
- A. 2 percent.
- B. 7 percent.
- C. 12 percent.
- D. 17 percent.
- E. 22 percent.

15. Canada last experienced *deflation*
- A. during the Great Depression.
- B. in the 1980s, after a period of high inflation.
- C. during the recession of 2001.
- D. with the oil shocks in the 1970s.
- E. during World War II.

Self-Test: Short-Answer Problems
(Answers and solutions are given at the end of the chapter.)
1. Economic Growth and the Standard of Living
Use the data in the following table on output, employment, and population in Canada and the United States during 2000 to answer the questions below. Round answers to the nearest dollar.

Economic Variable	Canada	United States
Output (GDP)	$1,056,000 million	$11,760,000 million
Population	30.8 million	275.4 million
Employed persons	14.9 million	135.2 million

Source: Statistics Canada: *Canadian Economic Observer: Summary Statistics*, August 2001.

    A. Output per person in Canada during 2000 equalled *34 286* and in the United States equalled *42 702* .

    B. The average labour productivity in Canada during 2000 equalled *70 872* and in the United States equalled *86 982* .

    C. In general terms and based on the data in the table above, which country had the highest standard of living during 2000? *US* .

NOTE:

As will be discussed in Chapter 6 of the textbook, output per person and average labour productivity are usually taken as rough guides only to a difference in the standard of living.

2. Aggregation

Use the data in the following table on production in Macroland to answer the questions below.

NOTE:

For this question, assume that the population is the same in both years. As will be discussed in Chapter 6, there are a number of other indicators of living standards, such as education levels, mortality rates, and so on. Here, we are using differences in output per capita and output per worker as rough guides to differences in living standards.

Product	Price per Unit	Units Produced in 2002	Units Produced in 2003
Clothing	$ 5	1000	600
Food	2	5000	4000
Houses	100	250	800

    A. Macroland's total output in 2002 equalled *40 000* and in 2003 equalled *91 000* .

    B. Based on your answer to question 3A, in 2003, Macroland produced (more/less) *MORE* output than in 2002.

    C. The change in output from 2002 to 2003 would suggest that the Macroland economy experienced *Growth* , and thus, one could deduce that the Macrolandian standard of living had (improved/worsened) *improved* .

    D. The workers of Macroland are equally divided into three groups each of which specializes in producing a single good (i.e., clothing, food, or houses). Calculate the output produced by each group in 2002 and 2003. The clothing workers produced _____ output in 2002 and _____ in 2003, the food workers produced _____ output in 2002 and _____ in 2003, and the housing workers produced _____ output in 2002 and _____ in 2003.

E. Thus, the output and standard of living of the (clothing/food/housing) _____ workers of Macroland's increased, while the output and standard of living of (clothing/food/housing) _____ and (clothing/food/housing) _____ workers of Macroland's decreased.

F. Thus, the aggregation in question 3A obscures the fact that for a majority of Macroland workers, output and standard of living (decreased/increased) _____ in 2003 compared with 2002.

SOLUTIONS

Quick Quiz

1. B.
2. E Average labour productivity = output/number of employed workers (i.e., $200,000/40 = $5,000).
3. B.
4. A.
5. C.
6. C.
7. D.
8. A.
9. D.
10. C.
11. E.
12. B.

Self-Test: Key Terms

1. fiscal policy
2. average labour productivity
3. aggregation
4. monetary policy
5. macroeconomic policy
6. structural policy
7. fallacy of composition

Self-Test: Multiple Choice

1. C.
2. D.
3. B.
4. E.
5. D Output per person = output/number of people in the economy (i.e., $200,000/50 = $10,000).
6. A.
7. A.
8. D.
9. C.
10. C.
11. B.
12. E.
13. D.
14. C.
15. A.

Self-Test: Short-Answer Problems

1. A. Output per person = Output divided by population $34,286; $42,702.
    B. Average labour productivity = Output divided by the number of employed persons $70,872; $86,982.
    C. The United States has the higher standard of living because both output per person and average labour productivity are higher than in Canada.

2. A. $(1,000 \times \$5) + (5,000 \times \$2) + (250 \times \$100) = \$40,000$;
    B. $(600 \times \$5) + (4,000 \times \$2) + (800 \times \$100) = \$91,000$
    C. more.
    D. economic growth; improved.
    E. $1,000 \times \$5 = \$5,000$; $600 \times \$5 = \$3,000$; $5,000 \times \$2 = \$10,000$; $4,000 \times \$2 = \$8,000$; $250 \times \$100 = \$25,000$; $800 \times \$100 = \$80,000$
    F. housing; clothing; food.
    G. decreased.

5 Measuring Economic Activity: GDP and Unemployment

OVERVIEW

Economists depend on economic data to make accurate diagnoses. Political leaders and policy makers also need economic data to help them in their decisions and planning. This chapter explains how economists measure two basic macroeconomic variables, gross domestic product (GDP) and the rate of unemployment. It also discusses how the measures are used and provides some insight into the debates over the accuracy of the measures.

Chapter Review

5.1 Gross Domestic Product: Measuring the Nation's Output

▶ **LO 1.** **Define GDP and its components.**

The *gross domestic product (GDP)* is the market value of the final goods and services produced in a country during a given period. To calculate GDP, economists aggregate, or add up, the market values of the different goods and services the economy produces. Economists, however, do not include the value of all goods and services in the calculation. Only the market values of *final goods and services*, the goods or services consumed by the ultimate user, are counted as part of GDP. The market values of *intermediate goods and services*, those used up in the production of final goods and services, are not included when calculating GDP because they are already included in the market value of the final goods and services. The distinction between final and intermediate goods is difficult to determine for some goods, for example, capital goods. Newly produced *capital goods*, long-lived goods that are used to produce other goods, are classified as final goods for the purposes of calculating GDP. Because GDP is a measure of domestic production, only goods and services produced within a nation's borders are included in its calculation. Similarly, because GDP is measured for a given period, only goods and services produced during the current year (or the portion of the value produced during the current year) are counted as part of the current year's GDP.

Quick Quiz

1. Which of the following would be included in the calculation of GDP for 1996?
   A. the price of a home built in 1991 and sold in 1996.
   B. the price of 100 shares of Canadian Pacific shares purchased in 1996.
   C. the price of a classic 1960 Thunderbird purchased in 1996.
   D. the price of a new punch press built and purchased in 1996 to replace a worn-out machine.
   E. the price of a used bicycle purchased.

5.2 Methods for Measuring GDP

There are three methods for measuring GDP: (1) by aggregating the value added by each firm in the production process, (2) by adding up the total amount spent on final goods and services and subtracting the amount spent on imported goods and services, and (3) by adding labour income and capital income. The *value added* by any firm equals the market value of its product or service minus the cost of inputs purchased from other firms. The value added by each firm represents the portion of the value of the final good or service that the firm creates in its stage of the production process. Summing the value added by all firms in the economy yields the total value of final goods and services, or GDP.

▶ **LO 2.** **Identify the components of the expenditure method and calculate GDP by this method.**

To calculate GDP using the expenditure method, economic statisticians add together consumption expenditures, private-sector investment, government purchases, and net exports. *Consumption (C)* is spending by households on goods and services. Consumption spending can be divided into three subcategories; (1) consumer durables, long-lived consumer goods, such as cars and furniture; (2) consumer nondurables, shorter-lived goods, such as food and clothing; and (3) services, including everything from haircuts to taxi rides to legal, financial, and educational services. *Private-sector Investment (I)* is spending by firms on final goods and services, primarily capital goods and housing. Private-sector investment is also divided into three subcategories: (1) investment in nonresidential structures and equipment, or nonresidential gross fixed capital formation. This includes business fixed investment, the purchase of new capital goods, such as machinery, factories, and office buildings; (2) residential investment, the construction of new homes and apartment buildings; and (3) inventory investment, changes in the value of unsold goods to company inventories. This change in inventories can be positive or negative. A positive change indicates an addition to inventories in the particular period, wheras if the change is negative, the value of unsold inventories will have decreased during the period. *Government purchases (G)* are purchases of final goods and services by the federal, provincial, and municipal governments. Government purchases do not include transfer payments (payments made by government for which no current goods or services are received), or interest paid on the public debt. In the foreign sector, *net exports (NX)* equal exports minus imports. Exports are domestically produced final goods and services that are sold abroad. Imports are purchases by domestic buyers of goods and services that were produced abroad. Using symbols for each of the components, the algebraic equation for calculating GDP (Y) is: **Y = C + I + G + NX.**

Quick Quiz

2. Which of the following is included when using the expenditure method to measure GDP?
   A. corporate profits.
   B. private-sector investment.
   C. capital income.
   D. net interest on the public debt.
   E. labour income.

5.3   GDP and the Incomes of Capital and Labour

▶ **LO 3.**   **Identify the components of the income method and calculate GDP by this method**

All three methods of measuring GDP result in the same overall value for GDP. The last method, measuring GDP by income, involves identifying the sources of income that are linked to spending in the economy. For example, spending on an automobile could lead, in part, to labour income in wages and salaries for factory and car sales workers; as well, it could lead, in part, to business and investor profits, which is referred to as capital income.

Quick Quiz

3. Which of the following is included when using the labour and capital income method to measure GDP?
   A. government purchases of goods and services.
   B. net exports of goods and services.
   C. personal consumption.
   D. private-sector investment.
   E. business profits.

5.4   Nominal GDP versus Real GDP

▶ **LO 4.**   **Define nominal GDP and Real GDP and calculate Real GDP.**

As a measure of the total production of an economy during a given period, GDP is useful in comparisons of economic activity in different places but cannot be used to make comparisons over time. To make comparisons of production in an economy over time, GDP must be adjusted for inflation. To adjust for inflation, economists differentiate between nominal GDP and real GDP. *Nominal GDP* measures the current dollar value of production, in which the quantities of final goods and services produced are valued at current-year prices. *Real GDP* adjusts nominal GDP for changes in the prices of final goods and services. If prices rise, then the increase in real GDP will be less than the increase in nominal GDP.

Quick Quiz

4. To calculate nominal GDP, the quantities of goods and services are valued at prices in the _____ year, but to calculate real GDP, they are valued at _____-year prices.
    A. current, base.
    B. base; current.
    C. current; current.
    D. base; base.
    E. current; last.

5.5   Real GDP Is Inappropriate as the Sole Economic Goal

▶ **LO 5.**   **Identify the strengths and weaknesses of Real GDP and GNP as indicators.**

We distinguish GDP from GNP. The gross national product is the market value of goods and services produced by factors of production owned by the residents of the country. The difference between GDP and GNP is that the latter includes investment income received by Canadian residents less the payments of profits, dividends, and interest flowing to foreigners. Due, in part, to the high degree of foreign ownership of corporations operating in Canada, the net foreign investment income figure has been negative, and so GNP has been less than GDP for Canada.

While economists and policy makers often assume that a higher GDP is better, real GDP is not intended to be a measure economic well-being. With the major exception of government-produced goods and services, real GDP captures only those goods and services that are priced and sold in markets. There are many factors that contribute to people's economic well-being that are not priced and sold in markets. Thus, at best, it is an imperfect measure of economic well-being. Some important factors that are excluded from real GDP are leisure time; environmental quality; resource depletion; nonmarket activities, such as volunteer services, home-grown foods, homemaker services, and underground economic activities from informal babysitting to organized crime; "quality of life" issues, such as crime, traffic congestion, civic organization, and open space; and income inequality. Clearly, in evaluating the effects of a proposed economic policy, considering only the likely effects on GDP is not sufficient. The correct way is to apply the cost-benefit principle. Nevertheless, real GDP per person does tend to be positively associated with many things people value, including a high material standard of living, better health and life expectancies, and better education.

Quick Quiz

5. GDP would be a better measure of economic well-being if it included
   A. the costs of education.
   B. the total value of intermediate goods.
   C. the market value of final goods.
   D. the sales of corporate shares.
   E. leisure.

5.6 But Real GDP per Capita Is Related to Living Standards

▶ **LO 6.** **Explain why per capita income reflects people's standards of living.**

Real GDP per capita tends to be positively associated with indicators of a higher standard of living, including such factors as improved health, longer life expectancy, lower infant mortality, and higher enrollment rates in school.

5.7 Quick Quiz

6. Which of the following is NOT a basic indicator of international living standards?
   A. life expectancy.
   B. infant mortality rate.
   C. number of vehicles owned.
   D. doctors per 100,000 people.
   E. female enrollment in secondary school.

5.7 The Unemployment Rate

▶ **LO 7.** **Explain and calculate the unemployment rate and the participation rate.**

A second macroeconomic measure that receives a great deal of attention from economists and policy makers, as well as the general public, is the rate of unemployment. In Canada, the unemployment rate is calculated by Statistics Canada by means of the monthly Labour Force Survey. Each person in those households selected who is 15 years and older is placed in one of three categories: employed, unemployed, or not in the labour force. A person is employed if he or she worked full time or part time during the week preceding the survey or is on vacation or sick leave from a regular job. A person is unemployed if he or she did not work during the week preceding the survey but made some effort to find work during the previous four weeks. All other persons are considered not in the labour force. To calculate the unemployment rate, Statistics Canada first calculates the total number of employed and unemployed people in the economy to determine the size of the labour force. The unemployment rate is then defined as the number of unemployed people divided by the labour force and expressed as a percentage. Another useful statistic calculated by Statistics Canada is the *participation rate*, or the ratio of the labour force to the population 15 years of age and older, or the proportion of the working-age population that is in the labour force.

▶ **LO 8.** **Discuss the costs of unemployment.**

Unemployment imposes economic, psychological, and social costs on a nation. The main economic cost, borne by both the unemployed individuals and society, is the output that is lost because the workforce is not fully utilized. The psychological costs of unemployment are felt primarily by the unemployed workers and their families and include loss of self-esteem, feelings of loss of control over one's life, depression, and suicidal behaviour. The social costs, borne by both the unemployed individuals and society, include increases in crime, domestic violence, drug abuse, and other social problems. Thus, long spells of unemployment can be especially detrimental.

▶ **LO 9.** **Discuss criticisms of the unemployment rate.**

The official rate of unemployment published by Statistics Canada is calculated in accordance with international guidelines. But the official rate has been criticized, primarily for ignoring discouraged workers and involuntary part-time workers. *Discouraged workers* are people who say they would like to have a job but have not made an effort to find one in the past four weeks. Involuntary part-time workers are people who say they would like to work full time but are able to find only part-time work. Statistics Canada has responded to criticisms of the official unemployment rate by publishing supplementary measures that adjust the official rate for the underutilization of labour associated with discouraged workers and involuntary part-time workers. But movements in the supplementary measures are similar to movements in the official rate.

Quick Quiz

7. The official unemployment rate is calculated as
   A. the number of working-age people 15 years or older who are employed divided by the number of people in the labour force.
   B. all people 18 years of age or older who are employed plus all those unemployed who are actively seeking work.
   C. the percentage of the working-age population 15 years or older who are not working but are actively seeking work.
   D. the number of people 15 years and older who are not employed and are actively seeking work divided by the number of people in the labour force.
   E. all people 15 years of age or older who are employed plus all those unemployed who are actively seeking work, divided by the number of people in the labour force.

8. From an economic perspective, the main cost of unemployment is
   A. increased crime, domestic violence, alcoholism, and drug abuse.
   B. the opportunity cost of lost output and income because the labour force is not fully employed.
   C. increased stress, loss of self-esteem, and deterioration in the workers skills from lack of use.
   D. workers' loss of income and control over their lives.
   E. the increase in the cost of social programs to combat increased crime, alcoholism, drug abuse, and other social problems.

9. The accuracy of the official unemployment rate is criticized because
   A. unemployed homemakers and students who are not actively seeking employment are not included in the number of unemployed people.
   B. people who would like to work but have given up trying to find work are not included in the number of unemployed people.
   C. it fails to indicate how many people work at more than one job.
   D. people less than 15 years of age and over 70 years of age are excluded from the data.
   E. the Statistics Canada survey does not include all the households in Canada.

Self-Test: Key Terms

Use the terms below to complete the following sentences. (Answers are given at the end of the chapter.)

capital good	labour force
consumption	net exports
discouraged workers	nominal GDP
final goods and services	participation rate
government purchases	private-sector investment
GDP deflator	real GDP
gross domestic product (GDP)	unemployment rate
gross national product (GNP)	value added
intermediate goods and services	

1. Purchases of final goods by the federal, provincial, and municipal governments are included in the expenditure method of calculating GDP as _____ .

2. Dividing the number of people in the labour force by the working-age population equals the

   _____ .

3. Exports minus imports equals _____ .

4. To compare a nation's production over time, economists calculate _____ .

5. To calculate GDP, economists include the market value of _____ but exclude the market value of _____goods and services.

6. Statistics Canada adds together the total number of employed and unemployed people in the economy to determine the size of the _____.

7. The market value of a firm's product or service minus the cost of inputs purchased from other firms equals the firm's _____ .

8. Some critics have argued that a more accurate picture of the labour market would be achieved if _____ were counted as unemployed.

9. When valuing the quantities of final goods and services produced in an economy at current-year prices, we are calculating _____ .

10. In the expenditure method of calculating GDP, inventory expenditure is included as _____spending.

11. The largest component in the expenditure method of calculating GDP is _____ .

12. Despite the fact that it is not exactly a final good nor an intermediate good, economists conventionally classify a newly produced _____ as a final good for the purpose of calculating GDP.

13. The market value of the final goods and services produced in a country during a given period is the definition of _____. If we subtract net foreign investment income from this figure, we have _____.

14. The number of unemployed people divided by the labour force equals the _____ .

15. When nominal GDP is adjusted for changes in the general price level, we have _____ .

16. A measure of the price level of goods and services included in GDP is the _____ .

Self-Test: Multiple Choice

1. Which of the following is an intermediate good and, therefore, would be excluded from the calculation of GDP?
   A. a new set of tires sold to a car owner.
   B. a new set of tires purchased by Ford to install on a new Explorer.
   C. 100 shares in Microsoft.
   D. a new home.
   E. a preowned automobile.

2. The value-added method eliminates the problem of
   A. differentiating between final and intermediate goods and services.
   B. inflation when comparing GDP over time.
   C. determining whether capital is a final good or intermediate good.
   D. double-counting intermediate goods.
   E. aggregation.

3. Consumption is subdivided into several categories, including
   A. consumer durables, semidurables and nondurables, and new homes.
   B. consumer services, consumer durables and semidurables, and new homes.
   C. consumer durables, consumer semidurables and consumer nondurables, and services.
   D. exports, imports, consumer durables, and services.
   E. consumer durables, consumer nondurables, services, and net exports.

4. If the value of imports is greater than the value of exports, then
   A. net exports are negative.
   B. net exports are positive.
   C. net exports are zero.
   D. net exports are not, under such circumstances, included in the calculation of GDP.
   E. net exports cannot be determined from the information provided.

5. One shortcoming of GDP by income as a measure of production is that it fails to measure the
   A. growth in productivity.
   B. increase in the quantity of goods.
   C. underground activity.
   D. change in the price level.
   E. increase in the number of imported goods.

6. Real GDP is GDP adjusted for
   A. changes in the quality of goods and services.
   B. value added during a previous year.
   C. price changes over time.
   D. imports.
   E. changes in the cost of intermediate goods and services.

7. In the monthly survey conducted by Statistics Canada, a person who was not working and was not actively seeking work during the last four weeks is classified as
   A. employed.
   B. unemployed.
   C. underemployed.
   D. part-time employed.
   E. not a member of the labour force.

8. The cost of unemployment that is almost exclusively borne by workers and their families is the _____ cost.
   A. economic.
   B. social.
   C. psychological.
   D. historical.
   E. total.

9. The participation rate is
   A. the number of people actively looking for work during the period of the survey.
   B. the ratio of the number of people unemployed to the total population.
   C. the labour force as a percentage of the population 15 years of age and older.
   D. the number of discouraged workers relative to the labour force population.
   E. the number employed.

10. The unemployment rate
   A. rises during recessions.
   B. falls during recessions as does the level of GDP.
   C. is a period during which an individual is continuously unemployed.
   D. is shorter for the chronically unemployed than it is for the long-term unemployed.
   E. is of less importance to macroeconomics than the costs of unemployment.

11. Government transfer payments enter the government budget
   A. and are included in the expenditure method of GDP.
   B. and are included in the value-added approach to GDP.
   C. but are not part of government current purchases for purposes of national income accounting.
   D. and are included in current nominal GDP, since they are payments for current production.
   E. and are included in real GDP as part of base-year production.

12. Real GDP per person is associated with indicators of living standards because it tends to be positively associated with
   A. crime, pollution, and economic inequality.
   B. better education, health, and life expectancy.
   C. poverty, depletion of nonrenewable resources, and congestion.
   D. unemployment, availability of goods and services, and better education.
   E. a lower quantity of goods and services available.

13. Home gardening which goes toward the households' own subsistence
   A. is counted as consumption in GDP by expenditure.
   B. is counted as wages and salaries in GDP by income.
   C. is a nonmarket activity, not counted in the GDP.
   D. comprises a major proportion of the GDP in Canada.
   E. is of no interest in valuing economic activity.

14. In the case of a loaf of bread you buy at the grocery store,
   A. only the value of the bread is included in the GDP.
   B. only the value of the flour and the loaf of bread are included in the GDP.
   C. the wheat and the flour used to make the bread, as well as the loaf of bread, are included in the GDP.
   D. only the value of the wheat and the flour are included in the GDP.
   E. only activities resulting in wage income are included in the GDP.

15. The purchase of a new house is included as
   A. a consumption durable in GDP by expenditure.
   B. investment in GDP by expenditure.
   C. only the costs of materials in GDP by expenditure, since wages and salaries fall under GDP by income.
   D. a consumption semidurable in GDP by expenditure.
   E. a value-added item under consumption.

16. Capital consumption allowances relate to
   A. business investments in new machinery.
   B. capital that is used up during the process of production.
   C. financial capital used in new investments.
   D. depreciation of fixed capital.
   E. capital that is used by consumers, for example, in home carpentry.

17. Nominal GDP is measured using
   A. rolling averages of prices.
   B. base-year prices.
   C. constant prices.
   D. deflated prices.
   E. current prices.

18. The GDP deflator may be calculated by
   A. multiplying nominal GDP by real GDP.
   B. dividing nominal GDP by real GDP, times 100.
   C. multiplying real GDP by 100.
   D. dividing real GDP by nominal GDP, times 100.
   E. dividing constant prices by current prices.

19. Canadian "gross national product" would include
   A. the same things as GDP.
   B. the value of all goods and services produced on Canadian soil.
   C. the value of goods and services by production factors owned by Canadians.
   D. the value of all Canadian intermediate goods.
   E. the value of all purchases by the Government of Canada.

20. "Involuntary part-time workers" are
   A. people who would rather not be working by are forced to take a part-time job.
   B. people who were only employed part of the year.
   C. people with seasonal work.
   D. people forced to work, such as military reservists and prisoners.
   E. people who would like to work full time but are only able to find part-time work.

Self-Test: Short-Answer Problems

1. The Expenditure Approach to GDP
This problem will give you practice calculating GDP using the expenditure method. From the data in the following table, answer the questions below:

Expenditure Components	Year 2001($ Billions)
Nonresidential structures	52.0
Machinery and equipment	84.6
Durable goods	84.0
Exports	469.4
Government current expenditure on goods and services	199.8
Imports	413.7
Business investment in Inventories	-6.0
Nondurable goods	148.0
Residential structures	51.7
Services	333.3
Semidurable goods	54.6
Government gross fixed capital formation and inventories	26.4
Statistical Discrepancy	0.3

Source: Statistics Canada: *Gross Domestic Product, Expenditure-Based*. Web site:
http://www.statcan.ca/english/Pgdb/Economy/Economic/econ04.htm

   A. Total consumption spending in the Canadian economy during the year 2001 equalled
      $_____ billions.
   B. Total investment spending in the Canadian economy during the year 2001 equalled
      $_____billions.
   C. Net export spending in the Canadian economy during the year 2001 equalled $_____
      billions.
   D. Total government purchases in the Canadian economy during the year 2001 equalled
      $_____ billions.
   E. The expenditure method of calculating GDP indicates that Gross Domestic Product for the
      Canadian economy during the year 2001 equalled $ _____ billions.

2. The Income Approach to GDP

This problem will give you practice calculating GDP using the income approach. Use the data in the following table to answer the questions below.

Income Components	Year 2001 ($ Billions)
Wages and salaries*	559.1
Corporate profits (and inventory adjustment)	119.4
Interest and investment income	53.5
Unincorporated enterprise profits**	78.5
Taxes and subsidies on factors	56.2
Taxes and subsidies on products	75.3
Capital Consumption Allowance (CCA)	142.5
Statistical discrepancy	0.3

Source: Statistics Canada: *Gross Domestic Product, Income-Based.*
http://www.statcan.ca/English/Pgdb/Economy/Economic/econ03.htm
   *Includes supplementary labour income.
   **Includes Unincorporated Business profits ($65.7 billions), farm profits ($3 billions),
      and government enterprise profits ($9.8 billions).

A. The net domestic income at basic prices for the year 2001 is $_____billions.
B. The income method indicates that GDP (at market prices) for the Canadian economy during the year 2001 equalled $ _____ billions.
C. Net Domestic Product (NDP) in 2001 is $_____billions.
D. Suppose that Gross National Product (GNP) at market prices is $ 1056.8 billions for 2001. The difference between GDP above and GNP for 2001 of $ _____billions is the item _____.

3. Nominal and Real GDP

This problem will give you practice calculating GDP using the value-added method and adjusting nominal GDP to calculate real GDP using base-year price weights.

A. Mr. Jones harvested logs (with no inputs from other companies) from his property in British Columbia that he sold to Fraser Mill for $1,500. The Fraser Mill cut and planed the logs into lumber and sold it for $4,000 to the Mesa Company. The Mesa Company used the lumber in producing 100 tables that they sold to customers for $70 each. Complete the table below to calculate the value added by each firm.

Company	Revenues	Cost of Purchased Inputs	Value Added
Mr. Jones			
Fraser Mill			
Mesa Company			

The total value added in the production of the tables equals $_____. This is equal to the _____ of the 100 tables.

B. If Mr. Jones had harvested the logs in October 2000 but did not sell them to the Fraser Mill until January 2001, which then sold the lumber to Mesa Company that produced the tables in June 2001, the contribution to GDP in 2000 would equal $ _____ and in 2001 would equal $ _____ .

C. The nation of Mandar specializes in the production of various types of vehicles involved in transportation. The table below provides data on the prices and quantities of the vehicles produced in 2001 and in 2005. Assume that 2001 is the base year. In 2001, nominal GDP equals $_____, and in 2005, it equals $_____. In 2001, real GDP equals $_____, and in 2005, it equals $_____.

This question, which is unrelated to parts A, B, and C, gives you practice in the basic concepts involved in calculating real and nominal GDP.

	Bicycles		Automobiles		Trucks	
Year	Quantity	Price	Quantity	Price	Quantity	Price
2001	1,000	$50	100	$10,000	400	$15,000
2005	1,500	$60	50	$12,500	500	$15,000

4. Measures of Employment

This problem will give you practice in calculating employment measures. Use the data in the following table to answer the questions below. (The figures are in '000s).

Year	Employed	Unemployed	Not in Labour Force	Working - Age Population	Labour Force	Unemployment Rate (%)	Participation Rate (%)
1996	13,676	1,469	5,927				
1997	13,941	1,413	6,160				
1998	14,410	1,278	8,266				
1999	14,531	1,190	8,244				
2000	14,910	1,089	8,278				
2001	15,077	1,170	8,372				

Source: Statistics Canada: *Canadian Economic Observer*, Statistical Summary, August, 2001. (Catalogue no. 11-010-XPB) Table 8. Update for 2001 from Statistics Canada's Web site: http://www.statcan.ca/english/Pgdb/Economy/Economic/econ10.htm

A. Calculate the working-age population for 1996 through 2001 to complete the fifth column of the table.

B. Calculate the size of the labour force for 1996 through 2001 to complete the sixth column of the table.

C. Calculate the official unemployment rate for 1996 through 2001 to complete the seventh column of the table. (Round your answers to the nearest tenth of a percent.)

D. Calculate the participation rate for 1996 through 2001 to complete eighth column of the table. (Round your answers to the nearest tenth of a percent.)

SOLUTIONS

Quick Quiz

1. D. The punch press is a newly produced capital.
2. B.
3. E. Profit is a component of capital income.
4. A.
5. E.
6. C.
7. D.
8. B.
9. B.

Self-Test: Key Terms

1. government purchases.
2. participation rate.
3. net exports
4. real GDP.
5. final goods and services; intermediate goods and services.
6. labour force.
7. value added.
8. discouraged workers.
9. nominal GDP.
10. private-sector investment.
11. consumption expenditure.
12. capital good.
13. gross domestic product (GDP) (nominal); gross national product (GNP).
14. unemployment rate.
15. real GDP.
16. GDP deflator.

Self-Test: Multiple-Choice Questions

1. B. The set of tires was purchased to be used in the production of an Explorer (i.e., an intermediate good) and, therefore, is not included in GDP.
2. D.
3. C.
4. A.

5. C.
6. C.
7. E.
8. C.
9. C.
10. A.
11. C.
12. B.
13. C.
14. A.
15. B.
16. D.
17. E.
18. B.
19. C.
20. E.

Self-Test: Short-Answer Problems

1. A. $84.0 + 54.6 + 148.0 + 333.3 = \$619.9$ billions.
   B. $52.0 + + 84.6 + (- 6.0) + 51.7 = \$182.3$ billions.
   C. $469.4 - 413.7 = \$55.7$ billions.
   D. $199.8 + 26.4 = \$226.2$ billions.
   E. $619.9 + 182.3 + 226.2 + 55.7 = \$1,084.1$ billions.

2. A. NDP at basic prices is $559.1 + 119.4 + 78.5 + 53.5 + 56.2 = \$866.7$ billions.
   B. GDP at market prices $= \$866.6 + 75.3 + 142.5 - 0.3 = \$1084.1$ billions.
   C. NDP at market prices $= \$1084.1 - 142.5 = \$941.6$ billions $=$ GDP at market prices less capital consumption allowance.
   D. $1084.1 - \$1056.8 = \$27.3$ billions. [GDP – GNP = net foreign investment income. Thus, for Canada, GNP – (– 27.3) = GDP or 1056.8 – (–27.3) = 1084.1 billions.]
   [Note, slight discrepancies between the figures in questions 1 and 2 and in the Statistics Canada tables are due to rounding.]

3. A.

Company	Revenues	Cost of Purchased Inputs	Value Added
Mr. Jones	$1,500	$0	1,500
Fraser Mill	$4,000	$1,500	$2,500
Mesa Company	$7,000	$4,000	$3,000

   B. $7,000; total market value.
   C. $1,500; $2,500 + $3,000 = $5,500.
   D. Nominal GDP in 2001 is $(1,000 \times \$50) + (100 \times \$10,000) + (400 \times \$15,000) = \$7,050,000$;

Nominal GDP in 2005 is (1,500 × $60) + (50 × $12,500) + (500 × $15,000) = $8,215,000;
Real GDP in 2001 is (1,000 × $50) + (100 × $10,000) + (400 × $15,000) = $7,050,000;
Real GDP in 2005 is (1,500 × $50) + (50 × $10,000) + (500 × $15,000) = $8,075,000.

4. (Note that the figures in the table and the answers for this question are in '000s).
   A. Working-age population = number of persons employed + number of persons unemployed + number of persons not in the labour force. (For example, 2000: 14,910 + 1,089 + 8,278 = 24,277).
   B. Labour force = number of persons employed + number of persons unemployed. (For example, 2000: 14,910 + 1,089 = 15,999).
   C. Unemployment rate = (number of persons unemployed divided by number of persons not in the labour force) times 100. (For example, 2000: (1,089 × 15,999) × 100 = 6.8%).
   D. Participation rate = (the labour force as a percentage of the population 15 years of age and older) times 100. (For example, 2000: (15,999 × 24,277) × 100 = 65.9%).

Year	Employed	Unemployed	Not in Labour Force	Working-Age Population	Labour Force	Unemployment Rate (%)	Participation Rate (%)
1996	13,676	1,469	5,927	21,072	15,145	9.7	71.9
1997	13,941	1,413	6,160	21,514	15,354	9.2	71.4
1998	14,140	1,278	8,266	23684	15,418	8.2	65.5
1999	14,531	1,190	8,244	23,965	15,721	7.6	65.6
2000	14,910	1,089	8,278	24,277	15,999	6.8	65.9
2001	15,077	1,170	8,372	24,619	16,247	7.2	66.0

6 Measuring the Price Level and Inflation

OVERVIEW

The topics discussed are measurement of the general price level, adjustment of nominal dollar amounts to eliminate the effects of inflation, use of a price index to maintain the constant real value of a variable, distinction between nominal and real interest rates, types of price changes, and the consequences of various types of inflation.

Chapter Review

6.1   The Consumer Price Index: Measuring the Price Level

▶ **LO 1.**   **Define price index, consumer price index, inflation, and deflation.**

The basic tool economists use to measure the price level and inflation in the Canadian economy is the consumer price index, or the CPI. The CPI is a *price index*, a measure of the average price of a given class of goods and services relative to the price of the same goods and services in a base year.

▶ **LO 2.**   **Explain how the Consumer Price Index is measured.**

The *consumer price index* measures the cost, for any period, of a standard basket of goods and services relative to the cost of the same basket of goods and services in a fixed year, called the base year. Statistics Canada determines the goods and services to include in the standard basket from family expenditure surveys. Then each month, thousands of stores are surveyed to determine the current prices of the goods and services. The formula for calculating the CPI is "cost of the base-year basket of goods and services in the current year" divided by the "cost of the base-year basket of goods and services in the base year."

Quick Quiz

1. The Consumer Price Index is a measure of the change in prices of
   A. a standard basket of all goods and services.
   B. a standard basket of goods determined by family expenditure surveys.
   C. a standard basket of agricultural goods determined by the agricultural expenditure surveys.
   D. a standard basket of selected items in wholesale markets.
   E. a standard basket of machinery, tools, and new plant.

2. A price index is a measure of
   A. a list of prices in a given year relative to the list of prices in a base year.
   B. the cost of a given goods and/or services in a base year.
   C. the average price of given goods and/or services relative to the price in the base year.
   D. price changes of given goods and/or services over the course of a year.
   E. the average goods and/or services purchased and how much they cost.

6.2   Inflation

▶ **LO 3**   **Define inflation, rates of inflation and deflation, and calculate the rate of inflation from price indices.**

Inflation measures how fast the average price level is changing over time. The *rate of inflation* is defined as the annual percentage rate of change in the price level as measured, for example, by the CPI. To calculate the inflation rate, we take the change in the price level from one time period to another divided by the price level in the initial time period. *Deflation* is a situation in which the prices of most goods and services are falling over time so that the rate of inflation is negative.

Quick Quiz

3. Inflation exists when
   A. and only when the prices of all goods and services are rising.
   B. the purchasing power of money is increasing.
   C. the average price level is rising, although some prices may be falling.
   D. the prices of basic necessities are increasing.
   E. wages and the price of oil are rising.

6.3 Adjusting for Inflation

► **LO 4.**   **Calculate a real quantity from a nominal quantity, and vice versa.**

The CPI not only allows us to measure changes in the cost of living but can also be used to adjust economic data to eliminate the effects of inflation, a process called *deflating*. To adjust *nominal quantity*, a quantity that is measured at its current dollar value, we divide the nominal quantity by a price index for the period. The adjusted value is called a *real quantity*, that is, a quantity measured in physical terms. Such real quantities are also sometimes referred to as inflation-adjusted quantities. For example, nominal wages for two different periods can be adjusted using the CPI to determine the change in real wages over time. The *real wage* is the wage paid to workers measured in terms of real purchasing power. To calculate the real wage, we divide the nominal (dollar) wage by the CPI for that period. The CPI can also be used to convert real quantities to nominal quantities. The practice of increasing a nominal quantity according to changes in a price index in order to prevent inflation from eroding purchasing power is called *indexing*. For example, some labour contracts provide for indexing of wages, using the CPI, in later years of a contract period.

► **LO 5.**   **Compare deflating using the CPI versus the GDP deflator.**

In addition to the CPI, sometimes the GDP deflator is used. It is a price index for all the goods and services included in the GDP. Over long periods of time, it will generally make little difference whether one deflates with the CPI or with the GDP deflator. Because they include different things, there can be substantial differences between the CPI and the GDP deflator from year to year or between quarters.

Quick Quiz

4. When comparing the money wages of today's workers to money wages workers earned 10 years ago, it is necessary to adjust the nominal wages by
   A. indexing the money wages in each period to today's price index.
   B. deflating the money wages in each period with today's price index.
   C. indexing the money wages in each period with the price indexes of the respective periods.
   D. deflating the money wages in each period with the price indexes of the respective periods.
   E. deflating the money wages in each period with the price index of the past period.

5. The "GDP deflator" is
   A. a price index for all the goods and services making up GDP.
   B. a measure of the change of prices from year to year.
   C. the same as the CPI, except that it uses a different base year.
   D. used when prices are falling.
   E. very different in the long run from the CPI.

6.4   Nominal versus Real Interest Rates

▶ **LO 6.   Define nominal and real interest rates.**

An important aspect of inflation is its effect on interest rates. To understand the relationship between inflation and interest rates, economists differentiate between the nominal interest rate and the real interest rate. The *nominal interest rate* (also called the market interest rate) is the annual percentage increase in the nominal value of a financial asset. The *real interest rate* is the annual percentage increase in the purchasing power of a financial asset and is equal to the nominal interest rate minus the inflation rate.

▶ **LO 7.   Discuss the relationship between anticipated inflation and interest rates.**

To obtain a given real interest rate, lenders must charge a higher nominal interest rate as the inflation rate rises. This tendency for nominal interest rates to rise when the inflation rate increases is called the *Fisher effect.* This tendency is linked to expectations. If the outcome is as people expect, then economists refer to the outcome as *anticipated*, otherwise the outcome is *unanticipated*. Nominal interest rates will be high if anticipated inflation is also high.

Quick quiz

6. The real interest rate can be written in mathematical terms as
    A. $r = i - \pi$.
    B. $r = \pi - I$.
    C. $r = i + \pi$.
    D. $r = \pi + I$.
    E. $r = i / \pi$.

7. The Fisher effect is explained by the fact that
    A. borrowers want to maintain the same real rate of interest.
    B. commercial banks insist on standard interest rates.
    C. most inflation is unanticipated.
    D. high nominal interest rates cause higher prices.
    E. lenders want to maintain the same real rate of interest.

6.5   Controversy over the "True" Inflation Rate

▶ **LO 8.   Define "quantity adjustment bias" and "substitution bias."**

Using the CPI to measure inflation has not been without controversy. Because the CPI has been used to index Social Security benefits, the U.S. government commissioned a report on the subject. The Boskin Commission concluded that the official CPI inflation overstates the true inflation rate by as much as 1 to 2 percent per year. The CPI may overstate inflation because of the quality adjustment bias and the substitution bias.

Quick Quiz

8. The Boskin Commission reported that the official inflation rate, based on the CPI, might overstate true inflation. It identified two reasons, including the
    A. quality adjustment bias and the indexing bias.
    B. quality adjustment bias and substitution bias.
    C. substitution bias and the indexing bias.
    D. quality adjustment bias and the deflation bias.
    E. indexing bias and deflation bias.

6.6 Types of Price Changes

▶ **LO 9. Define types of price changes and inflation.**

To understand the consequences of inflation, we need to distinguish between the price level and the relative price of a good or service. The *price level* is a measure of the overall level of prices in the economy at a particular point in time, as measured by a price index (e.g., the CPI). The *relative price* of a specific good or service is its price in comparison with the prices of other goods and services. Inflation is an increase in the overall price level, not an increase in the relative price of a good or service.

In describing the overall price changes, economists distinguish between zero inflation, stable inflation, accelerating inflation, and disinflation:
*   With *zero inflation*, **the price level stays roughly constant from one year to the next.**
*   **If the economy is characterized by** *stable inflation*, **the inflation rate stays constant from one year to the next.**
*   **If the rate of inflation rises from one year to the next, there is** *accelerating inflation*, **while we have** *disinflation* **if the rate of inflation falls from one year to the next.**

There are also terms to distinguish the differing intensity of inflation:
*   *Low inflation* usually refers to inflation between 1 and 3 percent per year.
*   *Moderate inflation* sees rates in the range of 3 to 6 percent per year.
*   *High inflation* is characterized by inflation greater than 6 percent.
*   *Hyperinflation* typically refers to rates greater than 500 percent per year.

Quick Quiz

9. If the Consumer Price Index is 135 at the end of 2001 and at the end of 2002 it is 142, then during 2002, the economy experienced
   A. accelerating inflation.
   B. moderate inflation.
   C. hyperinflation.
   D. indexing.
   E. low inflation.

6.7 The Economic Consequences of Various Types of Inflation

▶ **LO 10. Explain the income effects of unanticipated and anticipated inflation.**

Inflation creates "noise" in the price system that obscures the information transmitted by prices, reduces the efficiency of the market system, and imposes costs on the economy. Similarly, inflation produces unintended changes in the tax people pay and distorts the incentives in the tax system that may encourage people to work, save, and invest. Another concern about inflation is that if it is unanticipated, it arbitrarily redistributes wealth from one group to another (e.g., between lenders and borrowers and between workers and employers). As a result, a high inflation economy encourages people to use resources in trying to anticipate inflation to protect themselves against losses of wealth.

▶ **LO 11. Discuss the effects of inflation on economic growth.**

Another cost of inflation is its tendency to interfere with the long-run planning of households and firms. These effects follow from the *price signal distortion hypothesis,* and are a basis for zero or low inflation. Other economists favour moderate inflation. Where it is believed that low inflation hampers flexibility of real wages, we have the *downward nominal wage rigidity hypothesis.* The second argument for moderate inflation is based on the *zero bound on nominal interest rates hypothesis.*

While any inflation imposes some costs on the economy, *hyperinflation,* a situation in which the inflation rate is extremely high, greatly magnifies the costs. When an economy suffers from hyperinflation, there are serious consequences for economic growth. Transaction costs, such as shoe-leather costs and menu costs, increase. It is widely accepted that macroeconomic policy should avoid the extremes of deflation and hyperinflation. The latter has often led to economic collapse. High and accelerating inflation should also be avoided.

Quick Quiz

10. If, in a given period, the rate of inflation turns out to be lower than lenders and borrowers anticipated, the effect is that
   A. the real payments by the borrowers will be lower than expected.
   B. the nominal income of lenders will be higher than expected, but their real income will be lower than expected.
   C. the nominal income of the lenders will be as expected, but their real income will be higher than expected.
   D. both the nominal and real income of lenders will be higher than expected.
   E. the real income of lenders will be higher than expected, but their nominal income will be lower than expected.

11. The claim that the central bank may be unable to stimulate the economy with interest rate cuts if the official interest rate is low to begin with is known as
   A. the zero bound on the nominal interest rate hypothesis.
   B. the downward nominal price rigidity hypothesis.
   C. the downward nominal wage rigidity hypothesis.
   D. the zero bound on the real interest rate hypothesis.
   E. a substitution bias.

Self-Test: Key Terms

Use the terms below to complete the following sentences. (Answers are given at the end of the chapter.)

accelerating inflation
anticipated inflation
consumer price index (CPI)
deflating (a nominal quantity)
deflation
disinflation
downward nominal wage rigidity
   hypothesis
Fisher effect
high inflation
hyperinflation
indexing
low inflation
moderate inflation

nominal interest rate
nominal quantity
price index
price signal distortion hypothesis
price level
rate of inflation
real interest rate
real quantity
real wage
relative price
stable inflation
unanticipated inflation
zero bound on nominal interest rate hypothesis
zero inflation

1. Economists measure the change in the average price of a given class of goods or services relative to the price of the same goods and services in a base year by calculating a _____.

2. The tendency for nominal interest rates to rise when the inflation rate increases is called the _____.

3. Inflation is an increase in the overall _____, not an increase in the _____ of a good or service.

4. When the rate of inflation is negative, there is _____.

5. Some labour contracts provide for the _____ of wages, using the CPI, in later years of a contract period.

6. An inflation-adjusted quantity is a quantity measured in physical terms and is referred to as a _____.

7. The real interest rate is equal to the _____ minus the inflation rate.

8. The costs of inflation are greatly magnified when an economy experiences an extremely high inflation rate called _____.

9. The cost, for any period, of a standard basket of goods and services that the typical household purchases relative to the cost of the same basket of goods and services in the base year is measured by the _____.

10. Statistics Canada calculates the annual percentage rate of change in the price level as measured, for example, by the CPI to determine the _____.

11. Indexing is the practice of increasing a _____ according to changes in a price index in order to prevent inflation from eroding purchasing power.

12. A worker's money wages for two different periods can be adjusted using the CPI to determine his/her real wages by _____ the money wage.

13. The annual percentage increase in the real purchasing power of a financial asset's "return" is the _____.

14. The wage paid to workers measured in terms of real purchasing power is the _____.

15. In support of moderate inflation, we have the _____ hypothesis and the _____ hypothesis.

16. Where inflation is between 3 and 6 percent per year, we have _____ inflation, whereas if inflation is over 6 percent, we have _____ inflation.

17. If the inflation rate rises from one year to the next, we have _____.

18. If the inflation rate stays roughly constant from one year to the next, we have _____.

19. If the price level stays constant from one year to the next, we have _____.

20. If the inflation rate falls from one year to the next, the economy experiences

_____.

Self-Test: Multiple-Choice Questions

Circle the letter that corresponds to the best answer. (Answers are given at the end of the chapter.)

1. If the CPI is 125 at the end of 2000 and equals 150 at the end of 2001, then the inflation rate for 2001 would equal
   A. 15 percent.
   B. 20 percent.
   C. 25 percent
   D. 125 percent.
   E. 150 percent.

2. If the Consumer Price Index (CPI) decreases between periods
   A. the purchasing power of money increases.
   B. a dollar will buy fewer goods and services.
   C. real income equals nominal income.
   D. there is inflation.
   E. there is deflation.

3. If you borrow money at what you believe is an appropriate interest rate for the level of expected inflation, but the actual inflation rate turns out to be much higher than you had expected
   A. you will be paying the loan back with dollars that have much less purchasing power than you had expected.
   B. you will be paying the loan back with dollars that have much higher purchasing power than you had expected.
   C. you will be paying the loan back with dollars that have the same purchasing power as the dollars you borrowed.
   D. you, the borrower, will not gain from an intended redistribution of wealth.
   E. you, the borrower, will unintentionally redistribute wealth to the lender.

4. If the Consumer Price Index (CPI) overstates the true rate of inflation, the use of the CPI to adjust nominal incomes results in
   A. understating gains in real incomes.
   B. overstating gains in real incomes.
   C. an accurate statement of gains in real incomes.
   D. nominal values equalling real values.
   E. an arbitrary redistribution of income.

5. The CPI for a given year measures the cost of living in that year relative to
   A. what it was in the base year.
   B. what it was in the previous year.
   C. the cost of the basic goods and services need to sustain a typical household.
   D. the amount spent on goods and services by the randomly selected families in the family expenditure surveys.
   E. the cost of the basic goods and services in the base year.

6. The practice whereby it is ensured that a nominal payment represents a constant level of purchasing power is referred to as
   A. nominal wage rigidity.
   B. deflating.
   C. indexing.
   D. adjustment bias.
   E. disinflation.

7. A period of deflation is characterized by
   A. a rising price of oil relative to the CPI.
   B. the CPI falling from one period to the next.
   C. the rate at which the price level increases has declined but the price level does not drop.
   D. where the inflation rate changes from accelerating to decelerating but is still positive.
   E. zero inflation.

8. In which situation should policy makers be concerned most about major impacts on income distribution (in the absence of indexing)?
   A. deflation.
   B. moderate inflation.
   C. low inflation.
   D. unanticipated inflation.
   E. zero inflation.

9. If the price level stays roughly constant from one year to the next, we have
   A. disinflation.
   B. stable inflation.
   C. zero inflation.
   D. deflation.
   E. moderate inflation.

10. Suppose the level of nominal GDP in the current year is $995 billions. The GDP deflator is 104.2 (based on 1997 = 100). The real GDP (in billions of 1997 dollars) is
    A. 890.88.
    B. 1034.05.
    C. 954.89.
    D. 1012.5.
    E. 100.

11. Disinflation refers to a period where
  A. the price level increases at an increasing rate.
  B. the CPI falls between periods.
  C. where there is no change in the CPI between periods.
  D. the rate of inflation declines but the price level, as measured by the CPI, does not drop.
  E. the rate of change at which the CPI is increasing increases.

12. Suppose the National Accounts records the nominal GDP for Canada in 1998 as $778.5 billions. In the same year, the real GDP (1997 base year) is $799 billions. The implicit price index (GDP deflator) in 1998 is
  A. 102.7.
  B. 100.
  C.   87.1.
  D. 117.2.
  E.   97.4.

13. Workers would want to have their wages indexed in order to
  A. ensure that they receive a promotion.
  B. maintain their same purchasing power.
  C. protect themselves from falling nominal wages.
  D. ensure that they are paid the minimum wage.
  E. make the same money as other workers.

14. Financial investors and lenders do best when the real interest rate is
  A. lower than the nominal rate.
  B. the same as the nominal rate.
  C. high, since they get a better return.
  D. low because they benefit from low rates.
  E. negative.

15. The Consumer Price Index is calculated by
  A. [(cost of standard basket in the current year) divided by (cost of standard basket in the base year)] times 100.
  B. [(cost of standard basket in the base year) divided by (cost of standard basket in the current year)] times 100.
  C. (cost of a standard basket in the current year) minus (cost of a standard basket in the base year).
  D. (cost of a standard basket in the base year) minus (cost of a standard basket in the current year).
  E. [(cost of a standard basket in the current year) minus (cost of a standard basket in the base year)] times 100.

16. The inflation rate may be calculated, using the consumer price index, as
  A. [(new CPI) divided by (old CPI)] times 100.
  B. [(old CPI) divided by (new CPI)] times 100.

    C. [(new CPI – old CPI) divided by old CPI] times 100.
    D. [(new CPI – old CPI) divided by new CPI] times 100.
    E. (new CPI – old CPI) times 100.

17. The term "disinflation" means that
    A. inflation has become negative.
    B. the change in prices has become negative.
    C. prices have gone back to base-year level.
    D. consumer prices are rising more slowly than producer prices.
    E. prices are increasing, but at a decreasing rate.

18. The nominal wage of hourly paid employees in Canada has been higher than their real wage
    since the base year because
    A. unions have become stronger since the base year.
    B. employers have raised wages at an increasing rate since the base year.
    C. the minimum wage has kept nominal wages higher.
    D. prices have risen since the base year, and hence the purchasing power of real wages has
        been less.
    E. the number of hourly workers has decreased.

19. Consider that lenders wish to maintain a real interest rate of 5 percent If the nominal interest
    rate has been 7 percent and the rate of inflation has been 2 percent—but now inflation rises to
    4 percent—what will have to happen to keep lenders satisfied?
    A. the real interest rate must fall.
    B. the nominal interest rate must fall.
    C. the inflation rate must rise further.
    D. the nominal interest rate must rise.
    E. both the nominal interest rate and the real interest rate must rise.

20. The measured rate of growth of information technology investment has been much higher in
    the United States than in Germany because
    A. methods if measurement were different.
    B. the United States is a younger economy.
    C. the American government provides better incentives.
    D. the United States is a bigger economy.
    E. the German private sector has other interests.

Self-Test: Short-Answer Problems
(Answers and solutions are given at the end of the chapter.)

1. The Consumer Price Index and Inflation
In this question, you use CPI to adjust a nominal income for inflation.

Suppose that you are given the following data for the consumer price index and the after-tax income for the given years.

Year	Consumer Price Index	Inflation Rate (%)	After-Tax Income	After-Tax Real Income
2001	116.4		$29,603	
2000	113.5		28,193	
1999	110.5		26,850	
1998	108.6		25,609	
1997	107.6		24,405	

A. Complete the third column of the table by calculating the inflation rates for 1997–2001. (The CPI was taken from the CANSIM II database, where 1996 is the base year. The CPI for 1996 was 105.9).

B. Suppose the after-tax income for an average (hypothetical) household in nominal terms is given in the fourth column. Complete the fifth column of the table, using the CPI as in the second column, to adjust the nominal income to calculate after-tax real income of the typical household.

C. In which of the years from 1997 to 2001 was the typical household in Canada economically best off? _____. In which of the years from 1997 to 2001 was the typical household in Canada economically worst off? _____.

2. Costs of Higher Education
This question provides practice in taking into account the effects of inflation.

Suppose that a Canadian student is planning to study in the United States. In making the decision to attend a state university or a private college, cost of living expenses will be important. The following problem draws on a study by an accounting firm in the United States, which estimated average costs of attending college during 1994–95 for public and private institutions. The data are shown in the table below.

Categories	State Universities	Private Colleges
Tuition and fees	$2,686	$11,709
Books and supplies	578	585
Room and board	3,826	4,976
Transportation	592	523
Other	1,308	991
Total Cost	**$8,990**	**$18,784**

A. In the year 2000–01, it has also estimated that the total cost of attending a state university was $14, 266 and a private college was $33, 277. Using 1994–95 as the base year, calculate the price index for attending the state university and the private college.

Price index for the state university in 1994–95 _____
Price index for the private college in1994–95 _____
Price index for the state university in 2000–01_____
Price index for the private college in 2000–01 _____

B. What was the percentage increase in the cost of attending a state university between 1994 and 1995 and between 2000 and 2001? _____ percent.
   What was the percentage increase in the cost of attending a private college between 1994 and 1995 and between 2000 and 2001? _____ percent.

C. Sam attended a state university in his home state beginning in 1994–1995 and graduated in 2000–01. He paid the cost of his education by working part time and summers as a firefighter. When he entered college, his nominal (money) income was $13,000, and the year he graduated his nominal income had risen to $15,500. Because the cost of college includes all his living expenses, the price index for attending a state university represents his cost of living index. Thus, his real income (measured in 1994–95 dollars) in 1994–95 was $_____ and in 2000–01 it was $_____ .

D. Was Sam economically better off during the year he graduated or the first year he entered college? Explain your answer.
   _____

E. Sue attended private college beginning in 1994–95 and she also graduated in 2000–01. She paid the cost of her education by working part time and summers as a consultant to businesses designing Web pages. When she entered college, her nominal (money) income was $40,000. Because the cost of college includes all her living expenses, the price index for attending a college represents her cost of living index. If her real income was to remain constant from 1994–95 through 2000–01, her nominal income in 2000–01 would have had to rise to $_____.

3. **Nominal and Real Interest Rates**

Answer the questions below based on the data in the following table. The table shows the inflation rate in Canada, measured by the CPI, and nominal short-term interest rates (3-month treasury bills), taken from the CANSIM II database. (Assume that the treasury bills are held until maturity.)

Year	Inflation Rate	Interest Rate
1982	10.9	13.8
1985	4.0	9.5
1989	5.0	12.0
1991	5.6	8.8
1994	0.2	5.4
1999	1.7	4.7

A. Of the years listed in the table, in what year was the real interest rate on the short-term bond the highest? _____

B. From the years in the table, what year did the financial investors who bought the short-term bonds get the best deal? _____

C. In what year was the real interest rate on the short-term bond the lowest but still positive? _____

D. In what year did the financial investors who bought the short-term bonds get the worst deal? _____

E. What was the real interest rate on short-term bonds in 1999? _____ percent.

SOLUTIONS

Quick Quiz

1. B.
2. C.
3. C.
4. D.
5. A.
6. A.
7. E.
8. B.
9. B.
10. C.
11. A.

Self-Test: Key Terms

1. price index.
2. Fisher effect.
3. price level; relative price.
4. deflation.
5. indexing.
6. real quantity.
7. nominal interest rate.
8. hyperinflation.
9. consumer price index (CPI).
10. rate of inflation.
11. nominal quantity.
12. deflating.
13. real interest rate.
14. real wage.
15. downward nominal wage rigidity hypothesis, zero bound on nominal interest rate hypothesis.

16. moderate inflation, high inflation.
17. accelerating inflation.
18. stable inflation.
19. zero inflation.
20. disinflation.

Self Test: Multiple Choice Questions

1. B.
2. A.
3. A.
4. A.
5. A.
6. C.
7. B.
8. D.
9. C.
10. C.
11. D.
12. E.
13. B.
14. C.
15. A.
16. C.
17. E.
18. D.
19. D.
20. A.

Self-Test: Short-Answer Problems

1.
A. inflation rate = (CPI in year – CPI in previous year) ÷ CPI in previous year. (For example, 2001 inflation rate = [(116.4 – 113.5) ÷113.5] × 100% = 2.6%.

B. real income (after tax) = nominal income (after tax) ÷ price index. (For example, 2001: after-tax real income = ($29,603 ÷ 116.4) × 100 = $25,432.).

Year	Consumer Price Index	Inflation Rate (%)	After-Tax Income	After-Tax Real Income
2001	116.4	2.6	$29,603	$25,432
2000	113.5	2.7	28,193	$24,840
1999	110.5	1.8	26,850	$24,299
1998	108.6	1.0	25,609	$23,581
1997	107.6	1.6	24,405	$22,681

C. 2001; 1997.

2. A. price index = $8,990 ÷ $8,990 = 1.00; $14,266 ÷ $8,990 = 1.59; 1.00; 1.77.
   B. percentage change = ($14,266 − $8,990) ÷ $8,990 = 58.7%; 77.2%.
   C. real income = $13,000 ÷ 1.00 = $13,000; $9,748.
   D. during his first year, since from question 2C, his real income his higher in 1994–95.
   E. to determine by how much her income would need to rise, you need to index her income during the first year of university by multiplying it times the price index for university during the year she graduated, (i.e., $40,000 × 1.77 = $70,800).

3. A. 1989.
   B. 1989.
   C. 1982.
   D. 1982.
   E. 3% (= 4.7 − 1.7).

7 Economic Growth, Productivity, and Living Standards

OVERVIEW

Over the past two centuries, a radical transformation has occurred in the living standards of people in the industrialized countries that has resulted from a remarkable rise in the economic growth rates of those nations. This chapter explores the sources of economic growth and rising standards of living in the modern world. Secondary issues discussed include government policies to promote economic growth, the costs of rapid economic growth, and whether there may be limits to economic growth.

Chapter Review

7.1 The Remarkable Rise in Real GDP Per Capita

▶ **LO 1.** Compare rates of growth in real GDP per person among countries during the nineteenth and twentieth centuries.

Despite the recognition that it is an imperfect measure, economists have focused on real GDP per person as a key measure of a country's living standard and stage of economic development. As discussed in Chapter 5, real GDP per person is positively related to a number of pertinent variables, such as life expectancy, infant health, and literacy. During the nineteenth century, the annual percentage change in real GDP per person began to increase in a number of industrializing countries, and during the latter half of the twentieth century, the rate of economic growth increased again. As a result of the power of compound growth, real GDP in these countries is anywhere from 4 to 25 times greater than it was a century ago.

Quick Quiz

1. The increase in average labour productivity is important to the economy because
   A. without it, real GDP per person cannot increase.
   B. without it, real GDP per person must decrease.

C. it is a key to improving living standards in the long run.

D. the fraction of the total population that is employed is constant over time and, thus, real GDP per person is solely dependent upon average labour productivity.

E. it implies more resources are being employed to produce less output.

7.2   Why "Small" Differences in Growth Rates Matter

▶ **LO 2.**   **Differentiate simple and compound interest and calculate compound interest.**

The increases in the growth rates of real GDP during the last half of the twentieth century were relatively small in comparison with the previous 80 years, but the *power of compound growth* resulted in large changes in real GDP over time. A specific instance of the power of compound growth is *compound interest*, which is the payment of interest not only on the original deposit but also on all previously accumulated interest. This is distinguished from simple interest, in which interest is paid only on the original deposit. When interest is compounded, small differences in interest rates or growth rates matter a lot. As in the case of the industrializing countries during the late nineteenth and twentieth centuries, relatively small differences in growth rates, among the countries and during different time periods ultimately produced very different living standards.

Quick Quiz

2. If on the day you were born, your parents deposited $1,000 into a savings account that would earn an annual compound interest rate of 5 percent, what would the value of the account be on your twentieth birthday?
   A. $1,100.
   B. $2,653.30.
   C. $3,325,256.73.
   D. $1,500.
   E. $1,050.

7.3   Why Nations Become Rich: The Crucial Role of Average Labour Productivity

▶ **LO 3.**   **Discuss the relationship of real GDP per person to average labour productivity and share of working population.**

The rate of economic growth over time is an extremely important variable, and therefore, understanding the sources of economic growth is very important. Real GDP per person can be expressed as the product of two terms: average labour productivity and the share of the population that is working. Real GDP per person can only grow if there is growth in worker productivity and/or the fraction of the population that is employed. In Canada, for example, during 1960–2000, the fraction of the population employed increased as women entered the labour force in greater proportions and as the coming of age of the "baby boomers" increased the share of the population that was of working age. This contributed to the increased growth in real GDP per capita in Canada during that time. In the long run, however, it is unlikely that this trend will continue as demographic changes take place. Average labour productivity is, therefore, the more important determinant of increases in living standards in the long run. In simple terms, the more people produce, the more they can consume.

Quick Quiz

3. Which of the following could contribute to a growth in real GDP per person?
   A. growth in worker productivity.
   B. growth in the fraction of the population that is employed.
   C. both A and B.
   D. neither A not B.

7.4 The Determinants of Average Labour Productivity

▶ **LO 4.** **Discuss the determinants of average labour productivity.**

There are six factors that appear to account for the major differences in *average labour productivity* among countries and among generations:

- *Human capital*, the talents, education, training, and skills of workers, is the first factor that affects average labour productivity. In general, people acquire additional education and skills when the difference in the additional wages paid (marginal benefit) to skilled workers is greater than the marginal cost of acquiring the skills.

- A second determinant of average labour productivity is *physical capital*—machines, equipment, and buildings. More capital generally increases average labour productivity. There are, however, *diminishing returns to capital* (i.e., if the amount of labour and other inputs employed is held constant, then the greater the amount of capital already in use, the less an additional unit of capital adds to production). Diminishing returns to capital is an illustration of the principle of increasing opportunity cost.

- The third determinant of average labour productivity is the availability of *land* and other resources. In general, an abundance of natural resources increases the productivity of the workers that use them. Because resources can be obtained through trade, however, countries need not possess large quantities of them within their own border to achieve economic growth.

- A fourth determinant is *technology*. A country's ability to develop and apply new, more productive technologies will increase its workers' productivity. More importantly, new technologies can improve productivity in industries other than the one in which they are introduced.

- *Entrepreneurship* is a fifth determinant of average labour productivity. Entrepreneurship refers to behaviour that results in new products, services, technological processes, or organizational innovations that are productivity-enhancing. Entrepreneurs are people who create new enterprises and are critical to the introduction of new technologies into the production of goods and services.

- *Government*, a sixth determinant, also has a role to play in fostering improved productivity. A key contribution of government is to provide a political and legal environment that encourages people to behave in economically productive ways. A stable government that provides a legal and political framework for innovative and productive economic activity is also an important determinant of a nation's average labour productivity.

Quick Quiz

4. In provinces like Saskatchewan and Alberta, an abundance of natural resources, such as arable land, raw materials, and energy
   A. within a province's borders is necessary to achieve economic growth.
   B. increases the productivity of workers who use them.
   C. results in economic growth only if the population increases at least as rapidly.
   D. results in economic growth only if an economy obtains them through international trade.
   E. seldom contributes to economic growth, as measured by percentage increases in real GDP per person.

7.5   The Productivity Slowdown

▶ **LO 5.   Explain the slowdown in productivity after 1973.**

In spite of the twentieth century increases in productivity, there has been a slowdown in the growth rates since 1973 that has puzzled economists and policy-makers alike. Some economists attribute a slowdown in technological innovation as the cause. There are signs of a possible recovery in productivity, however.

Quick quiz

5. Which of the following contributed to the worldwide slowdown in productivity since 1973?
   A. the increase in the price of oil that followed the Arab–Israeli war of 1973.
   B. the decline the quality of public education.
   C. the improvement in the measurement of productivity growth.
   D. a dearth of technological innovations during the 1970s.
   E. an increase in technological innovations during the 1970s.

7.6   Two Possible Costs of Economic Growth

▶ **LO 6.**   **Identify the costs of economic growth, applying cost-benefit analysis.**

While economic growth provides substantial benefits to society, it is not without costs. An increase in the rate of investment in new physical and human capital often requires that people save and, thus, consume less in the present. Alternatively, an increase in the rate of investment might be purchased at the cost of reduced leisure time or, possibly, reduced workers' health and safety. The fact that a higher living standard tomorrow must typically be purchased at the cost of current sacrifices is an example of the scarcity principle. The cost-benefit principle suggests that a nation should pursue additional growth only if the marginal benefits outweigh the marginal costs.

Quick Quiz

6. The cost-benefit principle suggests that higher economic growth
    A. is always desirable.
    B. is seldom desirable.
    C. should be pursued only if the marginal benefits outweigh the marginal costs.
    D. should be pursued only if the marginal costs outweigh the marginal benefits.
    E. should be pursued only if the marginal benefits equal the marginal costs.

7.7   Promoting Economic Growth

▶ **LO 7.**   **Discuss potential government policies that may promote economic growth.**

If a society decides to try to increase its rate of economic growth, policy makers can help achieve the goal by providing education and training programs or by subsidizing the provision of such programs by the private sector. In addition, governments can encourage high rates of investment in the private sector through tax incentives. Governments can also directly contribute to capital formation through public investment in infrastructure. Government financing of research and development activities, especially in the area of basic scientific knowledge, can promote a higher rate of economic growth. Government also plays an essential role in providing the framework within which the private sector can operate productively.

Quick Quiz

7. Most countries provide their citizens free public education through high school because
    A. the supply curve for education does not include all the social benefits of education.
    B. a market in equilibrium exploits all the gains achievable from collective action.
    C. the demand curve for education does not include all the social benefits of education.

D. educational vouchers that help citizens purchase educational services in the private sector have not proven to increase human capital.

E. direct government control over the standards and quality of education is necessary to increase human capital.

7.8   Are There Limits to Growth?

▶ **LO 8.**   **Discuss the criticisms of the "limits to growth" thesis.**

While economic growth accelerated during the nineteenth and twentieth centuries, an influential book, *The Limits to Growth*, published in 1972, reported the results of computer simulations that suggested continued growth would deplete natural resources, drinkable water, and breathable air. Critics of the limits to growth thesis point out that its underlying assumption is that growth implies producing more of the same type of goods. A second criticism is that it overlooks the fact that increased wealth expands a society's capacity to safeguard the environment. Additionally, it is argued that markets and government action can deal with the depletion of natural resources through new sources and conservation. Despite these shortcomings and also that not all concerns about limits to growth are valid, economic growth does give rise to environmental problems.

Quick Quiz

8. One criticism of the "limits to growth" thesis is that the market can generally deal with shortages of natural resources that may result from economic growth through price changes that induce
    A. consumers to consume more and suppliers to produce less of the resources.
    B. consumers to consume less and suppliers to produce more of the resources.
    C. a slowdown in the rate of economic growth.
    D. government actions to allocate public funds to preserve open space and reduce air pollution.
    E. an optimal level of environmental quality on a global scale.

Self-Test: Key Terms
Use the terms below to complete the following sentences. (Answers are given at the end of the chapter.)

compound interest   human capital
diminishing returns to capital   power of compound growth
entrepreneurship   rule of 72
labour productivity

1. The greater the amount of capital already in use, the less an additional unit of capital adds to production if the amount of labour and other inputs employed is held constant because of

    _____ .

2. Innovative behaviour that results in new products, services, technological processes, or organizational innovations that are productivity-enhancing, is known as

    _____.

3. The payment of interest on all previously accumulated interest the payment of interest and on the original deposit is called _____ .

4. An increase in the level of _____, such as skills of workers, tends to raise _____ and hence output per worker.

5. Applying the _____ , an economy will take about 12 years for its GDP per capita to double if the latter is growing at 6 percent a year.

6. According to the _____, small differences in growth rates can have large long-run effects.

Self-Test: Multiple-Choice Questions

Circle the letter that corresponds to the best answer. (Answers are given at the end of the chapter.)

1. The rate of growth in real GDP per person in Canada, the United States, Japan, Australia, and the major European economies was highest during the period of
    A. 1870–98.
    B. 1950–98.
    C. 1973–79.
    D. 1979–97.
    E. 1960–73.

2. Compound interest differs from simple interest in that compound interest is interest paid on
    A. the original deposit only, whereas simple interest is interest paid on not only on the original deposit but also on all previously accumulated interest.
    B. all previously accumulated interest, whereas simple interest is interest paid on not only on the original deposit but also on all previously accumulated interest.
    C. the original deposit only, whereas simple interest is interest paid only on all previously accumulated interest.
    D. the original deposit and on all previously accumulated interest, whereas simple interest is interest paid on all previously accumulated interest.
    E. the original deposit and on all previously accumulated interest, whereas simple interest is interest paid on the original deposit only.

3. International data on the relationship between the amount of capital per worker and average labour productivity indicate that there is a
    A. positive relationship between the two variables.
    B. negative relationship between the two variables.
    C. no relationship between the two variables.

    D. positive relationship between the two variables for some countries but a negative relationship between the two variables for other countries.

    E. positive relationship between the two variables for some countries but no relationship between the two variables for other countries.

4. The country which achieved the highest growth rate during the twentieth century was

    A. Australia.

    B. Canada.

    C. Germany.

    D. Japan.

    E. United States.

5. The faster the rate of technological change, the

    A. lower is the rate of growth in productivity.

    B. lower is the rate of economic growth.

    C. higher is the rate of unemployment.

    D. higher is the rate of growth in productivity.

    E. higher is the rate of capital accumulation.

6. For a given number of workers, as the amount of capital is increased output will

    A. increase at a diminishing rate.

    B. increase at an increasing rate.

    C. increase at a constant rate.

    D. decrease at a diminishing rate.

    E. decrease at an increasing rate.

7. Entrepreneurship is

    A. easy to teach in schools and colleges.

    B. not affected by government policies.

    C. more important than management in determining average labour productivity.

    D. hindered by few regulatory barriers in Canada.

    E. believed to be largely absent in Japan.

8. The scarcity principle implies that the cost of a higher economic growth rate is

    A. less future capital accumulation.

    B. less current consumption.

    C. greater future capital consumption.

    D. greater current consumption.

    E. greater future consumption.

9. The general thesis of the book *The Limits to Growth* was that continued pursuit of economic growth would soon

    A. cease when all the workers were employed.

    B. consume all available natural resources, drinkable water, and breathable air.

    C. cause the principle of scarcity to no longer be an issue.

    D. increase the living standard of the poorest nations to that of the richest nations.

   E. limit our desire to increase the production of goods and services.

10. Critics of the "limits to growth" thesis argue that
   A. economic growth will always take the form of more of what we have now, rather than newer, better, and cleaner goods and services.
   B. the market is not capable of adjusting to shortages of resources.
   C. the more economically developed a country becomes, the easier it will be to keep the environment clean.
   D. government action spurred by political pressure is the only best way to avoid the depletion of natural resources and pollution of the environment that results from economic growth.
   E. all the problems created by economic growth can be dealt with effectively through the market or the political process.

11. The increase in the percentage of people employed in Canada from 33 percent in 1961, to 50 percent in 2003, was most importantly a result of
   A. a rise in the minimum wage.
   B. the immigration of workers from other countries.
   C. an increase in the number of women working outside the home.
   D. a rise in the number of teenagers employed.
   E. a later average retirement age.

12. On-the-job training to teach office staff to use additional computer software would be an example of boosting labour productivity through
   A. human capital.
   B. physical capital per worker.
   C. new innovations in technology.
   D. entrepreneurship.
   E. diminishing returns to capital.

13. Which of the following would NOT encourage entrepreneurship?
   A. low status in society of nonprofit activities.
   B. creativity.
   C. low barriers to starting new businesses.
   D. leadership skills.
   E. complementary government policies.

14. Productivity growth recovered somewhat in the 1990s in the United States and Canada, which the textbook says can be attributed, in part, to:
    A. increased immigration.
    B. higher real wages.
    C. advances in computers.
    D. a decline in leisure time.
    E. the growth of technology shares.

15. During the 1980s and 1990s in Canada, hourly *real* wages
    A. tripled.
    B. doubled.
    C. stayed the same.
    D. decreased slightly.
    E. fell by half.

16. Using the "GDP by income" method of valuing national production, labour's share of national income
    A. has risen continually since 1961.
    B. rose until the late 1970s and then fell.
    C. has stayed the same the last 40 years.
    D. has fallen continually since 1961.
    E. has fluctuated, with no overall trend.

17. The rule of 72 is important for understanding
    A. how fast a country's GDP has grown since the oil shocks of the 1970s.
    B. why the world's 72 most industrialized countries have grown faster.
    C. how fast it will take a country's GDP to double.
    D. a country's rate of growth in the past 30 years.
    E. how high a growth rate a country must achieve in order to double its GDP.

18. In order to maintain growth in the income per capita, in a country where the percentage of participation in the workforce is falling, then
    A. the solution would be to raise immigration.
    B. the mandatory retirement age should be lowered.
    C. the solution would be to allow workers more leisure time.
    D. average labour productivity would have to grow commensurately.
    E. the country's living standards will rise.

19. Which of the following is NOT a determinant of average labour productivity?
    A. size of the workforce.
    B. amount of physical capital.
    C. amount of natural resources.
    D. introduction of new technology.
    E. compatibility of legal and political environment.

20. According to the textbook, the decline of the percentage of compensation to labour in GDP by income in Canada is related to
  A. unionization of labour.
  B. stagnation of real wages.
  C. apathy of workers.
  D. replacement of office staff by computers.
  E. increased leisure time of employees.

Self-Test: Short-Answer Problems
(Answers and solutions are given at the end of the chapter.)

1. **Compounding Economic Growth Rates**
   The table below shows the output per person for selected countries in 2000 and the economic growth rates of the countries for 1990–2000. Use the data in the table to answer the following questions. (*Take your answers to the nearest cent. Make your own columns for 50 and 100 years in the future*).

Country	2000 GNP per Capita[1]	1990 – 2000 Growth Rate	2010 GNP per Capita	2020 GNP per Capita
Canada	$27,330	2.9%		
France	24,470	1.7%		
Germany	25,010	1.5%		
Italy	23,370	1.5%		
Mexico	8,810	3.1%		
New Zealand	18,780	3.0%		

Source: *World Development Report*, 2002, Tables 1 and 3.

[1] Calculated in 2000 dollars and using the purchasing power parity method to adjust the value of output across countries.

  A. Assuming that each country's economy continues to grow at the same rate that it did during 1990–2000, complete the last two columns of the table by calculating the GNP per capita (person) for 2010 and 2020.

  B. On the graph below, plot the level of GNP per capita for the remaining countries for 10, 20, 50, and 100 years later, assuming a compound growth rate equal to that of 1990–2000,

Compound Economic Growth

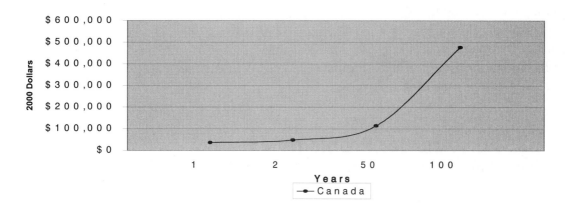

C. Approximately how many decades would it take for Mexico's output per person to equal that of Italy's output per person? _____ decades.

D. Approximately how many decades would it take for France's output per person to equal that of Canada's output per person? _____ decades.

E. Approximately how many decades would it take for Italy's output per person to equal that of Germany's output per person? _____ decades.

2. **Why Nations Become Rich**
   This problem will help you understand the relationship among how much workers produce, how many people are working, and the quantity of goods and services available to consume. All data are for 1998, and the Real GDP and productivity are measured in 1998 dollars. (*Take your answers to the nearest dollar.*)

Country	Real GDP per Person	Average Labour Productivity	Share of the Population Employed
Canada	$25,496		47.5
France	$22,255	$56,722	
Japan	$24,170		51.2
Norway		$54,007	51.1
United States		$65,888	49.2

A. Complete the table above by calculating the average labour productivity for Canada and Japan, the value of real GDP per person for the United States and Norway, and the share of the population employed in France during 1998.

B. The data indicate that workers in France produce considerably more output per year than do workers in Norway, and yet the average Norwegian has a higher real GDP per person.

Explain why.

_____

_____

C. A larger share of the population in Japan is employed than in Canada, and yet the average Canadian has a higher real GDP per person than the Japanese do. Explain why.

_____

_____

_____

D. The population in Japan is aging faster than the population in Canada, and thus, by the early twenty-first century the share of the population employed in Japan will decline as the elderly retire. If the share of the population employed in Japan falls to the level of Canada, which country would have the higher real GDP per capita, assuming no other changes? Explain your answer.

_____

_____

_____

3. The Costs of Economic Growth

The following table shows the GNP per capita and air pollution, as proxied by carbon dioxide (CO_2) emissions from energy use of selected countries in 1997. The developed countries are Canada, Japan, and the United States, whereas the newly industrialized countries are Korea, Mexico, and Turkey.

Country	GNP per Capita		CO_2 Emissions	
	1997 (US$)	Change 80–97 (%)	1997 (million tonnes)	Change 80–97 (%)
Canada	19,290	90.4	477	11.0
Japan	37,850	282.7	1,173	27.9
Korea	10,550	594.7	422	237.0
Mexico	3,680	76.1	346	39.2
Turkey	3,130	112.9	187	156.6
United States	28,740	153.0	5,470	14.3

A. Is there a relationship between GNP per capita and air pollution? If so, describe it based on the cost-benefit principle.

_____

_____

_____

B. Among the developed countries, is there a relationship between the changes in GNP per capita and the changes in air pollution over the period 1980–97?

_____

_____

_____

C. Among the newly industrialized countries, is there a relationship between the changes in GNP per capita and the changes in air pollution over the period 1980–97?

_____

_____

_____

D. From B and C above, what can you say about the cost of economic growth based on the cost-benefit principle?

_____

_____

_____

E. Give an economic reason to explain why the percentage increases in air pollution in the developed countries are lower than those in the newly industrialized countries?

_____

_____

_____

SOLUTIONS

Quick Quiz

1. C.
2. B.
3. C.
4. B.
5. D.
6. C.
7. C.
8. B.

Self-Test: Key Terms

1. diminishing returns to capital.
2. entrepreneurship.
3. compound interest.
4. human capital, labour productivity.

5. rule of 72.
6. power of compound growth.

Self-Test: Multiple-Choice Questions

1. E. Compare the growth rates for each of these periods in Table 7.3 and Figure 7.1.
2. E.
3. A. See Figure 7.4.
4. D.
5. D.
6. D.
7. E.
8. B.
9. B.
10. C.
11. C.
12. A.
13. A.
14. C.
15. C.
16. B.
17. C.
18. D.
19. A.
20. B.

Self-Test: Short-Answer Problems

1.

A.

Country	2000 GNP per Capita	2010 GNP	2020 GNP
Canada	$27,330.00	$36,374.19	$48,411.34
France	$24,470.00	$28,963.00	$34,280.96
Germany	$25,010.00	$29,025.13	$33,684.84
Italy	$23,370.00	$27,121.84	$31,476.00
Mexico	$8,810.00	$11,955.35	$16,223.67
New Zealand	$18,780.00	$25,238.75	$33,918.77

B.

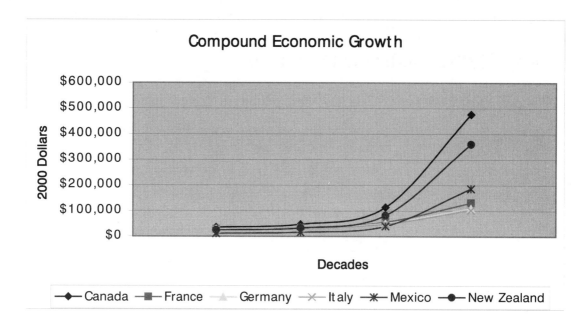

C. About six decades.
D. Never, because France's output per person in 2000 is lower than that of Canada and it is growing at a slower rate.
E. Never, because both are growing at the same rate but Germany has a higher GNP per capita in 2000.

2.

A.

Country	Real GDP per Person	Average Labour Productivity	Share of the Population Employed
US	$32,413	$65,888	49.2
Canada	$25,496	$53,675	47.5
France	$22,255	$56,722	39.2
Japan	$24,170	$47,207	51.2
Norway	$27,598	$54,007	51.1

B. Because a larger share of the population is employed in Norway than is employed in France, the average person in Norway has a higher real GDP per person than the French.

C. The average labour productivity in Canada is higher than that of Japan and thus, despite the fact that a smaller share of the population is employed in Canada, its citizens have a higher real GDP per person.

D. Canada. If the share of the population employed in Japan declines to Canada's current level, that is, 47.5 percent, Japan's real GDP per person will drop to about $22,423. The real GDP per person for the average Canadian will remain higher than that of the Japanese because of Canada's higher average labour productivity.

3.

A. In general, the data show a positive relationship between GNP per capita and CO_2 emissions—the higher the level of GNP per capita, the higher is the level of CO_2 emission. In this case, the cost of maintaining a higher GNP per capita is more air pollution.

B. There is a positive relationship, as can be seen by ranking the countries in terms of changes in GNP per capita and of changes in CO_2 emissions. In both cases, the rankings are: Japan, the United States, and Canada, with Japan having the highest increases.

C. There is again a positive relationship. The rankings are: Korea, Turkey, and Mexico.

D. One of the costs of economic growth is that it causes environmental problems (air pollution in our example here).

E. One reason is that the developed countries can afford extra income for environmental protection at home.

8 Saving and Capital Formation

OVERVIEW

In this chapter, saving and its links to the formation of new capital are discussed. The concepts of saving and wealth and the connections between them are presented in the first part of the chapter. This is followed by a discussion of why people save, and the relationship between economywide saving and wealth.

Chapter Review

8.1 Saving and Wealth

▶ **LO 1.** **Define saving, saving rate, wealth, assets, liabilities, stocks, and flows.**

Saving by an economic unit (e.g., a household, business, or nation) is its current income minus its spending on current needs. It can be expressed as a *saving rate* by dividing the amount of saving by the amount of income. Saving by an economic unit is closely related to its *wealth*, the value of its assets minus its liabilities. *Assets* are anything of value that is owned, while *liabilities* are the debts that are owed. Accountants list the assets and liabilities of an economic unit on a balance sheet to determine its net worth. Saving and wealth are related because saving contributes to wealth. This relationship is best understood by distinguishing between stocks and flows. A *flow* is a measure that is defined per unit of time, and a *stock* is a measure that is defined at a point in time. In many cases, a flow is the rate of change in a stock. For example, the flow of saving causes the stock of wealth to change at the same rate.

▶ **LO 2.** **Explain the link between saving and wealth.**

Higher rates of saving, therefore, lead to faster accumulation of wealth and a higher standard of living. Although saving increases wealth, it is not the only factor that determines wealth.

▶ **LO 3.** **Define capital gains and capital losses.**

Wealth also changes because of changes in the values of the real and financial assets owed by an economic unit. If the value of existing assets increases, the owner has a *capital gain*, but if the value of existing assets decreases, then there is a *capital loss*. In summary, changes in wealth equal the amount of saving plus capital gains minus capital losses.

Quick Quiz

1. When a person owns a chequing account that would be listed on their balance sheet as
    A. an asset.
    B. a liability.
    C. net worth.
    D. saving.
    E. wealth.

2. Luis had accumulated $5,000 in wealth at the end of a year. At the beginning of the next year, he deposits all his wealth in a saving account that will earn 5 percent interest per year. If there are no changes in his liabilities, at the end of the next year, his wealth will have
    A. increased by $5,250.
    B. decreased by $5,250.
    C. increased by $250.
    D. decreased by $250.
    E. not changed.

3. If, in a given year, the saving in an economy decreases by an amount equal to the net capital gains, the economy's
    A. wealth will decrease.
    B. wealth will increase.
    C. wealth will remain unchanged.
    D. assets will decrease.
    E. liabilities will decrease.

8.2   Why Do People Save?

► **LO 4.**   **Identify three broad reasons for household saving.**

People save part of their income, rather than spending all they earn, for three reasons. First, they save to meet certain long-term objectives, such as retirement or the purchase of a home. This is called *life-cycle saving*. A second reason people save is called *precautionary saving*, saving to protect against unexpected setbacks. The third reason for saving is *bequest saving*, saving for the purpose of leaving an inheritance. Although most people save for one of these three reasons, the amount that they save depends on the economic environment. There are some who argue that despite these rational reasons for saving, some people lack the self-control to do what is in their own best interests. In spite of having good intentions to save, for example, some lack the necessary self-control to put aside as much of their income as they would like. This *self-control hypothesis* suggests that consumer credit arrangements that make borrowing and spending easier may reduce the amount that people save. Similarly, the demonstration effect suggests that additional spending by some people causes others to spend more to maintain a lifestyle commensurate with their peer group. On the other hand, many Canadians enjoyed significant capital gains from the bull market.

▶ **LO 5.** **Explain the relationship between household saving and the real interest rate.**

One economic variable of some importance in saving decisions is the real interest rate, r. The real interest rate is the reward for saving. Because of the power of compound interest in the long run, a higher real interest rate causes a dramatic increase in the real value of a saver's wealth. On the other hand, a higher real interest rate reduces the amount people need to save each year to reach a given wealth target. Nonetheless, empirical evidence suggests people are willing to save more the higher the real interest rate, all else being equal. Another economic variable that may have some importance for savings decisions is the scale of capital gains or losses in the economy. Significant capital gains increase the wealth of households and lessen their incentives to save.

Quick Quiz

4. One reason that household saving in Japan is higher than household saving in Canada is that
   A. the average Japanese income is higher than it is in Canada.
   B. housing in Canada is more expensive and, therefore, Canadians spend more of their income on housing and save less.
   C. Japanese workers continue working until they are much older and, therefore, they can save more.
   D. the Japanese save more for precautionary reasons because they have, in general, less job security than Canadian workers.
   E. the higher cost of housing and larger down payments required to purchase a house in Japan results in higher life-cycle saving.

5. If the real interest rate on saving accounts increases from 3 percent to 5 percent, all other things being equal
   A. business investment spending for new capital will increase.
   B. business investment spending for new capital will remain unchanged.
   C. households will tend to save less.
   D. households will tend to save more.
   E. the amount households save will remain unchanged.

8.3 Economywide Saving and Wealth

The above discussion pertains to individual saving, but macroeconomists are interested primarily in saving and wealth for the country as a whole. As for any economic unit, a nation's saving equals its current income less its spending on current needs. The current income of a country is its GDP, or *Y*, the value of the final goods and service produced within the country's borders during the year. Identifying the part of total expenditures that corresponds to a country's current needs is more difficult. Because investment spending is done to improve the future productive capacity, it is clearly not a part of spending on current needs. For consumption and government spending, some portion is for current needs while another portion is for future needs. Determining how much should be attributed to each portion is extremely difficult.

▶ **LO 6.   Define national saving, nonresident saving, and private saving.**

Gross saving is the total saving from all sources to support *gross investment* in an economy. In an open economy, like Canada, where there are international flows of capital, gross saving is the sum of *national saving* and *nonresident saving*. The latter is the balance between saving provided to the Canadian economy and saving provided to foreign economies by residents of Canada. National saving can be divided into two major components: *private saving* and *public saving* by government. Private sector saving can be further broken down into household saving and corporate saving.

Since the early 1980s, decreases in private household saving in Canada have been partially offset by increases in corporate saving. The relatively low Canadian household saving rate is not a problem from a macroeconomic perspective because national saving and nonresident saving, not household saving alone, determine the capacity of an economy to invest in new capital goods and continue to improve its standard of living. Although household saving is low, corporate saving remains significant and rising and in recent years, and government saving has also partly offset the fall in household saving. As a result, the low household saving rate does not constraint the level of economywide investment.

▶ **LO 7.   Define public saving, government budget deficit, and surplus and explain the relationships among them.**

Public saving, or saving of the government sector, is closely related to government sector budget balance. A *government budget deficit* is the excess of government spending over tax collections, whereas a *government budget surplus* is the excess of government tax collections over spending. Government spending here consists of government current purchases of goods and services, government investment (government fixed capital formation and government investment in inventories), and government *transfers* (government transfer payments and interest payments on the public debt). In calculating net government saving, however, the government purchases concept does not include government investment.

Overall, Canada's national saving rate has been reasonably stable, although it has declined slightly over the last four decades. Despite the fact that Canada's saving rate is low by international standards, business investment in machinery and equipment, which is closely related to productivity growth, does not show a downward trend.

► **LO 8.** **Define national wealth, national net worth, and net foreign liabilities.**

A concept closely related to saving and capital formation is *national wealth*, defined as the total value of real assets in a country. *National net worth* is national wealth adjusted for a country's net foreign liabilities. A country has *net international liabilities*, or net foreign debt, when the value of financial claims of nonresidents on its wealth exceeds the value of financial claims of its residents against foreign wealth.

Quick Quiz

6. Private saving
  A. can be broken down into household saving and corporate saving.
  B. can be broken down into transfers and household saving.
  C. rises when net taxes increase.
  D. falls when income rises.
  E. rises when government spending decreases.

7. An increase in net taxes (i.e., taxes paid by the private sector to government minus transfer payments and interest payments made by government to the private sector) will
  A. increase private saving.
  B. decrease public saving.
  C. increase public saving.
  D. reduce investment in new capital equipment.
  E. cause crowding out.

8. If a country has real assets of $4 billion, financial assets of $6 billion, and financial liabilities of $7 billion, then the national net worth is
  A. $17 billion.
  B. $13 billion.
  C. $10 billion.
  D. $4 billion.
  E. $3 billion.

8.4 Investment and Capital Formation

► **LO 9.** **Apply cost-benefit analysis to the investment decision.**

Firms' willingness to invest depends on the expected cost of using the capital and the expected benefit, measured as the marginal product, of the capital. On the cost side, two important factors are the price of capital goods and the real interest rate. The more expensive the capital goods, the less willing businesses are to invest in them. The real interest rate measures the opportunity cost of a capital investment. Since an increase in the real interest rate increases the opportunity cost of investing in new capital, it lowers the willingness of firms to invest. On the benefit side, the key factor in determining business investment is the value of the marginal product of the new capital, calculated net of operating costs, maintenance expenses, and taxes paid on the revenues the capital generates. The value of the marginal product of capital is affected by several factors, including technological improvement and the relative price of the good or service that the capital is used to produce. Technological improvements and increases in the price of the good or service raise the marginal product of capital and increase the willingness of businesses to invest. Apart from these factors, government taxation and subsidies also affect firms' investment in new capital.

Quick Quiz

9. Samantha has $5,000 in a GIC account paying 5 percent interest. It will mature in a few weeks, and the bank told her that interest rates on GICs were decreasing. She is thinking of spending it on a new computer and software that she will use to start a bookkeeping service. If she were to do so, she would have to quit her job where she makes $15,000 per year in after-tax income. She has estimated that the bookkeeping service will earn a net income of $15,250 after taxes, and maintenance and operating costs (including the depreciation of the computer and software).
   A. since the interest rate is declining, Samantha would be better off using the money to buy the computer.
   B. if the interest rate on the new GIC is 7 percent or greater, she should leave the money in the GIC.
   C. if the interest rate on the new GIC is 2.5 percent or greater, she should buy the computer.
   D. if the interest rate on the new GIC is 2 percent or less, she should leave the money in the GIC.
   E. if the interest rate on the new GIC is 5 percent or greater, she should leave the money in the GIC.

SELF-TESTS

Key Terms
Use the terms below to complete the following sentences. (Answers are given at the end of the chapter.)

assets	national saving
bequest saving	national wealth
capital gains	net international liabilities
capital losses	nonresident saving
corporate saving	precautionary saving
flow	saving
government saving	saving rate
liabilities	stock
life-cycle saving	transfers
national net worth	wealth

1. Excluding the international sector, GDP less consumption expenditures and government purchases of goods and services equals _____.

2. In accounting, the debts that one owes are recorded as _____.

3. A decrease in the value of existing assets causes _____.

4. Positive _____ corresponds to an international capital inflow.

5. Payments government makes to the public for which it receives no current goods or services in return are _____.

6. Gross _____ consists of capital consumption allowances, undistributed profits, and inventory adjustment.

7. The type of saving that is done for certain long-term objectives, such as retirement or the purchase of a home, is _____ .

8. Current income minus spending on current needs represents the _____ _____ of an economic unit.

9. Net tax payments minus government purchases and investment equals net

    _____ .

10. Saving done for the purpose of leaving an inheritance is _____ .

11. A measure that is defined per unit of time is a(n) _____ .

12. Dividing the amount of saving by the amount of income equals the _____ .

13. To protect against unexpected setbacks, people maintain _____.

14. The value of assets minus liabilities equals _____ .

15. In many cases, a flow equals the rate of change in a(n) _____ .

16. Anything of value that one owns is a(n) _____ .

17. If the value of existing assets increases, the owner has _____.

18. The total value of real assets in a country is its _____.

19. When Canadians borrow from abroad more than they lend to foreigners, Canada's

    _____ increase.

20. _____ equals the total value of real assets in a country less its net foreign debt.

Multiple-Choice Questions

Circle the letter that corresponds to the best answer. (Answers are given at the end of the chapter.)

1. The strong Canadian bull market of the late 1990s ended (at least temporarily) in 2000, as the Toronto Stock Exchange 300 Index fell about 20 percent during the third quarter of 2000. As a result, many Canadians
    A. suffered capital losses and increases in their wealth.
    B. suffered capital losses and decreases in their wealth.

C. enjoyed capital gains and increases in their wealth.

D. enjoyed capital gains and decreases in their wealth.

E. suffered capital losses and decreases in their liabilities.

2. Which of the following provide(s) incentives for Canadians to save more?
   A. Registered Pension Plans (RPPs).
   B. Registered Retirement Savings Plans (RRSPs).
   C. Employment Insurance (E.I.).
   D. both A and B.
   E. all of the above.

3. The low and declining Canadian household saving rate is
   A. a macroeconomic problem because it reduces the amount of funds available for investment and, thus, reduces the standard of living.
   B. not a macroeconomic problem because the national saving rate has been stable and sufficient.
   C. a microeconomic problem because it reduces the amount of funds available for investment and, thus, reduces the standard of living.
   D. not a microeconomic problem because the national saving rate has been stable and sufficient.
   E. not a microeconomic problem because the booming stock market has increased the wealth of Canadians and reduced income inequality.

4. The investment demand curve indicates that there is a(n)
   A. positive relationship between the real interest rates and the level of investment spending, all other things being equal.
   B. inverse relationship between the real interest rates and the level of investment spending, all other things being equal.
   C. direct relationship between the real interest rates and the level of investment spending, all other things being equal.
   D. inverse relationship between the determinants of investment and the level of investment spending, holding interest rates constant.
   E. positive relationship between the determinants of investment and the level of investment spending, holding interest rates constant.

5. Rafael's current income is $100 more per month than his current consumption needs. He decides to use the $100 to reduce his credit card debt. As a result, his
   A. liabilities will decrease and his wealth will increase.
   B. liabilities and his wealth will decrease.
   C. assets will decrease and his wealth will increase.
   D. assets and his wealth will decrease.
   E. assets and his wealth will increase.

6. During a conversation with her mother about her financial circumstances, Sylvia complained that she could not afford to save because she wanted to maintain a lifestyle similar to that of her friends. Her mother suggested that if she would save more now, she would not only have

more wealth, but she would also have a higher standard of living than her friends' in the future. Her mother's argument was

A. incorrect because if she saved, her standard of living would be lower than that of her friends.

B. incorrect and probably an attempt to confuse her daughter in order to get her to begin saving some of her income.

C. correct because of the power of compound interest her income would increase to a level that would allow her to save and consume more.

D. correct because the more saving, the higher the standard of living.

E. irrelevant because daughters never listen to what their mother tells them.

7. In national income accounting, government saving is

A. increased when the government budget deficit rises.

B. not identical to the government budget surplus.

C. less important to national saving than private saving.

D. more important to national saving than private saving.

E. unimportant in determining the capacity of an economy to invest in new capital.

8. Based on the information given in Quick Quiz question 8, the country has

A. net international liabilities of $7 billion.

B. net international liabilities of $3 billion.

C. net international liabilities of $1 billion.

D. net international assets of $6 billion.

E. net international assets of $4 billion.

9. As the cost of capital goods falls relative to other prices, the

A. demand for investment in new capital will shift to the left.

B. demand for investment in new capital will shift to the right.

C. amount of investment in new capital will increase.

D. amount of saving will rise.

E. amount of saving will fall.

10. Which of the following is NOT a source of saving in Canada?

A. saving by Canadians deposited in other countries' banks.

B. personal saving.

C. corporate saving.

D. government saving.

E. net borrowing from abroad.

11. Which of the following factors would NOT cause people to decrease their savings?

A. spending by other consumers, giving a demonstration effect.

B. a lack of self control.

C. availability of credit card debt.

D. increased availability of home-equity loans.

E. a payroll saving plan.

12. Which of the following is NOT included in calculating net Government saving?
   A. government purchases of goods and services.
   B. government investment.
   C. interest payments on the public debt.
   D. employment insurance.
   E. government transfer payments.

13. The difference between gross saving and national saving is
   A. government saving.
   B. personal saving.
   C. corporate saving.
   D. nonresident saving provided to the Canadian economy and Canadian saving provided to foreign economies.
   E. taxes paid on saving.

14. Which is the largest source of saving in the Canadian economy?
   A. corporate.
   B. government.
   C. household.
   D. nonresident.
   E. personal.

15. Government saving tends to decline during recessions because
   A. government purchases of goods and services always rise.
   B. income tax revenues fall.
   C. transfer payments rise.
   D. both B and C.
   E. all of the above.

16. Canada experienced "positive nonresident saving" most of the past 40 years, meaning that
   A. foreigners put their money into Canadian banks.
   B. Canadians bought a large amount of foreign bonds.
   C. capital inflows were needed to supplement national saving.
   D. Canadians were investing a large amount in foreign countries.
   E. there was a surplus of Canadian saving.

17. The largest component of corporate saving is
   A. corporate savings accounts.
   B. corporate income taxes.
   C. capital consumption allowances.
   D. inventory valuation adjustment.
   E. undistributed profits.

18. Interest rates affect the amount of government saving because
   A. government has to borrow more from commercial banks.
   B. government investment has to compete with private investment.
   C. government may have to refinance the debt it carries.
   D. government likes to save more at higher interest rates.
   E. government can more easily pay down its debts at high interest rates.

19. Which of the following is NOT a reason for personal saving?
   A. precautionary saving.
   B. bequest saving.
   C. life-cycle saving.
   D. inventory adjustment.
   E. saving to buy a house or other large item.

20. A person who uses $10 of savings per week to pay down her credit card balance is adding to her
   A. saving.
   B. liabilities.
   C. stock of wealth.
   D. rate of saving.
   E. capital losses.

Self-Test: Short-Answer Problems
(Answers and solutions are given at the end of the chapter.)

1. Savings and Wealth
In this problem, you will identify an individual's assets and liabilities to determine his wealth. You will also calculate the effect of saving on wealth over time.

At the end of the year 2000, Franklin prepares for the new millennium by writing down all his assets and liabilities. His list includes a car with a market value of $7,500 but with $6,000 left on the car loan; his home with a market value of $125,000 and a mortgage of $122,500; a chequing account with $750 in it; a credit card balance of $1,000; 8,000 shares of the ABC Corporation with a current price of $12 per share; and a debt of $2,500 on a student loan.

A. Construct Franklin's balance sheet below, and calculate his wealth.

Franklin's Balance Sheet:

Assets	Liabilities
Total	Total
	Net Worth

B. Upon returning to his job after the new year 2001, his boss informs him that he has been awarded a bonus of $1,000. He has decided he will not spend it on consumption but rather will use it to increase his wealth. His alternatives are to put it into a deposit account paying 7.5 percent annual interest, pay off his credit card debt that has an annual interest charge of 11 percent, or pay off his student loan that has a 7 percent annual interest charge, or pay off his mortgage that has a 5 percent annual interest charge. What would you recommend that he do with his bonus to maximize the increase in his wealth? Why?

_____

_____

_____

C. After reviewing his net worth, Franklin decides that he has insufficient wealth to achieve his goal of retiring in 20 years. He decides to begin saving $500 per year in an RRSP retirement account (that is not subject to taxes until after he retires). After investigating all the options, Franklin settles on depositing his RRSP funds into a money market account paying 5 percent annual interest. Assume that the interest rate remains unchanged and that Franklin deposits $500 on January 1 in each year, and calculate the value of his retirement account at the end of each of the following periods: 1 year _____, 2 years _____, 3 years _____ , 4 years _____, 5 years _____ .

D. At the end of the fifth year, Franklin reviews his retirement account and discovers that had he deposited the RRSP funds in a stock fund rather than in the money market account, he would have earned an average of 10 percent in capital gains each year. Recalculate the value that his retirement account would have reached, if he had chosen the stock fund, at the end of 1 year _____, 2 years _____, 3 years _____ , 4 years _____, and 5 years _____ .

2. Cost-Benefit Analysis for Investment Decisions

This problem focuses on the use of cost-benefit analysis in making investment decisions. You will calculate the marginal product of capital, determine the marginal benefit and marginal cost of capital, and decide whether to make an investment. You will also analyze the effects of changes in taxation, the cost of capital, and expected income on the investment decision.

Thelma is thinking of going into the business of translating documents for international businesses. In order to do so, she needs to borrow $10,000 to buy computer equipment. She has estimated that she will net $50,000 per year, after deducting operating and maintenance costs. The tax rate on her business profit each year would be 15 percent, and the annual interest rate on the loan would equal 12 percent. Her best job alternative would be teaching Spanish in high school with an after-tax income of $40,000.

A. Assume that the computer equipment does not lose value over time. Calculate the marginal product of the computer equipment. $ _____

B. Calculate the amount of the annual interest that Thelma would have to pay on the loan. $_____

C. Should Thelma invest in the computer equipment and start the translation business? Why, or why not? _____

_____

D. If the government increases the tax rate on business profits to 19%, and the computer equipment does not lose value over time, calculate the marginal product of the computer equipment. $ _____

E. After the tax increase in Question D, should Thelma to buy the computer equipment and start the translation business? Why? _____

_____

F. If the cost of the computer equipment decreased to $4,000, should Thelma buy the computer equipment and start the translation business? Why, or why not?

_____

_____

_____

G. If the computer equipment was less productive than Thelma thought, so that her net income was $45,000 per year, should Thelma buy the computer equipment and start the translation business? Why, or why not? _____

_____

3. Tabulating Saving and Investment
After the untimely departure of a statistician, you have been called in to complete the following table and answer questions.

A. Fill in the data in this table. There are no "statistical discrepancies."

I. Saving	
A. Domestic saving	
1. Persons and unincorporated businesses	
2. Corporations and government business enterprises	
3. Government	
B. Capital consumption allowances	
C. Saving of nonresidents	
Gross Saving	
II. Investment in Fixed Capital and Inventories	
D. Persons and unincorporated businesses	
E. Corporations and government business enterprises	
F. Government	
Gross Investment	

Capital consumption allowances	14
Corporations and government business enterprises investment	120
Corporations and government business enterprises saving	you solve
Domestic saving	you solve
Government investment	11
Government saving	12
Inventory adjustment	−1
Persons and unincorporated businesses investment	you solve
Persons and unincorporated businesses saving	2
Saving of nonresidents	−22
Undistributed corporation profits	151
Unremitted profits of government business enterprises	3

B. What is the total Gross Saving?_____
C. What is the total Gross Investment? _____
D. What is total "net saving"? _____

SOLUTIONS

Quick Quiz
1. A.
2. C.
3. C.
4. E.
5. D.
6. A.
7. C.

8. E. $6 + $4 − $7 = $3 billion.

9. E. The financial benefit of the computer is $250. If the interest rate on the GIC is less than 5 percent, the financial cost of the capital ($5,000 times the interest rate) would be less than the financial benefit of the computer. Therefore, if the interest rate on the GIC is less than 5 percent, she should buy the computer.

Key Terms

1. national saving.
2. liabilities.
3. capital losses.
4. nonresident saving.
5. transfers.
6. corporate saving.
7. life-cycle saving.
8. saving.
9. government saving.
10. bequest saving.
11. flow.
12. saving rate.
13. precautionary saving.
14. wealth.
15. stock.
16. assets.
17. capital gains.
18. national wealth.
19. net international liabilities.
20. national net worth.

Self-Test: Multiple-Choice Questions

1. B.
2. D.
3. B.
4. B.
5. A. Debt is a type of liability, and reducing liabilities increase wealth.
6. C.
7. B.
8. C. National wealth = $4 billion, national net worth = $ 3 billion, and so net worth − national wealth = 3 − 4 = −1 (net foreign liabilities).
9. B.
10. C.
11. A.

12. E.
13. B.
14. D.
15. A.
16. D.
17. C.
18. E.
19. C.
20. D.
21. C.

Self-Test: Short-Answer Problems

1. A. Franklin's Balance Sheet:

Assets		Liabilities	
Car	$7,500	Car loan	$6,000
Home	125,000	Mortgage	122,500
Chequing account	750	Credit card balance	1,000
ABC Corp. shares	96,000	Student loan	2,500
Total	$ 229,250	Total	$132,000
		Net Worth	$ 97,250

B. He should pay off his credit card debt because it will reduce his liabilities and, thus, increase his wealth. The credit card debt has a higher opportunity cost (interest rate) than the student loan, and he will save more in interest payments than he would earn on the deposit account.

C. $525(= $500 + [$500 × 0.05]); $1,076.25 (= 525 + 500 + [1,025 × 0.05]); $1,655.06; $2,262.81; $2,900.95.

D. $550; $1,155; $1,820.50; $2,552.55; $3,357.80.

2. A. $2,500 (Thelma would have to pay $7,500 [$50,000 × 0.15] in profit taxes, leaving her an after-tax income of $50,000 – $7,500 = $42,500. Subtracting the Spanish teacher's salary [$40,000] that she must forgo to start the translating business from the after-tax income [$42,500] equals the marginal product of the computer equipment.)

B. $1,200 (= $10,000 × 0.12)

C. Yes; because the financial cost ($1,200 interest payment) is less than the financial benefit ($2,500 marginal product of the computer equipment).

D. $500 (The solution is the same as in 2A, except the tax rate is now 0.19.)

E. No, because the financial cost ($1,200) is greater than the financial benefit ($500).

F. Yes, because the financial cost ($480) is less than the financial benefit ($500).

G. No, because the financial benefit has become negative ($ –3,550) and, therefore, is less than the financial cost.

3. A.

I. Saving	
A. Domestic saving	167
1. Persons and unincorporated businesses	2
2. Corporations and government business enterprises	153
3. Government	12
B. Capital consumption allowances	14
C. Saving of non-residents	-22
Gross Saving	159
II. Investment in Fixed Capital and Inventories	
D. Persons and unincorporated businesses	29
E. Corporations and government business enterprises	120
F. Government	11
Gross Investment	160

Capital consumption allowances	14
Corporations and government business enterprises investment	120
Corporations and government business enterprises saving	you solve
Domestic saving	you solve
Government investment	11
Government saving	12
Inventory adjustment	−1
Persons and unincorporated businesses investment	you solve
Persons and unincorporated businesses saving	2
Saving of nonresidents	−22
Undistributed corporation profits	151
Unremitted profits of government business enterprises	3

B. What is the total Gross Saving?   **159**

C. What is the total Gross Investment?   **160**

D. What is total "net saving"?   **145 (Gross investment – capital consumption allowance = net saving)**

9 Money, Banks, and Central Banking

OVERVIEW

The concept of money is introduced and measuring the quantity of money in the economy is discussed in the first part of this chapter. The second part introduces major central banks—the Bank of Canada, the Federal Reserve, and the European Central Bank. The third section discusses how central banks use some of their policy tools.

Chapter Review

9.1   Money and Its Uses

▶ **LO 1. Define money and barter.**

Money is any asset that can be used in making purchases. Without money, all economic transactions would have to be in the form of *barter* that is, the direct trade of goods and services for other goods and services. Barter is inefficient because it requires that both parties to a trade have something the other party wants, a so-called "double coincidence of wants." Money facilitates more efficient transactions and permits individuals to specialize in producing particular goods and services.

▶ **LO 2. Define and discuss the three functions of money.**

Money has three principal uses: it serves as a medium of exchange, a unit of account, and a store of value. Money serves as a *medium of exchange* when it is used to purchase goods and services. As a *unit of account*, money is the basic yardstick for measuring economic value. As a *store of value*, money serves as a means of holding wealth.

▶ **LO 3.   Identify and calculate the components of M1 and M2.**

When measuring the quantity of money in the economy, economists vary as to how they define the concept of money. The narrowest definition of the amount of money in Canada is called *M1*, the sum of currency outstanding and balances held in chequing accounts. A broader measure of the money supply is *M2*, which includes all the assets in M1 plus personal savings deposits and nonpersonal notice deposits held at banks. M1 and M2 differ substantially in magnitude. Because the definition of the money supply includes both currency and bank deposits, the amount of money in the economy depends, in part, on the behaviour of commercial banks and their depositors. When households or businesses deposit currency into a bank, the currency becomes a part of the bank reserves.

Quick Quiz

1. Double coincidence of wants is avoided if money is used as a
   A. medium of exchange.
   B. measure of value.
   C. standard of deferred payment.
   D. store of value.
   E. tool of monetary policy.

2. Money serves as a basic yardstick for measuring economic value (i.e., a unit of account), allowing
   A. people to hold their wealth in a liquid form.
   B. governments to restrict the issuance of private monies.
   C. easy comparison of the relative prices of goods and services.
   D. goods and services to be exchanged with a double coincidence of wants.
   E. private money to be issued for local use.

3. M1 differs from M2 in that
   A. M1 includes currency and balances held in chequing accounts that are not included in M2.
   B. M2 includes savings deposits, small-denomination time deposits, and money market mutual funds that are not included in M1.
   C. M2 includes personal savings accounts and nonpersonal notice deposits at banks that are not included in M1.
   D. M1 is a broader measure of the money supply than M2.
   E. the assets in M2 are more liquid than the assets in M1.

9.2   Commercial Banks and the Creation of Money

▶ **LO 4.**   **Define bank reserves, 100 percent reserve banking, reserve–deposit ratio, and fractional reserve banking system.**

Bank reserves are cash or similar assets held by commercial banks for the purpose of meeting depositor withdrawals and payments. When banks must keep bank reserves equal to the amount of their deposits, it is referred to as a *100 percent reserve banking* system. If banks can maintain a *reserve/deposit ratio* (bank reserves divided by deposits) of less than 100 percent, then it is referred to as a *fractional-reserve banking system*. In a fractional-reserve banking system, the amount of the money supply is expanded when banks make loans in the form of new deposits. Today, the Bank of Canada does not set reserve requirements, which were abolished in 1992.

▶ **LO 5.**   **Calculate bank reserve–deposit ratio.**

The reserve–deposit ratio is found by dividing the amount of money held by a bank by the total amount of money held by that bank in deposits, and multiplying by 100 to obtain a percentage answer.

▶ **LO 6.**   **Calculate the maximum amount of bank deposits held in the banking system, as a result of the lending of money not being held on reserve.**

By dividing the total amount of money *introduced* for reserves (the initial deposits held by banks) by the desired reserve deposit ratio, the total deposits which can ultimately be supported by the banking system is determined. In the textbook's example, $1,000,000 of initial deposits are available to the banking system, and banks wish to hold 10 percent of these deposits on reserve. After the money not held on reserve is on-lent to its maximum extent, the deposits now supported equals $1,000,000 divided by 0.10 (the decimal equivalent of 10 percent), or $10,000,000.

Quick quiz

4. A bank operating under a "fractional-reserve" system must be holding
   A. fewer deposits than other banks.
   B. less money on reserve than it has in deposits.
   C. less deposits than what it has in reserves.
   D. an inadequate amount of money on reserve.
   E. a greater percentage of money on deposits than other banks.

5. According to the Bank of Canada, the amount of money (in millions of dollars) held by banks in Canada in February 2003 on deposit was $100,184, and the amount of money held on reserve was $3,622. The reserve deposit ratio was therefore
   A. $96,562 million.
   B. 96 percent.
   C. $3,622.
   D. 2766 percent.
   E. 3.6 percent.

6. When a bank makes a loan by crediting the borrower's chequing account balance with an amount equal to the loan
   A. money is created.
   B. the bank gains new reserves.
   C. the bank immediately loses reserves.
   D. money is destroyed.
   E. the Bank of Canada has made an open-market purchase.

9.3 Central Banking

▶ **LO 7.** **Discuss the history and responsibilities of the Bank of Canada and other central banks.**

Central banks are usually responsible for monetary policy, oversight and regulation of financial markets, providing central banking services, issuing bank notes, and administering government debt. *The Bank of Canada* is the central bank in Canada, but it does not have a large regulatory role. The Canadian economy is influenced by not only the monetary policy of the Bank of Canada but also those of the *Federal Reserve System*, often called the Fed, and the *European Central Bank*, respectively the central banks of the United States and of the euro-zone countries of the European Union. Within the Bank of Canada, decisions about monetary policy are made by the Governing Council, which is made up by the Governor (who is appointed by the Board for a term of seven years), the Senior Deputy Governor, the Deputy Minister of Finance, and 12 outside directors.

▶ **LO 8.** **Define key policy rate and reserve requirements.**

The Bank of Canada's primary responsibility is making monetary policy, which typically involves decisions about changes to the Bank's official interest rate or *key policy rate*, the target for the overnight rate. In theory, the Bank of Canada can affect the amount of reserves held by commercial banks through several techniques to achieve its key policy rate. Some central banks affect the amount of reserves in the banking system by changing the reserve requirements. *Reserve requirements* are the minimum values of the ratio of bank reserves to bank deposits that commercial banks are allowed to maintain. Since 1992, the required reserve ratio in Canada has been set to zero, and the Bank of Canada has used other techniques to affect bank reserves.

▶ **LO 9.** **Explain open-market operations and how purchases or sales affect the amount of bank reserves.**

One of these techniques is *open-market operations*, which includes *open-market purchases* of government bonds ("securities") from the public for the purpose of increasing the supply of banks reserves, and *open-market sales* of government bonds to the public for the purpose of reducing bank reserves.

▶ **LO 10.** **Define government deposit shifting and how this affects the amount of bank reserves.**

Another technique, known as *government deposit shifting*, involves transfers of government deposits by the central bank between government's account at the central bank and government's accounts at the commercial banks. By shifting government deposits from a commercial bank to government's account with the Bank of Canada, the Bank of Canada can decrease bank reserves. Shifting government deposits in the opposite direction will increase bank reserves.

► **LO 11.** **Define bank panic and discuss the American experience during the Great Depression.**

Besides monetary policy, a central bank (along with other government agencies) has the responsibility to ensure that financial markets operate smoothly. This is because instability of the financial system may affect the money supply. A *banking panic* is an episode in which depositors, spurred by news or rumours of the imminent bankruptcy of one or more banks, rush to withdraw their deposits from the banking system. Although Canada was not gripped by a banking panic during the Great Depression of 1930–33, the United States experienced the worst and most protracted series of bank panics in its history. Fearing banking panics, American banks increased their reserve–deposit ratios, which tended to reduce the money supply.

Even in the absence of banking panics, the central bank cannot *directly* and *precisely* control the money supply at will. In the real world, many central banks, including the Bank of Canada, change their key policy rates so as to *indirectly* achieve their monetary policy objectives.

Quick Quiz

7. Which of the following is the monetary tool of the Bank of Canada?
   A. reserve requirement ratios.
   B. the dividends of banks.
   C. the key policy rate.
   D. the minimum net worth required of banks.
   E. market interest rates.

8. A central bank "reserve requirement" refers to
   A. the amount of reserves which commercial banks must hold with the central bank.
   B. the level of deposits which commercial banks must maintain.
   C. the central bank requirement that commercial banks must hold at least some cash on reserve.
   D. the central bank stipulation of a minimum percentage which commercial banks must hold on reserve.
   E. the amount of money which the central bank must hold on reserve at the commercial banks.

9. When the Bank of Canada sells government bonds, the banks'
   A. reserves will increase and lending will expand, causing an increase in the money supply.
   B. reserves will decrease and lending will contract, causing a decrease in the money supply.
   C. reserve requirements will increase and lending will contract, causing a decrease in the money supply.
   D. reserves/deposit ratio will increase and lending will expand, causing an increase in the money supply.

10. When the Bank of Canada transfers government deposits from its account to commercial banks
  A. bank reserves are increased and interest rates rise.
  B. the reserve/deposit ratio falls.
  C. bank reserves are increased and, ultimately, bank deposits and the money supply increase.
  D. bank reserves are decreased and, ultimately, bank deposits and the money supply increase.
  E. bank reserves are increased and, ultimately, bank deposits and the money supply decrease.

11. During the bank panic of 1930–33 in the United States, the public withdrew deposits from commercial banks, preferring to hold currency. As a result
  A. bank reserves decreased but were offset by an equal increase in currency, with no net effect on the money supply.
  B. bank reserves increased by less than the increase in currency, causing the money supply to decrease.
  C. bank reserves decreased by more than the increase in currency, causing the money supply to decrease.
  D. bank reserves decreased by less than the increase in currency, causing the money supply to increase.
  E. bank reserves decreased by an amount equal to the increase in currency, causing the money supply to decrease.

Self-Test: Key Terms

Use the terms below to complete the following sentences. (Answers are given at the end of the chapter.)

100 percent reserve banking	M2
bank reserves	medium of exchange
Bank of Canada	modern central banking theory
banking panic	money
barter	open-market operations
European Central Bank	open-market purchase
Federal Reserve System	open-market sale
fractional-reserve banking system	reserve requirements
Governing Council	reserve/deposit ratio
government deposit shifting	store of value
key policy rate	unit of account
M1	

1. Cash or similar assets held by commercial banks for the purpose of meeting depositor withdrawals and payments are called _____ .

2. One important tool of monetary policy is _____ , which occurs when the central bank buys and sells bonds or financial assets.

3. The sum of currency outstanding and balances held in chequing accounts equals

   _____ .

4. Monetary policy is the responsibility of _____ in Canada; its counterparts

   are _____ in the United States and _____ in the European

   Union.

5. By transferring government deposits, also known as _____, the Bank of Canada

   can change bank reserves.

6. When money serves as a means of holding wealth, it is serving the function of

   _____ .

7. Without money, all economic transactions would have to be in the form of

   _____ .

8. The Bank of Canada does not use _____ to alter the amount of bank

   reserves, although some central banks do use this policy tool.

9. In Canada, the assets in M1 plus personal savings deposits and nonpersonal notice deposits

   held at banks equal _____ .

10. If banks are permitted to maintain a reserve–deposit ratio of less than 100 percent, then a

    _____ exists.

11. In a _____, depositors rush to withdraw their deposits from the banking

    system.

12. The monetary policy of the Bank of Canada is decided by its _____ .

13. When banks must keep bank reserves equal to the amount of their deposits, it is referred to as

    a(n) _____ .

14. In order to reduce bank reserves, the Bank of Canada would undertake a(n)

    _____ of government bonds.

15. When money is used to buy a car, it serves the function of _____ .

16. The interest rate the Bank of Canada uses as a target in its monetary policy is called the

    _____ .

17. Bank reserves divided by deposits equals the _____ .

18. If the Bank of Canada wants to increase the supply of bank reserves, it should implement a(n)

    _____ .

19. Because money is the basic yardstick for measuring economic value, it serves as a(n)

    _____ .

Self-Test: Multiple-Choice Questions

Circle the letter that corresponds to the best answer. (Answers are given at the end of the chapter.)

1. If a bank's desired reserve–deposit ratio is 0.33 and it has deposit liabilities of $100 million and reserves of $50 million, it
    A. has too few reserves and will reduce its lending.
    B. has too many reserves and will increase its lending.
    C. has the correct amount of reserves and outstanding loans.
    D. should increase the amount of its reserves.
    E. should decrease the amount of its reserves.

2. If the reserve–deposit ratio is 0.25 and the banking system receives an additional $10 million in reserves, bank deposits can increase by a maximum of
    A. $10 million.
    B. $250 million.
    C. $400 million.
    D. $4 million.
    E. $40 million.

3. An open-market purchase of government bonds by the Bank of Canada will
    A. increase bank reserves, and the money supply will increase.
    B. decrease bank reserves, and the money supply will increase.
    C. increase bank reserves, and the money supply will decrease.
    D. decrease bank reserves, and the money supply will decrease.
    E. increase bank reserves, and the money supply will not change.

4. When an individual deposits currency into a chequing account
    A. bank reserves increase, which allows banks to lend more and, ultimately, increases the money supply.
    B. bank reserves decrease, which reduces the amount banks can lend thereby reducing the growth of the money supply.
    C. bank reserves are unchanged.
    D. bank reserves decrease, which increases the amount banks can lend thereby increasing the growth of the money supply.
    E. bank reserves increase, which reduces the amount banks can lend thereby reducing the growth of the money supply.

5. Which one of the following would NOT be a reason for people to hold cash as a store of value?
    A. it is anonymous.
    B. it is difficult to trace.
    C. it is a medium of exchange.
    D. it pays no interest.
    E. all of the above.

6. Canadian coins and paper currency are
   A. commodity money.
   B. fully backed by gold.
   C. minted by commercial banks.
   D. fiat money.
   E. barter.

7. Which of the following is not a use of money
   A. double coincidence of wants.
   B. medium of exchange.
   C. store of value.
   D. unit of account.

8. A major component of M1 is
   A. savings deposits.
   B. foreign currency deposits.
   C. chequing accounts.
   D. term deposits.
   E. caisses populaires.

9. The broadest measure of money, M3
   A. is about the same size as the total currency in circulation.
   B. includes nonpersonal notice deposits.
   C. contains more easily "usable" money than M1 or M2.
   D. comprises the only broadly accepted measure of money in the economy.
   E. includes credit card transactions.

10. The total money supply consists of currency, plus
   A. bank reserves/desired reserve–deposit ratio.
   B. desired reserve–deposit ratio/bank deposits.
   C. bank deposits/bank reserves.
   D. bank deposits/desired reserve–deposit ratio.
   E. desired reserve–deposit ration/bank reserves.

11. In order to stimulate the economy, a central bank could
   A. raise the key policy rate.
   B. shift government deposits from commercial banks back to itself.
   C. buy government bonds on the open market.
   D. ease reserve requirements for commercial banks.
   E. make more loans to the public.

12. When the Bank of Canada decreases its key policy rate, the predicted result would be
   A. a tendency for commercial banks to make more loans available, thus stimulating the economy.
   B. a compensating increase in the overnight rate.

   C. an increase in the government deposits in the Bank of Canada.

   D. a tendency for commercial banks to make fewer loans available, thus contracting the economy.

   E. uncertain because the policy rate does not affect the private sector.

13. A banking panic and large-scale withdrawals from commercial banks contract the economy because

   A. there is a smaller volume of coins and paper currency in circulation.

   B. commercial banks must increase the number of loans made to the public.

   C. commercial banks raise their lending rates.

   D. the central bank shifts government deposits to commercial banks.

   E. the money supply decreases, since banks have fewer deposits and thus less lending occurs.

14. The Bank of Canada is

   A. a subdivision of the federal Ministry of Finance.

   B. a semi-independent government agency.

   C. the largest commercial bank in Canada.

   D. a private regulatory institution.

   E. the Canadian branch of the International Monetary Fund (IMF).

15. "Commodity money" refers to

   A. home-produced articles historically used in barter, such as chickens and eggs.

   B. that part of the money supply utilized for private consumption.

   C. financial investments in commodity markets.

   D. an asset with intrinsic value which is accepted for payment, for example, a gold coin.

   E. income generated in key agricultural products, for example, wheat.

Self-Test: Short-Answer Problems

(Answers and solutions are given at the end of the chapter.)

1. Measuring the Money Supply

In this problem, you will practise calculating the measures of the Canadian money supply—Ml and M2.

Quarter/ Year	Currency	Personal Savings Deposits	Chequing Account Deposits	Nonpersonal Notice Deposits
1/2000	$32.5	$334.6	$68.0	$42.9
2/2000	33.5	336.9	70.6	45.3
3/2000	34.2	336.8	74.5	46.6
4/2000	35.0	341.5	81.1	49.7

Source: *Bank of Canada Banking and Financial Statistics.*
All figures are in millions of dollars.

A. Use the preceding data to complete the following table, calculating the amounts for Ml and M2 for the year 2000.

Quarter/Year	M1	M2
1/2000		
2/2000		
3/2000		
4/2000		

B. If the public transfers funds from their personal savings accounts at the Royal Bank of Canada to their chequing accounts at the Bank of Montreal, this will (increase/decrease/leave unchanged)_____ M1 and (increase/decrease/leave unchanged) _____ M2.

C. If the public deposits currency into their chequing accounts at the Bank of Montreal, this will (increase/decrease/leave unchanged) _____ Ml and (increase/decrease/leave unchanged) _____ M2.

2. Reserve–Deposit Ratio, Open-Market Operations, and Money Creation

Assuming there is only one type of deposit in the economy, in this problem, you will calculate reserve–deposit ratios, determine how much a bank can lend based on its reserves, deposit liabilities and reserve–deposit ratio, and determine the effect of open-market sales and purchases of government securities on a bank's ability to lend and create money. Each question refers back to the balance sheet of the Bank of Dollaria, a hypothetical bank, shown below (i.e., do NOT take into account the transaction indicated in a question, say, 3A, when answering another question, say, 3B, and so on.

Balance Sheet of the Bank of Dollaria

Assets	Liabilities
Currency (= reserves) $10,000	Deposits $10,000

A. If the Bank of Dollaria has a desired reserve–deposit ratio of 10 percent, it can make new loans of $_____ in the form of new _____. After making the new loans, The Bank of Dollaria will have total deposit liabilities of $_____ , currency (= reserves) of $_____ , and outstanding loans of $_____ . Its total assets will then equal $_____ , and its total liabilities will equal $_____ .

B. If the Central Bank of Dollaria imposes a minimum reserve–deposit ratio in the form of a 20 percent reserve requirement, the maximum amount of new loans the Bank of Dollaria could make would be $_____ . After making the new loans, the Bank of Dollaria would have total deposit liabilities of $_____ , currency (= reserves) of $_____ , and outstanding loans of $_____ . Its total assets would then equal $_____ , and its total liabilities would equal $_____ .

C. Assume the Central Bank of Dollaria buys $3,000 of government securities from Susan Slavin and she deposits the $3,000 in her chequing account at the Bank of Dollaria. Following the deposit, the Bank of Dollaria would have currency (= reserves) of $_____ and deposit liabilities of $_____ . Assuming the Central Bank of Dollaria maintains a minimum reserve–deposit ratio of 20 percent, the Bank of Dollaria could make new loans of $_____ . By doing so, it would (increase/decrease) _____ the money supply by $_____ .

D. Assume the Central Bank of Dollaria sells $3,000 of government securities to the Bank of Dollaria, which it pays for out of its reserves. After the sale of the government securities, the Bank of Dollaria would have currency (= reserves) of $_____ and deposit liabilities of $_____ . Assuming the Central Bank of Dollaria maintains a minimum reserve–deposit ratio of 20 percent, the Bank of Dollaria could make new loans of $_____ . By doing so, it would (increase/decrease) _____ the money supply by $_____ .

E. In comparing the answers to questions 3B and 3D, by selling $3,000 of government securities to the Bank of Dollaria, the Central Bank of Dollaria would be able to reduce the growth in the supply of money by $_____ .

SOLUTIONS

Quick Quiz

1. A.
2. C.
3. C.
4. B.
5. E.
6. A.
7. C.
8. D.
9. B.
10. C.
11. E.

Self-Test: Key Terms

1. bank reserves.
2. open-market operations.
3. M1.
4. bond.
5. The Bank of Canada, the Federal Reserve System (or Fed), the European Central Bank.
6. store of value.
7. barter.
8. reserve requirements.
9. M2.
10. fractional-reserves banking system.
11. banking panic.
12. Governing Council.
13. 100 percent reserve banking system.

14. open-market sale.
15. medium of exchange.
16. key policy rate.
17. reserve–deposit ratio.
18. open-market purchase.
19. unit of account.

Self-Test: Multiple-Choice Questions

1. B.
2. E.
3. A.
4. A.
5. D.
6. D.
7. A.
8. C.
9. B.
10. A.
11. C.
12. A.
13. E.
14. B.
15. D.

Self-Test: Short-Answer Problems

1.
A.

Quarter/Year	M1	M2
1/2000	$100.5	$478.0
2/2000	104.1	486.3
3/2000	108.7	492.1
4/2000	116.1	507.3

B. increase; leave unchanged (because the components of M1 are also included in M2).
C. leave unchanged; leave unchanged (currency and chequing deposits are included in both M1 and M2. Thus, depositing currency into a chequing account does not change the amount of M1 or M2).

2.

A. $90,000 (Because the desired reserve/deposit ratio is 0.10 the $10,000 in reserves can support $10,000/0.10 = $100,000 in deposits. Thus, $100,000 minus the existing $10,000 in deposits = $90,000); chequing deposits; $100,000; $10,000; $90,000; $100,000; $100,000.

B. $40,000 (Now that the Central Bank of Dollaria has imposed a reserve requirements of 0.20, the $10,000 in reserves can support $10,000/0.2 = $50,000. Thus, the bank can make new loan of $40,000); $50,000; $10,000; $40,000; $50,000; $50,000.

C. $10,000 + $3,000 = $13,000; $13,000; $52,000 ($13,000/0.2 = $65,000 from which the existing $13,000 is subtracted, allowing new loans of $52,000); increase; $52,000.

D. $10,000 − $3,000 = $7,000; $7,000/0.2 = $35,000 from which the existing $10,000 is subtracted, allowing new loans of $25,000; increase; $25,000.

E. $50,000 − $25,000 = $25,000.

10 Financial Markets and International Capital Flows

OVERVIEW

The major financial markets and institutions and their role in directing saving to productive use are discussed in the first part of this chapter. The chapter concludes by examining the crucial role of international capital flows in modern economies.

Chapter Review

10.1 The Financial System and the Allocation of Funds to Real Investment

▶ **LO 1.** **Explain how financial systems improve the allocation of saving.**

A successful economy not only saves but also uses its saving to invest in projects that are likely to be the most productive. In a market economy, like that of Canada, a financial system improves the allocation of funds by providing financial investors information about the uses of their funds that are most likely to prove profitable, and by helping financial investors share the risks of lending by allowing them to diversify their financial investments. Three key components of a financial system are discussed in this chapter: (1) the banking systems, (2) the bond market, and (3) the stock market.

▶ **LO 2.** **Discuss the role of financial intermediaries.**

Financial intermediaries are firms that extend credit to borrowers using funds raised from savers. Commercial banks, already discussed in Chapter 9, are the most important financial intermediaries in the banking system. Savers are willing to hold bank deposits because banks (and other financial intermediaries) have a comparative advantage in information-gathering about lending opportunities that results in lower costs and better results than individual savers could achieve on their own. Banks also make it easier for households and businesses to make payments for goods and services. Other examples of financial intermediaries are trust companies, credit unions, and caisses populaires.

►LO 3.   **Explain bond principal amount, present value, future value, and coupon rate and coupon payment.**

Corporations and governments seeking funds are not required to rely solely on banks. They can also obtain funds in the bond market. Corporations and governments frequently raise funds by issuing bonds and selling them to savers. A *bond* is a legal promise to repay a debt, usually including both the *principal amount* (the amount originally lent) and regular interest payments. The promised interest rate when a bond is issued is called the *coupon rate*, which is paid to the bondholder in regular interest payments called *coupon payments*. The coupon rate must be sufficiently attractive to savers, depending on the term, or length of time before the debt is fully repaid, and the risk that the borrower will not repay the debt. Bondholders do not have to hold bonds until they are to be repaid by the issuer because they can sell them in the bond market.

► LO4.   **Discuss the relationship between bond prices and interest rates.**

The price (or market value) of a bond at any point in time is inversely related to interest rates being paid on comparable newly issued bonds. For example, if the present price of a bond is $95, and the bond's future value is $100, then the effective interest rate is about 5.26 percent. If investors become less interested in bonds, and the price of the same bond falls to $93, then the effective interest rate increases to about 7.53 percent.

► LO 5.   **Explain stock, dividend, and risk premium.**

Another important way of raising funds, but one that is restricted to corporations, is by issuing shares to the public. A share of *stock*, also called equity, is a claim to partial ownership of a firm. Stockholders receive returns on their financial investment in a firm through dividend payments and capital gains (the increase in the price of the stock). A *dividend* is a regular payment received by stockholders for each share that they own, as determined by the firm's management and is usually dependent on the firm's recent profits. The price of a share of stock at any point in time depends on the expected future dividends and capital gain, adjusted for the risk premium. *Risk premium* is the rate of return that financial investors require to hold risky assets minus the rate of return on safe assets.

Quick Quiz

1. Which of the following is NOT a part of the Canadian financial system?
   A. Revenue Canada.
   B. the stock market.
   C. the bond market.
   D. commercial banks.
   E. financial institutions.

2. A feature common to all financial intermediaries is that they
   A. buy and sell information about savers and borrowers.
   B. have a comparative advantage in gathering and evaluating information about borrowers.
   C. act as agents for buyers and sellers in the money market.
   D. shift the risk of investing from borrowers to savers.
   E. collect funds from a few savers and distribute the funds to many borrowers.

3. The "future value" (FV) of a bond is
   A. the value of a bond in the initial period.
   B. the amount of interest which will be paid on a bond.
   C. the present value of the bond, compounded at a given interest rate.
   D. the present value of the bond minus the interest paid on the bond.
   E. the amount at which the bond could be resold on the bond market.

4. Antonio holds a two-year bond issued by the Jetson Corporation with a principal amount of $10,000. The annual coupon rate is 6 percent. He considered selling it after receiving the first coupon payment a week ago at a price of $9,390. Since that time, the coupon rate on new bond issues has risen from 6.5 to 7 percent. If he were to sell the bond today, the price would be
   A. $10,000.
   B. higher than it was a week ago.
   C. the same at it was a week ago.
   D. lower than it was a week ago.
   E. impossible to determine from the information given.

5. The price of a share of corporate stock varies over time depending on stockholders' expectations about the future
   A. coupon rate, risk premium, and coupon payment.
   B. dividend, stock price, and coupon rate.
   C. coupon payment, dividend and risk premium.
   D. coupon rate, coupon premium and dividend.
   E. dividend, stock price, and risk premium.

10.2 Bond Markets, Stock Markets, and the Allocation of Savings

▶ **LO 6.**   **Explain diversification and how mutual funds help individual savers to diversify financial assets.**

Like banks, bond and stock markets provide a means of channelling funds from savers to borrowers with profitable investment opportunities. Savers and their financial advisers search for high returns in the bond and stock markets and, thus, provide a powerful incentive to potential borrowers to use the funds for profitable investment opportunities. The markets also give savers a means to diversify their financial investments. *Diversification* is the practice of spreading one's wealth over a variety of different financial investments in order to reduce overall risk. From society's perspective, diversification makes it possible for risky but worthwhile projects to obtain funding without individual savers having to bear too much risk. For the typical saver, a convenient way to diversify is to buy stocks and bonds indirectly through mutual funds. A *mutual fund* is a financial intermediary that sells shares in itself to the public, and then uses the funds raised to buy a wide variety of financial assets.

Quick Quiz

6. Which of the following is the best example of diversification?
   A. buying all blue chip stocks.
   B. keeping money in a savings account.
   C. buying shares in a foreign company.
   D. investing in gold.
   E. purchasing shares in a mutual fund.

10.3 International Capital Flows

▶ **LO 7.** **Explain the difference between a closed economy and an open economy.**

A *closed economy* is one that does not trade with the rest of the world, while an *open economy* is one that does trade with the rest of the world. Financial markets in which borrowers and lenders are residents of different countries are called *international* financial markets.

▶ **LO 8.** **Define international real financial capital flows, including capital inflows and outflows.**

Purchases or sales of real and financial assets across international borders are known as *international capital flows*. From the perspective of a particular country, purchases of domestic assets by foreigners are called *capital inflows*, and purchases of foreign assets by domestic households and firms are called *capital outflows*. Net capital inflows are related to real interest rates and investment risk in a country. The higher the real interest rate in a country and the lower the risk of investing there, the higher is its net capital inflows. Net capital inflows expand a country's pool of saving, allowing for more domestic investment and economic growth. A drawback, however, to using capital inflows to finance domestic investment is that the interest and dividends on the borrowed funds must be paid to foreign savers rather than domestic residents. Also, if some countries are experiencing positive net capital inflows, other countries must be experiencing negative net capital inflows, or net capital outflows. An economy experiencing net capital outflows will have a higher real interest rate than would otherwise prevail and a lower level of investment.

▶ **LO 9.   Discuss trade balance and trade surplus and deficit.**

The *trade balance* refers the amount of a country's exports, less its imports. A *trade surplus* refers to a situation when exports exceed imports, and a *trade deficit* means that imports exceed exports.

▶ **LO 10.   Explain the relationship among the current account, net capital inflows, saving, and private sector investment.**

There is a precise link between the current account balance and international capital flows. In any given period, the current account balance and net capital inflows add up to zero, or CA (current account balance) + *KI* (net capital inflows) = 0. This link suggests that the primary cause of a current account deficit is a country's low rate of national saving relative to its rate of investment (or conversely, a country's high rate of investment relative to national saving). A country with a low rate of national saving relative to its rate of investment is likely to import more and export less than a country with a high rate of national saving relative to its rate of investment. It is also likely to have higher real interest rates, attracting net capital inflows. Because the sum of the current account balance and net capital inflows is zero, a high level of net capital inflows is consistent with a large current account deficit.

▶ **LO 11.   Identify the roles of returns and risk as determinants of international capital flows.**

The availability of higher investment returns in terms of higher interest rates at home will cause a net inflow of capital. The opposite is true of risk, where a higher degree of risk at home will cause a net outflow of capital.

▶ **LO 12.   Explain the loanable funds model and compare determination of the real interest rate in a closed economy and in an open economy.**

The loanable funds model explains how interaction between the desired gross investment in an economy interacts with the available savings to determine the equilibrium real interest rate. In a closed economy, the saving must come entirely from within the economy, whereas in an open economy, the flow of financial capital combines with domestic saving. When the home real interest rate is relatively high, there will be an inflow of financial capital, resulting in a total higher level of available saving; the equilibrium real interest rate will thus be lower than if the economy had been closed.

Quick Quiz

7. The Canadian economy is
   A. an autarky.
   B. fairly closed.
   C. fairly open.

D. opposed to most foreign trade.

E. characterized by only capital inflows.

8. From the Canadian perspective, which of the following transactions would cause a capital outflow?

A. the import of goods into Canada.

B. the purchase of Canadian securities by an American company.

C. the purchase of European securities by a Canadian company.

D. the import of shipping services.

E. the export of Canadian goods and services.

9. Since 1978, Canadian exports have generally

A. been less than imports.

B. exceeded imports.

C. comprised a minor portion of its GDP.

D. resulted in a trade deficit.

E. undercut the Canadian economy.

10. The current account is defined as

A. merchandise exports minus merchandise imports.

B. capital inflows less capital outflows.

C. net exports, net international investment income, and net international transfers.

D. transfers balance.

E. net investment income received.

11. If interest rates in Japan increase relative to international interest rate levels, all else being equal, Japan's net capital

A. inflows will tend to increase, and the pool of funds for domestic investment will tend to decrease.

B. inflows will tend to increase, and the pool of funds for domestic investment will tend to increase.

C. outflows will tend to increase, and the pool of funds for domestic investment will tend to decrease.

D. outflows will tend to increase, and the pool of funds for domestic investment will tend to increase.

E. inflows will tend to decrease, and the pool of funds for domestic investment will tend to decrease.

12. According to the loanable funds model, at a relatively low interest rate in the home open economy, neither foreign investors nor home investors are attracted to interest-bearing opportunities in the home market, and there will be a(n)

A. net outflow of financial capital.

B. net inflow of financial capital.

C. outflow of foreign financial capital only.

D. inflow of home financial capital only.

E. indeterminant change, since no one knows the nominal interest rate.

Self-Tests: Key Terms

Use the terms below to complete the following sentences. (Answers are given at the end of the chapter.)

bond
capital inflows
capital outflows
closed economy
consumption possibilities
coupon payments
coupon rate
current account
diversification
dividend
financial intermediaries

international capital flows
loanable funds model
mutual fund
open economy
principal amount
risk premium
stock (or equity)
trade balance
trade deficit
trade surplus

1. The promised interest rate when a bond is issued is called the _____ .

2. An investor can reduce the overall risk of investing through _____ .

3. The rate of return that financial investors require to hold risky assets minus the rate of return on safe assets is the _____ .

4. Unlike individuals, corporations and governments can frequently raise funds by issuing a _____ .

5. Firms that extend credit to borrowers using funds raised from savers are called _____ .

6. The price of a share of stock at any point in time depends on the expected future capital gain and the _____ , adjusted for the risk premium.

7. For the typical saver, a convenient way to diversify is buy stocks and bonds indirectly through a(n) _____ .

8. The regular interest payments paid to the bondholder are called the _____ .

9. An important way of raising funds, but one that is restricted to corporations, is by issuing _____ to the public.

10. The amount originally lent by a bondholder to a corporation or government is called the _____ .

11. A society that does not trade with the rest of the world has a(n) _____ .

12. From the perspective of a particular country, purchases of domestic assets by foreigners are called _____ .

13. A society that trades with the rest of the world has a(n) _____ .

14. Another term for a country's net exports is its _____ .

15. Purchases or sales of real and financial assets across international borders are known as

_____ .

16. When the value of a country's exports exceeds the value of its imports for a period, it has a(n)

_____ .

17. From the perspective of a particular country, purchases of foreign assets by domestic households and firms are called _____ .

18. If the value of a country's imports exceeds the value of its exports for a period, it has a(n)

_____ .

19. The record of payments and receipts arising from trade in goods and services, from international investment income, and from international transfers is the

_____.

20. An economic theory which explains the effect of capital flows, in an open economy, on the determination of the real rate of interest is the _____ .

Self-Test: Multiple-Choice Questions

Circle the letter that corresponds to the best answer. (Answers are given at the end of the chapter.)

1. According to the textbook, a financial system plays the role of
   A. reducing the risk faced by each saver.
   B. shifting the risk of investing from borrowers to savers.
   C. pooling the costs of gathering information about prospective borrowers.
   D. allowing financial investors to diversify the risk of financial investments.
   E. facilitating the direct lending of funds by savers to borrowers.

2. The informational role of the stock and bond markets provides incentives for savers and their financial advisers to
   A. direct funds to those borrowers that appear to have the safest investments.
   B. direct funds to those borrowers that appear to have the most profitable investments.
   C. diversify their investments by purchasing mutual funds.
   D. shift the risk of investing to the borrowers.
   E. avoid the cost of paying the financial intermediaries by going directly to the borrowers to make loans.

3. The difference between "real" and "financial" investment
   A. relates to adjustment for price changes.
   B. is a terminology difference between economists and accountants.
   C. has to do with purchases of Canadian versus foreign assets.
   D. is only semantic.
   E. is that "real" refers to new factories, equipment, inventories, and so on.

4. A good example of a financial intermediary would be a
   A. stockbroker selling mutual fund shares.
   B. major private investor engaging in a joint venture.
   C. a commercial bank using funds from savings accounts to provide loans.
   D. a financial analyst providing advice to investors.
   E. a legal trustee allocating funds on behalf of a client.

5. If you knew today's selling price (present value, PV) of a bond and its total future value (FV) with interest paid, you could calculate the effective interest rate (i) through the formula
   A. $i = PV/FV$.
   B. $i = FV/PV$.
   C. $1 + i = PV/FV$.
   D. $1 + i = FV/PV$.
   E. $i = FV/1+PV$.

6. Investors would be reluctant to buy "junk bonds" because they
   A. are illegal.
   B. have higher interest rates.
   C. are rated as risky.
   D. are longer term than regular bonds.
   E. are issued by private companies rather than governments.

7. Suppose that investors feel uncertain about prospects for stocks and thus increase their demand for bonds. Selling prices on the bond market would
   A. go up, and effective interest rates would increase.
   B. go up, and effective interest rates on bonds would decrease.
   C. go down, and interest rates would remain the same.
   D. go down, and effective interest rates on bonds would increase.
   E. go down, and effective interest rates on bonds would decrease.

8. Assuming equal initial purchase value, the advantage of holding a portfolio of government bonds instead of a portfolio of stocks is that the bonds
   A. are more volatile, and so future selling prices might rise considerably.
   B. make regular dividend payments.
   C. receive protection from the Canadian Deposit Insurance Corporation.
   D. are relatively safe.
   E. are not subject to capital gains tax when they are sold.

9. From the point of view of a new, high-risk company, there is an advantage when this company's stocks are contained in a mutual fund portfolio because
   A. investors might be reluctant to purchase this company's stocks solely.
   B. investors will not understand the risks involved.
   C. the company's own risk will decrease.
   D. the company's stocks will become less costly.
   E. the company can communicate directly with investors.

10. Capital flows are NOT counted as exports and imports in Canada because
   A. there is no way to keep track of them.
   B. most exports and imports occur with the United States, unlike capital flows.
   C. exports and imports involve payments from one country to another, whereas financial flows do not.
   D. capital flows do not involve trade in goods and services.
   E. government regulations prohibit it.

11. The current account and net capital flows
   A. vary in the same direction.
   B. may not be compared, since they involve different markets.
   C. must sum to zero.
   D. measure the same thing.
   E. indicate the degree of foreign ownership in Canada.

12. The relationship between "nonresident saving" and capital flows is that
   A. "positive nonresident saving" means that foreigners are bringing funds into Canada to invest.
   B. nonresident saving only refers to cash inflows into Canadian savings accounts.
   C. foreigners can have savings accounts without affecting capital flows.
   D. Canadians can maintain foreign savings accounts, thus causing a capital outflow.
   E. nonresident saving must equal capital inflows.

13. A low rate of national saving, relative to investment, is likely to cause a
   A. decline in national saving.
   B. current account deficit.
   C. rise in national investment.
   D. capital outflow.
   E. trade deficit.

14. When Canadian investors pay cash for stock in a French corporation, from the perspective of
   A. Canada, it is a capital inflow.
   B. France, it is a capital outflow.
   C. Canada, it is a capital outflow.
   D. France, it is a trade deficit.
   E. Canada, it is a trade deficit.

15. The sum of national saving and net capital inflows from abroad must equal
   A. domestic investment.
   B. net capital outflows.
   C. aggregate demand.
   D. aggregate supply.
   E. the current account surplus.

16. Canada's current account balance was often negative, but by the late 1990s, the current account was positive due to
   A. the poor performance of net exports.
   B. the strong performance of net exports.
   C. increased net capital inflows to Canada.
   D. the increase in the trade deficit.
   E. imports exceeding exports.

17. The effect of risk in the home country on capital flows is to
   A. increase both inflows and outflows.
   B. cause increased inflows of foreign capital.
   C. cause increased outflows of foreign capital.
   D. decrease both inflows and outflows.
   E. cause decreased outflows of home capital.

18. In the "loanable funds" model, gross investment is the same as
   A. net investment.
   B. national saving.
   C. the interest rate.
   D. the demand for saving.
   E. the equilibrium level of saving and investment.

19. If businesses suddenly became more enthusiastic about investing, the effect on the closed economy loanable funds model would be to
   A. shift the saving curve to the right.
   B. shift the gross investment curve to the left.
   C. increase the equilibrium real interest rate.
   D. decrease the amount of overall saving in the economy.
   E. leave the equilibrium real interest rate unaffected.

20. In the open economy loanable funds model, a higher level of home interest rates would trigger an
   A. inflow of foreign capital, higher total saving, and, thus, a lower real equilibrium interest rate.
   B. inflow of foreign capital, higher total saving, and, thus, a higher real equilibrium interest rate.
   C. outflow of foreign capital, lower total saving, and, thus, a lower real equilibrium interest rate.
   D. outflow of foreign capital, higher total saving, and, thus, a higher real equilibrium interest rate.
   E. uncertain change because the level of desired gross investment is unknown.

Self-Test: Short-Answer Problems
(Answers and solutions are given at the end of the chapter.)

1. Bond and Stock Prices
This problem will require you to calculate the effects of various factors on the prices of bonds and stocks.

A. Carley has purchased a newly issued bond from the SimonSays Corp. for $10,000. The SimonSays Corp. will pay the bondholder $750 at the end of years 1 through 4 and will pay $10,750 at the end of year 5. The bond has a principal amount of $_____, a term of _____ years, a coupon rate of _____ percent, and a coupon payment of $_____ .

B. After receiving coupon payments 1 through 4, Carley has decided to sell the bond. What price should she expect to receive if the one-year interest rate on comparable financial assets is 5 percent? $_____ What price should she expect to receive if the one-year interest rate on comparable financial assets is 8 percent? $_____

C. Justin has decided to buy 100 shares of stock in The Boot Company. He expects the company to pay a dividend of $3 per share in one year and expects the price of the shares will be $40 at that time. How much should he be willing to pay today per share if the safe rate of interest (i.e., the rate on low-risk assets like government bonds) is 7 percent and The Boot Company carries no risk? $_____

D. How much should Justin be willing to pay today per share if the safe rate of interest is 5 percent and The Boot Company carries no risk? $_____

E. How much should Justin be willing to pay today per share if the safe rate of interest is 5 percent and he requires a risk premium of 2 percent? $_____

2. Closed Economy Loanable Funds Model
In this problem, you will use the closed economy loanable funds model to analyze the financial market for saving and investment. You will determine the equilibrium real interest rate and quantity of saving and determine the effects of changes in the government budget and technology on the market equilibrium.

Answer the questions below based on the following the supply of saving and the gross investment (demand for saving) curves.

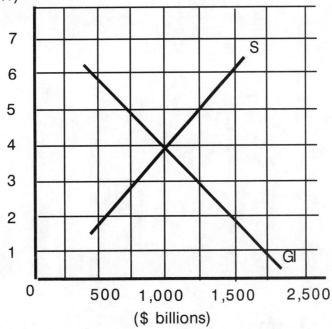

Real Interest
Rate (%)

0   500   1,000   1,500   2,500
              ($ billions)

A. The equilibrium real interest rate is _____ percent and the equilibrium quantity of saving/investment is $_____ billion.

B. An increase in the government budget surplus would cause the (saving/gross investment) _____ curve to (increase/decrease) _____ . On the above graph, draw a new curve that would reflect the change caused by the increased government budget surplus.

C. As a result of the increased government budget surplus, the equilibrium real interest rate _____ and the equilibrium quantity of saving/investment _____ .

D. The introduction of new technologies that increase the marginal product of new capital would cause the (saving/gross investment) _____ curve to (increase/decrease) _____ . On the above graph, draw a new curve that would reflect the change caused by the new technologies.

E. As a result of the new technologies, the equilibrium real interest rate _____ and the equilibrium quantity of saving/investment _____ .

SOLUTIONS

Quick Quiz

1. A.
2. B.
3. C.
4. D.
5. E.
6. E.
7. C.
8. C.
9. B.
10. C.
11. B.
12. A.

Self-Test: Key Terms

1. coupon rate.
2. diversification.
3. risk premium.
4. bond.
5. financial intermediaries.
6. dividend.
7. mutual fund.
8. coupon payments.
9. stock (or equity).
10. principal amount.
11. closed economy.
12. capital inflows.
13. open economy.
14. trade balance.
15. international capital flows.
16. trade surplus.
17. capital outflows.
18. trade deficit.
19. current account.
20. loanable funds model.

Self-Test: Multiple-Choice Questions

1. D.
2. B.
3. E.
4. C.
5. D.
6. C.
7. B.
8. D.
9. A.
10. D.
11. C.
12. A.
13. B.
14. C.
15. A.
16. B.
17. C.
18. D.
19. C.
20. A.

Self-Test: Short-Answer Problems

1.
A. $10,000; 5; 7.5%; $750.
B. $10,750 / 1.05 = $10, 238.10; $9,953.70.
C. $43 / 1.07 = $40.19.
D. $43 / 1.05 = $40.95.
E. $43 / (1.05 + 0.02) = $40.19.

2.
A. 4; $1,000 billion.
B. Saving; increase; (*see next page*).

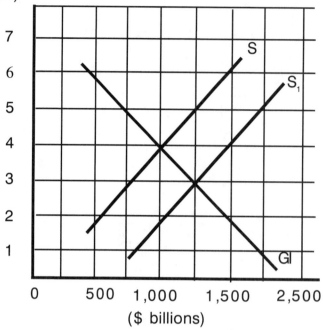

C. decreased; increased.
D. gross investment; increase;

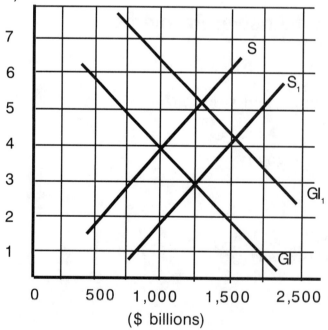

E. increased; increased.

11 Short-Term Economic Fluctuations: An Introduction

OVERVIEW

Short-run and medium-run fluctuations in economic conditions are important factors influencing the standard of living. The history, characteristics, and causes of the short-run fluctuations in economic conditions are discussed in this chapter.

Chapter Review

11.1 Recessions and Expansions

▶ **LO 1.**   **Define recession, depression, expansion, boom, peak, and trough.**

The short-run fluctuations in economic conditions are commonly known as recessions and expansions. A *recession*, or contraction, is a period in which the economy is growing at a rate significantly below normal. An extremely severe or protracted recession is called a *depression*. A more informal definition of a recession (often used by the mass media) is a period during which real GDP falls for at least two consecutive quarters. While the "two consecutive quarters" rule would not classify a slow-growth episode as a recession, many economists would argue that a period in which real GDP growth is significantly below normal should be counted as a recession. The beginning of a recession is called a *peak*, the high point of economic activity prior to a downturn. The end of a recession, marking the low point of economic activity prior to a recovery, is called the *trough*.

▶ **LO 2.**   **Identify the periods and characteristics of historically important recessions and expansions.**

By far the longest and most severe recession in Canada was during 1929–33. Since World War II, Canadian recessions have generally been short, lasting between 3 and 24 months. The opposite of a recession is an *expansion*, a period in which the economy is growing at a rate that is significantly above normal. A particularly strong and protracted expansion is called a *boom*. On average, expansions have lasted longer than recessions. The two longest expansions were during 1961–70, and the one following the trough of 1990–92. Expansions and recessions are not new, as they have been a feature of industrial economies since at least the late eighteenth century.

Quick Quiz

1. Periods during which the economy grows at a rate significantly below normal is referred to as
    A. expansions.
    B. troughs.
    C. booms.
    D. upturns.
    E. recessions.

2. The two most recent severe recessions occurred in
    A. the early 1980s and 1990–92.
    B. the early 1980s and 2001.
    C. the 1930s and the early 1980s.
    D. the 1930s and 1990–92.
    E. World War I and World War II.

11.2 Some Facts about Short-Term Fluctuations

▶ **LO 3.**   **Explain unemployment and inflation patterns during recessions and expansions.**

Short-run economic fluctuations, although they are sometimes referred to as business cycles, or cyclical fluctuations, do not recur at predictable intervals but rather are quite irregular in their length and severity. This irregularity makes it extremely hard to predict the dates of peaks and troughs. Expansions and recessions are felt throughout the economy, and even globally. Unemployment is a key indicator of short-term fluctuations, typically rising during recessions and falling (although more slowly) during expansions. Cyclical unemployment is the type of unemployment associated with recessions. In addition to rising unemployment, labour market conditions become more unfavourable during recessions, with real wages growing more slowly and workers less likely to receive promotions or bonuses. Inflation also follows a typical pattern during recessions and expansions, though not as sharply defined. Recessions tend to be preceded by increases in inflation and followed soon after by a decline in the rate of inflation. Durable goods industries tend to be more affected by recessions and expansions, while services and nondurable goods industries are less sensitive to short-term economic fluctuations.

Quick Quiz

3. Unemployment typically
    A. is unaffected by recessions and expansions.
    B. rises during recession and falls during expansions.
    C. falls during recessions and rises during expansions.
    D. rises during recessions and rises during expansions, as does inflation.
    E. falls during recessions and rises during expansions, as does inflation.

11.3 Measuring Fluctuations: Output Gaps and Cyclical Unemployment

▶ **LO 4.   Define potential output, output gap, recessionary gap, and expansionary gap.**

Economists measure expansions and recessions by determining how far output is from its normal level. The normal level of output is called *potential output* (also known as potential GDP or full-employment output): the amount of output (real GDP) that an economy can produce when using its resources, such as capital and labour, at normal rates. Actual output (real GDP) may be below or above potential output at any point in time. The difference between potential output and actual output is called the *output gap*. The output gap is expressed in symbols as $Y^* - Y$. A "positive output gap," when potential output is ABOVE actual output (resources are being utilized below-potential rates), is called a *recessionary gap*. A "negative output gap", when potential output is BELOW actual output (resources are utilized at above-potential rates), is called an *expansionary gap* (or *inflationary gap*).

▶ **LO 5.   Identify the causes of output gaps.**

Output gaps occur when the economy's resources, for example, labour and capital, are not being used at their potential rates. During a recession, resources may be underutilized for some reason. Similarly, resources may be pushed beyond their natural potential during periods of expansion.

▶ **LO 6.   Explain frictional, structural, seasonal, and cyclical types of unemployment and their relationship to the natural rate of unemployment.**

There are four categories of unemployment. The first, *frictional*, relates to the time taken to match workers with the available jobs. The second, *structural*, occurs when workers lack the skills required by jobs offered or do not live in regions where jobs are available. The third, *seasonal*, refers to workers who are only employed during certain seasons of the year. The fourth, *cyclical*, occurs during recessionary periods. Recessionary gaps are associated with below-normal utilization of labour resources. Frictional, structural, and seasonal types of unemployment are always present in the labour market. However, cyclical unemployment is present during recessions. In other words, there is extra unemployment during recessions.

Economists call that part of the total unemployment rate that is attributable to frictional, structural, and seasonal unemployment the *natural rate of unemployment*. The natural rate of unemployment can vary over time because of changes in frictional, structural, or seasonal unemployment. The natural rate of unemployment is the unemployment rate that prevails when cyclical unemployment is zero. This occurs when output is at its potential level. Cyclical unemployment can, therefore, be calculated as the difference between the actual unemployment rate (u) and the natural rate of unemployment (u^*).

► **LO 7.** **Explain Okun's Law on the relationship between cyclical unemployment and the output gap.**

During recessions, cyclical unemployment is positive (in that it is higher than the natural level), and during expansions, it is negative (lower than the natural level). The relationship between the output gap and the amount of cyclical unemployment is given by Okun's Law, which varies from country to country. *Okun's Law* states that each extra percentage point of cyclical unemployment is associated with about a two-percentage-point increase in the output gap, as it is believed to apply today to Canada and the United States. The output losses calculated according to Okun's Law suggest that recessions have significant costs (which are reflected, for example, in the importance that short-run economic fluctuations have on Canadian federal elections).

► **LO 8.** **Calculate the effect of cyclical unemployment on the output gap.**

As is the case with the potential GDP, the natural rate of unemployment cannot be measured exactly. Different organizations calculate potential GDP at varying levels. However, Okun's Law can be used to infer the corresponding natural rate of unemployment, based on a given estimate of potential GDP. For example, if the output gap is calculated at 4.6 percent, then the corresponding gap between actual unemployment and the natural rate of unemployment must be about 2.3 percent according to Okun's Law—in other words, unemployment is 2.3 percent higher than the natural rate. If actual unemployment were 10.3 percent, then 10.3 – 2.3% = 8% is the implied "natural rate of unemployment."

Quick Quiz

4. A recessionary gap occurs when
   A. total spending is abnormally high.
   B. total spending is at normal levels, but potential output is growing at abnormally high levels.
   C. total spending is low compared with what planned spending would be if output were at its potential.
   D. potential output is less than actual output.
   E. actual output is greater than potential output.

5. The cause of an inflationary gap might be increased demand for a country's products, resulting in
   A. increased unemployment.
   B. a fall in the inflation rate.
   C. lower than usual rates of unemployment.
   D. idle equipment in firms.
   E. spare capacity in factories.

6. An example of frictional unemployment would be
   A. a worker gets laid off during an economic slowdown.
   B. a secretary does not have the computer skills required by employers.
   C. a carpenter is so much in demand that he/she can pick and choose jobs.
   D. a new college graduate moves to Vancouver and looks for a job.
   E. an agricultural worker cannot find work during the winter.

7. Okun's Law states that each extra percentage point of cyclical unemployment is associated with about a two-percentage-point
   A. decrease in the output gap.
   B. increase in inflation.
   C. constant level of the natural rate of unemployment.
   D. increase in the recessionary output gap.
   E. structural change.

8. According to Okun's Law, if cyclical unemployment rises to 2.5 percent and potential output (GDP) equals $900 billion, the output gap would equal
   A. $225 billion.
   B. $45 billion.
   C. $900 billion.
   D. $877.5 billion.
   E. $922.5 billion.

11.4 Why Do Short-Term Fluctuations Occur? A Preview and Parable

▶ **LO 9.**   **Summarize causes and cures of output gaps.**

The chapter concludes with preview of the causes of recessions and expansions, which are discussed in greater detail in the next three chapters. First of all, in the short run, prices do not always adjust immediately to changing demand or supply as some producers vary the quantity of output rather than price, "meeting the demand" at a preset price. In the short run, therefore, changes in economywide spending comprise a primary cause of output gaps. Second, government may intervene to influence these fluctuations in output. Third, when firms eventually do adjust their prices in response to variations in demand, this affects the rate of inflation. Finally, these price changes set in motion a natural adjustment process back to potential output, although policy makers may intervene to hasten the return to potential.

Quick Quiz

9. An example of an event which would cause the economy to move AWAY from the potential output level would be
   A. policy makers cut government spending in an attempt to cool down an expanding economy.

B. firms respond to slack demand by eventually dropping their product prices.

C. firms respond to excessive demand by eventually raising their product prices.

D. a decline in American demand for Canadian exports leads firms to decrease their output.

E. a policy maker increases government spending in an attempt to stimulate a sluggish economy.

Self-Tests: Key Terms

Use the terms below to complete the following sentences. (Answers are given at the end of the chapter.)

boom	output gap
cyclical unemployment	peak
depression	potential output
expansion	recession
expansionary gap	recessionary gap
frictional unemployment	seasonal unemployment
natural rate of unemployment	structural unemployment
Okun's Law	trough

1. A particularly strong and protracted expansion is called a _____.

2. The amount of output (real GDP) that an economy can produce when using its resources, such as capital and labour, at normal rates is the _____.

3. A one-percentage-point increase in cyclical unemployment is associated with about a two-percentage point increase in the output gap, according to _____.

4. An extremely severe or protracted recession is called a _____.

5. When actual output is above potential output and resources are utilized at above-normal rates, there is a(n) _____ .

6. The end of a recession is marked by a(n) _____ .

7. The difference between potential output and actual output equals the _____ .

8. A period in which the economy is growing at a rate significantly below normal is a(n) _____ .

9. When cyclical unemployment is zero, the rate of unemployment equals the _____.

10. The high point of economic activity prior to a downturn is called a(n) _____ .

11. A period in which the economy is growing at a rate that is significantly above normal is a(n) _____ .

12. When Y* is greater than Y, a(n) _____ exists.

13. An avalanche-control technician who is idle during the summer is a victim of

_____.

14. The additional lack of jobs occurring during periods of slow economic activity is called

_____.

15. The short-term unemployment associated with the process of matching workers with jobs is

called _____.

16. When workers are unable to fill available jobs because they lack the skills or do not live in

available-job areas, they are experiencing _____.

Self-Test: Multiple-Choice Questions

Circle the letter that corresponds to the best answer. (Answers are given at the end of the chapter.)

1. Short-term economic fluctuations
   A. recur at predictable intervals.
   B. have a limited impact on a few industries or regions.
   C. contain peaks and troughs that are easily predicted by the professional forecasters.
   D. are irregular in their length and severity.
   E. have little impact on unemployment and inflation.

2. During a recession, or shortly after, inflation tends to _____ and unemployment tends to

_____
   A. rise, rise.
   B. fall, fall.
   C. fall, rise.
   D. no change, rise.
   E. rise, fall.

3. Cyclical unemployment refers to
   A. the portion of unemployment that rises during recessions.
   B. the unemployment due to labour market adjustment.
   C. the unemployment due to the changing structure of the economy .
   D. the rate of unemployment when the economy is at potential GDP.
   E. the level of unemployment that falls during recessions.

4. A particularly strong and protracted phase of an expansion is referred to as a(n)
   A. trough.
   B. peak.
   C. output gap.
   D. natural rate of unemployment.
   E. boom.

5. The actual rate of unemployment will exceed the natural rate
   A. during an expansionary gap.
   B. when potential output exceeds actual output.
   C. during a recessionary gap.
   D. when potential output equals actual output.
   E. during the boom phase of the business cycle.

6. During a recessionary gap,
   A. cyclical unemployment is positive, and we have a negative output gap.
   B. cyclical unemployment is negative, and the output gap is negative.
   C. cyclical unemployment is negative, and the output gap is positive.
   D. cyclical unemployment is positive, and the output gap is positive.
   E. we have the same unemployment as an expansionary gap.

7. During short-term economic fluctuations, inflation tends to
   A. rise following an economic peak and fall soon after the trough.
   B. fall following an economic peak and fall soon after the trough.
   C. rise following an economic peak and rise soon after the trough.
   D. fall following an economic peak and rise soon after the trough.
   E. move in the same direction as unemployment.

8. An expansionary gap implies that resources are
   A. not being fully utilized and the unemployment rate would be above the natural rate of unemployment.
   B. being utilized at above-normal rates and the unemployment rate would be above the natural rate of unemployment.
   C. not being fully utilized and the unemployment rate would be below the natural rate of unemployment.
   D. being utilized at above-normal rates and cyclical unemployment is positive.
   E. being utilized at above-normal rates and cyclical unemployment is negative.

9. The difference between the economy's potential output and its actual output at a point in time is the
   A. recession.
   B. natural rate of unemployment.
   C. output gap.
   D. potential GDP.
   E. equilibrium.

10. The beginning of a recession is called a(n)
    A. peak.
    B. trough.
    C. expansion.
    D. depression.
    E. recession.

11. Recessions and expansions have a greater impact on
   A. inflation than on unemployment.
   B. frictional unemployment than on cyclical unemployment.
   C. structural unemployment than on cyclical unemployment.
   D. industries that produce durable goods than on service and nondurable goods industries.
   E. industries that produce services and nondurable goods than on durable goods industries.

12. The difference between the total unemployment rate and the natural rate of unemployment
   A. is positive during a recession.
   B. is negative during a recession.
   C. is positive during an expansion.
   D. represents that portion of total unemployment that economists call frictional unemployment.
   E. represents that portion of total unemployment that economists call structural unemployment.

13. A key indicator of short-term economic fluctuations would be
   A. the level of GDP only.
   B. peaks.
   C. the rate of unemployment.
   D. troughs.
   E. the natural rate of unemployment.

14. On a graph of the growth of GDP (output) per year, the beginning of an expansionary period may be identified at the
   A. point where GDP growth levels off.
   B. highest point of economic activity.
   C. lowest point of economic activity.
   D. peak.
   E. point at which growth changes from positive to negative.

15. Which of these categories of unemployment is not associated with the "natural rate of unemployment"?
   A. cyclical.
   B. frictional.
   C. seasonal.
   D. structural.

Self-Test: Short-Answer Problems

(Answers and solutions are given at the end of the chapter.)

1. Actual Output and Potential Output

This problem utilizes data for a hypothetical economy on real GDP and potential GDP in billions of 1997 dollars, and will help you become more familiar with the concept of output gaps (recessionary and expansionary gaps).

Year	Real GDP	Potential GDP	Output Gap	Expansionary or Recessionary Gap?
1995	$762	$780		
1996	810	815		
1997	845	870		
1998	872	890		
1999	926	900		
2000	953	920		

A. Complete the fourth column of the above table by calculating the size of the output gap for 1995 through 2000 (be sure to include a plus sign if a positive gap or a minus sign if negative gap).

B. In the fifth column of the above table, identify whether the output gap was a recessionary gap or an expansionary gap for each year.

SOLUTIONS

Quick Quiz

1. E.
2. A.
3. B.
4. C.
5. C.
6. D.
7. D.
8. B. ($900 billion times 0.05 = $45 billion).
9. D.

Self-Test: Key Terms

1. boom.
2. potential output.
3. Okun's Law.
4. depression.

5. expansionary gap.
6. trough.
7. output gap.
8. recession.
9. natural rate of unemployment.
10. peak.
11. expansion.
12. recessionary gap.
13. seasonal unemployment.
14. cyclical unemployment.
15. frictional unemployment.
16. structural unemployment.

Self-Test: Multiple-Choice Questions

1. D.
2. C.
3. A.
4. E.
5. C.
6. D.
7. D.
8. E.
9. C.
10. A.
11. D.
12. A.
13. C.
14. C.
15. A.

Self-Test: Short-Answer Problems

1.

Year	Real GDP	Potential GDP	Output Gap	Expansionary or Recessionary Gap?
1995	$762	$780	$ 18	Recessionary gap
1996	810	815	15	Recessionary gap
1997	845	870	25	Recessionary gap
1998	872	890	18	Recessionary gap
1999	926	900	(26)	Expansionary gap
2000	953	920	(33)	Expansionary gap

12 Spending and Output in the Short Run

OVERVIEW

In this chapter, the basic Keynesian model is developed showing how recessions and expansions may arise from fluctuations in aggregate spending. The chapter first presents the two key assumptions of the model and then explains the important concept of planned aggregate expenditure, or total planned spending in the economy. After showing how planned aggregate expenditure helps determine the level of output, the use of government policies to reduce or eliminate output gaps is discussed.

Chapter Review

12.1 The Keynesian Model's Crucial Assumption: Firms Meet Demand at Preset Prices

▶ **LO 1.** **Explain the key assumption of the Keynesian model.**

The Keynesian model is based on the ideas first developed by John Maynard Keynes (1883–1946) who was responding to the unprecedented levels of unemployment in the early 1930s and the consequent decline in aggregate spending as discussed in the textbook. His views as to the remedies, which later formed the basis for the basic Keynesian model, were published in *The General Theory of Employment, Interest, and Money* (1936). The key assumption of the basic Keynesian model is that in the short run, firms meet the demand for their products at preset prices.

▶ **LO 2.** **Define menu costs and discuss how they affect the decision to change prices.**

Firms change prices only if the benefits of doing so outweigh the *menu costs* (the costs of changing prices).

Quick Quiz

1. Which of the following is *crucial* key assumption of the basic Keynesian model?
   A. planned aggregate expenditure is constant and has no bearing on the economy.
   B. in the short run, firms meet the demand for their products at preset prices.
   C. in the long run, firms meet the demand for the products at preset prices.
   D. in the short run, firms adjust price to changes in planned aggregate expenditure so as to clear the market.
   E. in the long run, firms do not adjust price to changes in planned aggregate expenditure so as to clear the market.

2. When firms apply the core principle of cost-benefit analysis to price changing decisions, they change the prices of their goods if
   A. menu costs are greater than or equal to the benefits of changing prices.
   B. menu costs are greater than or equal to the additional revenue derived from changing prices.
   C. additional revenue derived from changing prices is less than the menu costs.
   D. additional revenue derived from changing prices is greater than the menu costs.
   E. additional revenue derived from changing prices is less than or equal to the menu costs.

12.2 Planned Aggregate Expenditure

▶ **LO 3.** **Define planned aggregate expenditure.**

The most important concept of the basic Keynesian model is planned aggregate expenditure. Planned aggregate expenditure (PAE) is the total planned spending on final goods and services.

▶ **LO 4.** **Identify the components of PAE.**

PAE is composed of four components: (1) consumer expenditures, or simply consumption (C), is spending by households on final goods and services; (2) private-sector investment (I) is spending by firms on new capital goods, residential investment, and increases in inventories; (3) government purchases (G) is spending by the federal, provincial, and municipal governments on goods and services; and (4) net exports (NX), or exports minus imports, is sales of domestically produced goods and services to foreigners less purchases by domestic residents of goods and services produced abroad.

▶ **LO 5.** **Explain why planned spending may differ from actual spending.**

Total planned spending may differ from actual spending. If, for example, a firm sells more of its output than it planned to sell, actual private-sector investment will be greater than planned private-sector investment and total actual spending will be greater than total planned spending. When actual sales are greater than expected, inventories will be drawn down. When the opposite occurs, inventories will build up. Assuming that actual spending for consumption, government purchases, and net exports equals planned spending but that actual private-sector investment may not equal planned private-sector investment, the equation for planned aggregate expenditure is $PAE = C + I^P + G + NX$, where I^P is planned private-sector investment spending.

▶ **LO 6.** **Define consumption function, wealth effect, marginal propensity to consume, and average propensity to consume.**

Consumption, the largest component of PAE, is affected by many factors, the most important being after-tax, or disposable income. The relationship between consumption spending and its determinants, is referred to as the *consumption function* and is expressed by the equation $C = \overline{C} + c(Y - T)$, where $\overline{C}$ is a constant term intended to capture factors other than disposable income, and $(Y - T)$ represents disposable income, being national income, Y, less taxes, T, and c is a fixed number called the marginal propensity to consume. The *marginal propensity to consume*, or MPC, is the amount by which consumption rises when disposable income rises by one dollar, and is greater than 0 but less than 1 (i.e., $0 < c < 1$). The consumption function can also be show graphically, in which case $\overline{C}$ represents the intercept of the consumption function on the vertical axis and the MPC is the slope of the consumption function. The consumption function indicates that as disposable income rises, consumption spending will increase, but by a lesser amount. The *average propensity to consume* is consumption divided by disposable income.

▶ **LO 7.** **Explain the difference between autonomous and induced expenditure.**

Incorporating the consumption function into the equation for planned aggregate expenditure results in the expanded equation $PAE = [\overline{C} + c(Y - T)] + I^P + G + NX$. Assuming the nonconsumption components of PAE are fixed quantities (denoted by an overbar), the equation can be rewritten as $AD = [\overline{C} + c(Y - \overline{T})] + \overline{I} + \overline{G} + \overline{NX}$. Grouping together those terms that depend on output (Y) and those that do not, yields an equation of the form: $PAE = A_0 + cY$. This equation captures the key idea that as real output changes, demand changes with it in the same direction. It also shows that planned aggregate expenditure can be divided into two parts, one portion that is determined outside the model called *autonomous expenditure* and a second portion that is determined within the model (because it depends on output) called *induced expenditure*.

▶ **LO 8.** **Define short-run equilibrium output and explain how it is identified on a graph.**

In the basic Keynesian model, the *short-run equilibrium output* is the level at which output, Y, equals planned aggregate expenditure (PAE) and is the level of output that prevails during the period in which prices are predetermined. The short-run equilibrium output is determined where Y = PAE. The short-run equilibrium output can be determined graphically where the 45-degree line intersects the expenditure line. (Appendix 12A show how the level of output where Y = PAE can be determined algebraically).

▶ **LO 9.   Explain how firms respond when output differs from the equilibrium value.**

If output is less (greater) than the equilibrium level in the short run, when prices are preset and firms are committed to meeting their customers' demand, output will rise (fall).

▶ **LO 10.   Demonstrate how a decline in spending can cause a recessionary gap.**

A decrease in one or more of the components of autonomous planned aggregate expenditure will cause short-run equilibrium output to fall. If the economy began at potential output (Y*), the decreased spending will lead the economy into a recessionary gap. This is indicated on the graph by a downward shift of the PAE function. The result will be a new equilibrium of Y = PAE, but one which is lower than potential output (to the left of Y* on the graph)

▶ **LO 11.   Explain how a change in planned spending causes a larger change in actual output, through the multiplier.**

The effect of a one-unit increase (decrease) in autonomous planned spending will result in a larger increase (decrease) in equilibrium output because the initial spending causes incomes to increase (fall). This change in income triggers further increases (decreases) in spending, through an effect known as the *income–expenditure multiplier*, or the multiplier for short. (Appendix 12B provides an explanation of how, for a closed economy, the multiplier equals $1 \div (1 - c)$. The appendix shows how to calculate the multiplier.) Because the basic Keynesian model omits some important features of the real economy, however, it tends to yield unrealistically high values of the multiplier. Empirical estimates of multipliers indicate that they are less than 2.

Quick Quiz

3. "Planned aggregate expenditure" pertains to
   A. firms' spending on new capital goods and increases in inventories, and spending on new residences.
   B. foreign spending on domestically produced goods and services minus purchases by domestic residents of foreign goods and services.
   C. purchases by government.
   D. consumer spending.
   E. all of the above.

4. Planned aggregate expenditure is the sum of desired or planned
   A. consumption expenditures, private-sector investment, government purchases, and net exports.
   B. consumption expenditures, private-sector investment, government purchases, and imports.

    C. consumption expenditures, net private-sector investment, government purchases, and exports.

    D. consumption expenditures, net private-sector investment, government expenditures, and imports.

5. If a firm's PLANNED spending is greater than actual sales, the firm will find that it has
    A. produced too little and inventories are building up.
    B. produced too little and inventories are drawn down.
    C. produced too much and inventories are building up.
    D. produced too much and inventories are drawn down.
    E. produced an adequate amount because any extra inventories are useful for a rainy day.

6. The amount by which consumption rises each time disposable income increases by $1 is called
    A. the consumption function.
    B. the wealth effect.
    C. marginal propensity to consume.
    D. average propensity to consume.
    E. planned aggregate output.

7. The portion of planned aggregate expenditure that is determined within the model is called "induced" and includes
    A. all of household consumption, private-sector investment spending, government purchases, and net exports.
    B. all of household consumption.
    C. household consumption and private-sector investment spending.
    D. household consumption, private-sector investment spending, and government purchases.
    E. that part of expenditure that is dependent on income.

8. The short-run equilibrium in the basic Keynesian model occurs where
    A. actual inventories are greater than the level planned by businesses.
    B. actual inventories are less than the level planned by businesses.
    C. planned expenditure equals the potential output.
    D. planned expenditure equals planned output.
    E. planned expenditure is greater than output.

9. If actual output is lower than the planned aggregate expenditure and not enough actual output is available to meet the demand, then inventories are
    A. dropping, and firms will need to expand production.
    B. dropping, and firms will need to decrease production.
    C. building up, and firms will need to expand production.
    D. unchanged because the firms are selling all they are producing.
    E. building up, and firms will need to decrease production.

10. Which of the following events could cause the economy to enter a recessionary gap?
   A. a rise in autonomous consumption.
   B. a rise in net exports.
   C. a rise in investment.
   D. a fall in taxes.
   E. a fall in government spending.

11. If the value of the multiplier turned out to be 2 instead of 5, a REDUCTION in net export spending would lead to
   A. the same overall contraction of the economy as under the larger multiplier.
   B. a larger overall contraction of the economy than originally expected.
   C. a smaller overall contraction of the economy than originally expected.
   D. increased spending in the economy.
   E. a larger marginal propensity to consume.

12.3 Stabilizing Planned Spending: The Role of Fiscal Policy

▶ **LO 12.**   **Define stabilization policy, expansionary policies, and contractionary policies.**

To fight recessions caused by insufficient planned aggregate expenditure, policy makers can use stabilization policies. *Stabilization policies* are government policies that are used to affect planned aggregate expenditure, with the objective of eliminating output gaps. There are two major types of stabilization policy: monetary policy and fiscal policy. This chapter focuses on fiscal policy, that is, government spending and taxes. When government policy aims at increasing planned spending and output, this comprises an *expansionary policy*. On the other hand, actions designed to reduce planned spending and output are *contractionary*.

▶ **LO 13.**   **Demonstrate how an increase in government purchases can eliminate a recessionary gap or a decrease in government purchases can eliminate an expansionary output gap.**

A recessionary gap can be eliminated by increases in government spending. Government spending can be in the form of government purchases of goods and services. Graphically, when the economy is in a recessionary gap, a rise in government spending causes the PAE line to rise. This could continue until the recessionary gap closed, and the economy returned to potential output (Y*).

▶ **LO 14.**   **Explain how policies affecting taxes or transfer payments affect the change in planned aggregated expenditure a little differently from changes in government spending.**

While changes in government purchases directly change the amount of PAE, transfers and taxes only indirectly change PAE by altering the amount of disposable income. The change in PAE is equal to the change in taxes (or transfers) times the MPC. Because the MPC is a fraction, the change in taxes or transfer payments must be larger than the change in government purchases to cause the same change in PAE.

Quick Quiz

12. An implication of the basic Keynesian model is that
    A. changes in government spending can eliminate output gaps.
    B. stabilization policy has no role in eliminating cyclical unemployment.
    C. the classical adjustment mechanism operates perfectly.
    D. there is no role for changes in taxes to reduce or eliminate output gaps.
    E. the self-correcting process of the market can eliminate output gaps.

13. An expansionary output gap could be eliminated by
    A. an increase in government purchases.
    B. an increase in government transfer payments.
    C. a stabilization of government purchases.
    D. a decrease in government purchases.
    E. a decrease in tax rates.

14. A $100 increase in transfer payments or a $100 decrease in taxes will cause
    A. a smaller increase in planned aggregate expenditure than a $100 increase in government purchases.
    B. a larger increase in planned aggregate expenditure than a $100 increase in government purchases.
    C. the same increase in planned aggregate expenditure as would a $100 increase in government purchases.
    D. a smaller decrease in planned aggregate expenditure than a $100 increase in government purchases.
    E. a larger decrease in planned aggregate expenditure than a $100 increase in government purchases.

12.4 Fiscal Policy as a Stabilization Tool: Six Qualifications

▶ **LO 15.** **Discuss six qualifications related to the use of fiscal policy as a stabilization tool.**

While the basic Keynesian model suggests that fiscal policy can be used quite precisely to eliminate output gaps, in the real world, it is more complicated than that. (1) Using fiscal policy as a stabilization tool is complicated by the fact that fiscal policy may affect potential output as well as planned aggregate expenditure. Government spending, for example, on investments in public capital, (e.g., roads, airports, and schools) can play a major role in the growth of potential output. Taxes and transfer payments may affect the incentives and, thus, the economic behaviour of households and firms that, in turn, affect potential output. (2) Government spending and taxation affect factors other than output, such as quality of living. (3) Government spending can lead to budget deficits in some circumstances. (4) *Discretionary fiscal policy*, which pertains to policy changes made deliberately to stabilize planned expenditure, may take time to implement. (5) Recognition lags can also delay the onset of implementation. (6) There is some disagreement among economists as to the value of discretionary fiscal policy versus automatic stabilizers. The presence of *automatic stabilizers*, provisions in the law that call for automatic increases in government spending or decreases in taxes when real output declines helps increase PAE during recessions and reduce it during expansions, without the delays inherent in implementation lags.

Quick Quiz

15. Provisions in the law that imply automatic increases in government spending or decreases in taxes when real output declines are referred to as
   A. discretionary fiscal policy.
   B. automatic stabilizers.
   C. discretionary monetary policy.
   D. supply-side economics.
   E. natural rate of unemployment.

Self-Test: Key Terms

Use the terms below to complete the following sentences. (Answers are given at the end of the chapter.)

automatic stabilizers
autonomous planned aggregate
   expenditure
average propensity to consume
consumption function
discretionary fiscal policy
fiscal policy
income–expenditure multiplier

induced planned aggregate spending
marginal propensity to consume (MPC)
menu costs
monetary policy
planned aggregate expenditure (PAE; planned
   spending)
short-run equilibrium output
stabilization policies

1. The relationship between consumption spending and its determinants is referred to as the

   _____.

2. The sum of consumption, private-sector investment, government purchases, and net exports

   equals _____.

3. The slope of the consumption function is determined by the _____.

4. To fight recessions caused by insufficient planned spending, policy makers can use

   _____.

5. The effect of a one-unit increase or decrease in autonomous planned spending on the short-

   run equilibrium output is called the _____ .

6. Firms change the price of a product only if the benefits of doing so outweigh the _____ .

7. The portion of planned spending that is determined outside the model is the _____ .

8. The level of output that prevails during the period in which prices are predetermined is the _____ .

9. The changes in government spending and taxation deliberately made to stabilize PAE are known as _____ .

10. The portion of planned spending that is determined within the model (because it depends on output) is the _____ .

11. Government actions designed to reduce planned spending and output are _____ .

12. The tendency of changes in asset prices to affect households' spending on consumption goods and services is known as the _____ .

13. Government actions intended to increase planned spending and output are _____ .

14. A change in government spending is an example of _____ .

Self-Test: Multiple-Choice Questions

Circle the letter that corresponds to the best answer. (Answers are given at the end of the chapter.)

1. One of the key insights of John Maynard Keynes was that
   A. economies always operate at the natural rate of employment.
   B. there are always expansionary gaps, and he recommended the use of monetary policy to combat the resulting high inflation.
   C. a decline in aggregate spending may cause actual output to fall below potential output.
   D. prices adjust to clear all markets all the time.
   E. there is no need for government stabilization programs.

2. If a firms' actual sales are greater than expected sales
   A. actual inventories will be greater than planned inventories, and actual private-sector investment will be greater than planned private-sector investment.
   B. actual inventories will be less than planned inventories, and actual private-sector investment will be less than planned private-sector investment.
   C. actual inventories will be greater than planned inventories, and actual private-sector investment will be less than planned private-sector investment.

    D. actual inventories will be less than planned inventories, and actual private-sector investment will be greater than planned private-sector investment.

    E. planned inventories will be less than actual inventories, and planned private-sector investment will be greater than actual private-sector investment.

3. A decrease in consumers' disposable income will cause a(n)
    A. decrease in the consumption function and an increase in output.
    B. increase in the consumption function and a decrease in output.
    C. decrease in the consumption function and an increase in planned spending.
    D. increase in the consumption function and an increase in planned spending.
    E. decrease in the consumption function and a decrease in planned spending.

4. If autonomous consumption equals $250 billion, the marginal propensity to consume (MPC) is 0.6, private-sector investment equals $180 billion, government purchases equal $75 billion, taxes equal $200, and net exports equal minus $40 billion, the planned spending equation is
    A. PAE = $250 billion + 0.6Y.
    B. PAE = $585 billion + 0.6Y.
    C. PAE = $505 billion + 0.6Y.
    D. PAE = $625 billion + 0.6Y.
    E. PAE = $345 billion + 0.6Y.

5. If, in the short run, real output is less than the equilibrium level of output, firms will respond by
    A. increasing the prices of their products.
    B. decreasing the prices of their products.
    C. increasing their production.
    D. decreasing their production.
    E. producing the same amount of output.

6. The use of fiscal policy to eliminate output gaps is complicated by the fact that fiscal policy
    A. is more flexible than monetary policy.
    B. only affects planned spending but has no effect on potential output.
    C. affects both planned spending and potential output.
    D. there are no lags in the implementation of fiscal policy.
    E. includes not only government purchases but also transfer payments and taxation.

7. When we add net exports of the form, $NX = X_0 - M_0 - mY$, where Y is national income, m is the marginal propensity to import, and $X_0 - M_0$ is the autonomous component of net exports, the slope of the aggregate expenditure function is _____ and the open economy multiplier is _____ the case where there are no exports or imports.
    A. greater than, greater than.
    B. greater than, less than.
    C. less than, greater than.
    D. the same as, the same as.
    E. less than, less than.

8. Planned spending equals actual spending for households, governments, and foreigners in the basic Keynesian model, but for businesses
   A. planned spending equals actual inventories.
   B. planned spending equals planned inventories.
   C. actual private-sector investment may differ from planned private-sector investment.
   D. actual private-sector investment is always greater than planned private-sector investment.
   E. actual private-sector investment is always less than planned private-sector investment.

9. In the basic Keynesian model, when planned aggregate expenditure equals output
   A. inventories are zero.
   B. consumption equals private-sector investment.
   C. unplanned changes in inventories are positive.
   D. unplanned changes in inventories equal zero.
   E. unplanned changes in inventories are negative.

10. The "Keynesian cross" refers to
    A. the intersection of supply and demand.
    B. equilibrium in the market for financial assets.
    C. interaction between monetary and fiscal policies.
    D. a graph used to illustrate the dynamics of aggregate spending.
    E. the calculation of undesired inventories.

11. On a graph of the consumption function, the vertical intercept (C with a bar over it) is equal to
    A. factors other than disposable income that affect consumption.
    B. the marginal propensity to consume.
    C. the average propensity to consume.
    D. the wealth effect.
    E. planned aggregate expenditure.

12. The relationship between the amount of disposable income in Canada and the amount of consumption expenditure
    A. varies according to fluctuations in disposable income.
    B. is strongly negative.
    C. has no relationship because of fixed consumption needs.
    D. is strongly positive.
    E. depends on the size of the tax rate.

13. In the PAE model developed in this chapter, planned government spending and exports are examples of factors assumed to be
    A. negative.
    B. induced.
    C. variable.
    D. tools of government policy.
    E. autonomous.

14. The graph of planned aggregate expenditure includes a 45-degree line which corresponds to
   A. the highest possible level of output.
   B. equilibrium between planned spending and output.
   C. the marginal propensity to consume.
   D. the multiplier.
   E. the actual level of output at each price level.

15. If the income-expenditure multiplier were worth 2, a decrease in desired investment of $1 million would cause a(n) _____ in equilibrium output of _____.
   A. increase, $2 million.
   B. increase, $3 million.
   C. decrease, $2 million.
   D. decrease, $2 million.
   E. increase, $1 million.

Self-Test: Multiple-Choice—Appendices 12A and 12B

1. Assume that private-sector investment, government purchases, net taxes, and net exports are fixed. If the consumption function is $C = \$400 + 0.75Y$, then
   A. the MPC = 0.75, and the income-expenditure multiplier = 0.25.
   B. the MPC = 0.75, and the income-expenditure multiplier = 1.33.
   C. the MPC = 0.75, and the income-expenditure multiplier = 0.75.
   D. the MPC = 0.75, and the income-expenditure multiplier = 4.
   E. the MPC = 0.25, and the income-expenditure multiplier = 4.

2. Suppose we have derived relations for the economy such that autonomous consumption equals $250 billion, the marginal propensity to consume (MPC) is 0.6, private-sector investment equals $180 billion, government purchases equal $75 billion, taxes equal $200, and net exports equal minus $40 billion. Suppose also that potential output is estimated at $900 billion. The output gap is
   A. 0.
   B. $37.5 billion.
   C. – $ 100 billion.
   D. – $130.5 billion.
   E. + $50 billion.

3. If autonomous exports are equal to $25 billion, autonomous imports are equal to $5 billion, and the marginal propensity to import is 0.10, the net export function is
   A. $20 + 0.1Y$.
   B. $30 + 0.1Y$.
   C. $0.1Y$.
   D. $30 - 0.1Y$.
   E. $20 - 0.1Y$.

Self-Test: Short-Answer Problems

(Answers and solutions are given at the end of the chapter.)

1. The Consumption Function and Planned Aggregate Expenditure

This problem is designed to help you understand the relationship between the consumption function and planned aggregate expenditure. You will be asked to graph the consumption function, write the algebraic equation for planned aggregate expenditure, and differentiate between autonomous and induced planned aggregate expenditure.

A. On the graph below, plot the consumption function curve for disposable income levels $0 to $700 ($billions), assuming C = $175 billion (when Y = 0), the marginal propensity to consume (MPC) equals 0.75, and taxes equal $100 billion.

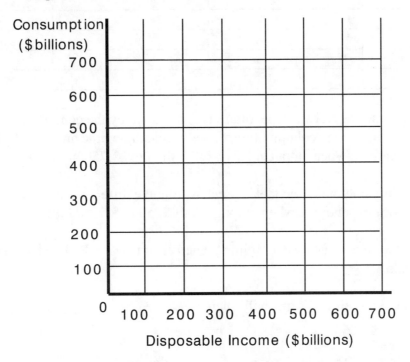

B. Assume that planned private-sector investment spending equals $50 billion, government purchases are $75 billion, and net exports equal – $75 billion. The algebraic equation for the planned aggregate expenditure curve would be PAE = $ _____ billion + _____ (Y – $_____ billion) + $ _____ billion + $ _____ billion + $ _____ billion. Combining the autonomous portions of PAE would result in a simplified equation, PAE = $_____ billion + _____ Y.

C. Plot the planned aggregate expenditure curve on the above graph, and label it PAE.

D. Autonomous planned aggregate expenditure equals $_____ billions and is graphically represented where the planned aggregate expenditure curve intersects the (vertical/ horizontal) _____ axis.

E. When disposable income equals $400 billions, the algebraic equation for the planned
    aggregate expenditure curve would be PAE = $ _____ billion + _____ (Y – $_____
    billion) + $ _____ billion + $ _____ billion + $ _____ billion.
    The induced planned aggregate expenditure equals $_____ billions.

2. Numerical Determination of Short-Run Equilibrium Output

The focus of this problem is the determination of the short-run equilibrium output within the
framework of a numerical table. (Figures are in billions.)

Output (Y)	Planned Aggregate Expenditure	Y – PAE	Y = PAE?
$ 250			
500			
750			
1,000			
1,250			
1,500			
1,750			

A. Assume that planned aggregate expenditure is determined by the equation PAE = $500 +
    0.6Y. Complete the second column of the table by calculating the amount of planned
    aggregate expenditure when output equals $250 billion to $1,750 billion.

B. Complete the third column of the table by calculating the difference between output and
    planned aggregate expenditure when output equals $250 to $1,750 billion.

C. Complete the fourth column by determining whether or not Y = PAE. The equilibrium level
    of output equals $_____.

D. If output equals $500 billion, firms will (increase/decrease) _____ the level of
    output.

E. If output equals $1,500 billion, firms will (increase/decrease) _____ the level of
    output.

3. The Basic Keynesian Model

This problem is designed to help you understand the fundamentals of the basic Keynesian model.
You will determine the equilibrium level of income (or output) and analyze the effects of
changes in private-sector investment spending on the equilibrium level of income (or output).

A. Assume that the consumption function is C = $200 billion + 0.8(Y – T), private-sector
    investment equals $150 billion, government purchases equal $200 billion, taxes equal $100
    billion, and net exports equal –$70 billion. Using this information, derive the aggregate
    expenditure function. PAE = $_____ billion + _____ Y.

B. On the graph below, plot the planned aggregate expenditure curve for level of output ranging from $0 billion to $5,000 billion (label the curve PAE).

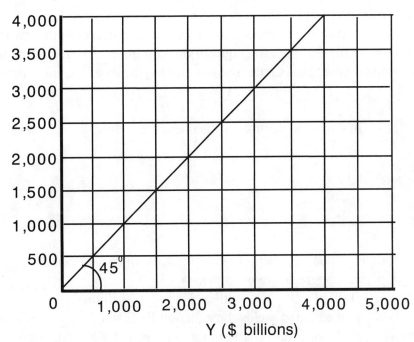

PAE
($billions)

Y ($ billions)

C. The equilibrium level of output equals $ _____ billion.

D. If firms produce $3,000 billion of output, planned aggregate expenditure would equal $ _____ billion. As a result, firms would have $ _____ billion of goods they intended to sell but did not. This would cause firms (increase/decrease) _____ their level of output. [In this question, you do not have to go back to the consumption function since you are told what firms are producing in aggregate. The consumption function could be given to you as a function of Y instead of (Y – T).]

E. The MPC equals _____, and the multiplier equals _____ .

F. If investment spending decreases by $100 billion, the planned aggregate expenditure curve will shift (upward/downward) _____, and the equilibrium output will (increase/ decrease) _____ by an amount equal to the change in planned aggregate expenditure times the multiplier.

G. On the graph above, draw the planned aggregate expenditure curve after a $100-billion decrease in investment spending (label it PAE$_1$). The new equilibrium output would equal $ _____ billion.

H. After investment spending has decreased and the new equilibrium output in question 3F is calculated, if the potential output (Y*) equals $2,000 billion, there would now be a (recessionary/expansionary) _____ gap in the economy.

4. Solving the Basic Keynesian Model Numerically

This problem uses algebraic equations to determine the short-run equilibrium output. You will derive the aggregate expenditure equation; calculate the short-run equilibrium real GDP, employing the equation for the short-run equilibrium condition; and determine the effect of changes in government purchases, taxes, and transfer payments of the short-run equilibrium output.

Use the following set of equations to answer the questions below. [The figures are in $billions.]
   $C = \$400 + 0.75(Y - T)$
   $T = \$200$
   $I^P = \$250$
   $G = \$300$
   $NX = \$50$

A. Using the information above, substitute into the equation the numerical values for each component of planned aggregate expenditure. Y= $_____ billion + _____(Y – $_____ billion) + $_____ billion + $_____ billion + $_____ billion.
B. After simplifying, that equation yields the equation PAE = $ _____ billion + _____Y.
C. The definition of short-run equilibrium output implies that Y = PAE. Replacing PAE with the equation found in question 4B yields Y = $ _____ billion + _____Y.
D. Now solve for Y in Y – ____ Y = $_____ billion, or Y = $ _____ billion.
E. Thus, the equilibrium output equals $ _____ billion.
F. If government purchases decrease by $100 billion, the new short-run equilibrium output will equal $ _____ billion.
G. Starting from the level of the short-run equilibrium output in question 4E, an increase in taxation of $100 (billion) will result in a new short-run equilibrium output of $ _____ billion.
H. If instead of decreasing government purchases by $100 billion in question 4F, the government decreased transfer payments by $100 billion, the new short-run equilibrium output would equal $ _____ billion.
I. In comparing the answers to questions 4F to H, it is apparent that a change in government purchases has a (greater/lesser/equal) _____ effect on the short-run equilibrium output than does an equal change in transfer payments or taxation.

SOLUTIONS

Quick Quiz

1. B.
2. D.
3. E.
4. A.
5. C.
6. C.
7. E.
8. D.
9. A.
10. E.
11. C.
12. A.
13. D.
14. A.
15. B.

Self-Test: Key Terms

1. consumption function.
2. planned aggregate expenditure.
3. marginal propensity to consume (MPC).
4. stabilization policies.
5. income–expenditure multiplier.
6. menu costs.
7. autonomous expenditure.
8. short-run equilibrium output.
9. discretionary fiscal policy.
10. induced expenditure.
11. contractionary policies.
12. wealth effect.
13. expansionary policies.
14. fiscal policy.

Self-Test: Multiple-Choice Questions

1. C.
2. B.
3. E.

4. E. [$250 billion + [0.6(Y - $200 billion)] + $180 billion + $75 billion + (-$40 billion) =
    $345 billion + 0.6Y].

5. C.

6. C.

7. C.

8. E.

9. C.

10. D.

11. D.

12. A.

13. D.

14. E.

15. B.

16. C.

Appendices 12A and 12B

1. D.

2. B.

3. E.

Self Test: Short-Answer Problems

1. A.

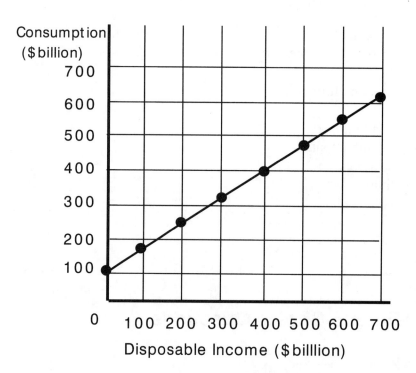

B. $175 billion + 0.75(Y – $100 billion) + $50 billion + $75 billion + (–$75) billion;
    $150 billion + 0.75Y

C.

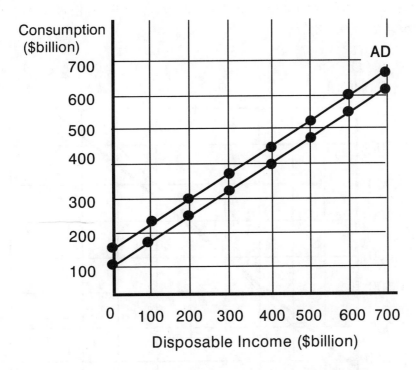

D. $150 billion (= $175 billion – $75 billion + $50 billion + 75 billion – $75 billion); vertical.

E. PAE = $175 billion + 0.75(Y – T) + $50 billion + $75 billion – $75 billion. With taxes (T) of $100 billion, and disposable income equal to $400 billion, this implies Y equals $500 billion. Therefore, the induced component of planned aggregate expenditure is $375 billion or 0.75 times $500 billion.

2. A.; B.

Output (Y)	Planned Aggregate Expenditure	Y– PAE	Y = PAE?
$ 250	$ 650	$–400	No
500	800	–300	No
750	950	–200	No
1,000	1,100	–100	No
1,250	1,250	0	Yes
1,500	1,400	100	No
1,750	1,550	200	No

C. $1,250.
D. increase.
E. decrease.

3.

   A. PAE = \$400 billion + 0.8Y.

   B.

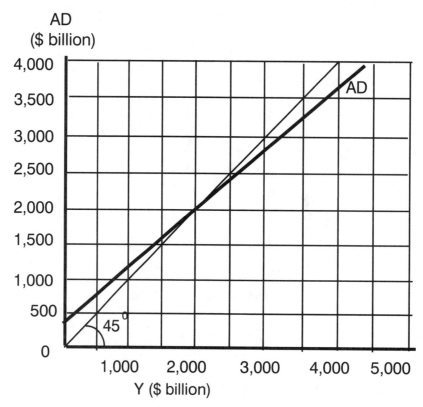

   C. \$2,000 billion.

   D. \$2,800 billion (= \$400 billion + 0.8(\$3,000 billion); \$200 billion (Y − PAE, or \$3,000 billion − \$2,800 billion); decrease.

   E. $0.8 \; ; 5 \; (= \dfrac{1}{1-0.8} = \dfrac{1}{0.2})$.

   F. downward; decrease; −\$500 billion or 5 times (− \$100 billion).

   G. the PAE curve after the change is labelled PAE_1 in the graph below.

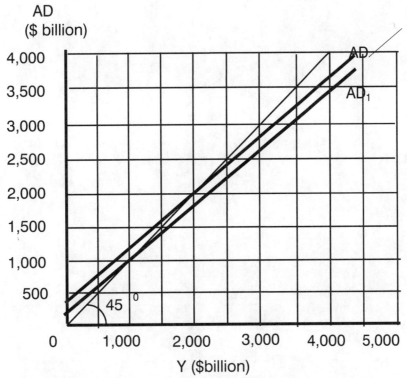

The new equilibrium output after the change is $1,500 billion.
(The change in equilibrium output is – $100 billion × 5 = – $500 billion. Subtracting the change in equilibrium output from the initial equilibrium output, $2,000 billion – $500 billion, gives us the new equilibrium output.)

H. Recessionary gap.

4.
    A. $400 billion + 0.75 (Y – $200 billion) + $250 billion + $300 billion + $50 billion.
    B. PAE = $850 billion + 0.75Y.
    C. Y = $850 billion + 0.75Y.
    D. Y*= $3,400 billion [Y* = $850 billion / 0.25].
    E. $3,400 billion.
    F. $3,000 billion [Y – 0.75Y = $750 billion, or 0.25Y = $750 billion, thus, Y = $3,000 billion].
    G. $3,100 billion [Y – 0.75Y = $675, or 0.25Y = $775 billion, thus, Y = $3,100 billion].
    H. $3,100 billion. [The effect a decrease in transfer payments is the same as an increase in taxation, and thus, the numerical derivation is identical to the answer to question 4G . That is, a decrease in transfer payments is like an increase in taxes.]
    I. greater.

13 Stabilizing the Economy: The Role of the Central Bank

OVERVIEW

This chapter examines the workings of monetary policy, one of the two major types of stabilization policy. The chapter begins with a discussion of how a central bank uses its ability to control or influence nominal and real interest rates with reference to two distinct views: the vertical money supply theory and the modern central banking theory. A main concern of this chapter is to use the basic Keynesian model to explain the effects of monetary policy and interest rates on planned aggregate expenditure and the short-run equilibrium output. The chapter ends with a discussion of the Bank of Canada's policy reaction function.

Chapter Review

13.1 The Vertical Money Supply Theory of Interest Rate Determination

► **LO 1.** Define vertical money supply theory.

As explained in Chapter 9, a central bank uses three tools to control the money supply. According to *vertical money supply theory* the central bank's control of the money supply involves changing interest rates by shifting a vertical money supply curve. The nominal interest rate is the price of money and is determined by the supply and demand for money.

► **LO 2.** Explain portfolio allocation decision and explain how it relates to the demand for money.

There are almost an infinite number of forms in which wealth can be held. The decision about the forms in which to hold one's wealth is called the *portfolio allocation decision*. People generally prefer a portfolio that pays high returns and does not carry too much risk.

▶ **LO 3.**   **Define demand for money and show a money demand curve.**

The demand for money is the result of choices made by households and businesses. The *demand for money* is the amount of wealth an individual chooses to hold in the form of money (principally, cash and chequing accounts). Households and businesses demand money to carry out transactions (i.e., use it as a medium of exchange) and as a way of holding wealth (i.e., the store of value function of money). Graphically, the *money demand curve* relates the aggregate quantity of money demand, M, to the nominal interest rate, i. Because an increase in the nominal interest rate increases the opportunity cost of holding money, which reduces the quantity of money demanded, the money demand curve slopes down.

▶ **LO 4.**   **Apply cost-benefit analysis to the money demand decision.**

How much money one chooses to hold is based on the costs and benefits of holding money. The opportunity cost of holding money is the interest that could have been earned if the person had chosen to hold interest-bearing assets instead of money. The higher the prevailing interest rate, the greater the opportunity cost of holding money and hence the less money individuals and businesses will demand. The principal benefit of holding money is its usefulness in carrying out transactions.

▶ **LO 5.**   **Discuss macroeconomic factors that affect the demand for money and the effects of changes on the money demand curve.**

The amount of money demanded to carry out transactions is affected at the macroeconomic level by real output and the price level. An increase in aggregate real output or income raises the quantity of goods and services that people and businesses want to buy and, thus, raises the demand for money. The higher the price of goods and services, the more dollars are needed to make a given set of transactions and, therefore, the higher the demand for money. This is reflected on a graph of money demand, where an increase in real output or the price level will cause the money demand curve to shift to the right, while a decrease in either will cause it to shift to the left. Other factors, such as technological and financial advances, also cause the money demand curve to shift.

▶ **LO 6.**   **Identify the money market equilibrium.**

According to vertical money supply theory of interest rate determination, the supply of money is controlled by the Bank of Canada (the central bank of Canada). Its primary tool for controlling the money supply is open-market operations. Because the Bank of Canada fixes the supply of money, the money supply curve is a vertical line that intercepts the horizontal axis at the quantity of money chosen by the Bank of Canada. The *equilibrium* in the market for money occurs at the intersection of the supply and demand for money curves. The equilibrium amount of money in circulation is the amount of money the Bank of Canada chooses to supply. The equilibrium nominal interest rate is the interest rate at which the quantity of money demanded by the public equals the fixed supply of money made available by the Bank of Canada.

▶ **LO 7.** **Explain what shifts money supply and how that affects interest rates.**

Only actions by the central bank shift the money supply curve. When the Bank of Canada increases the money supply, it lowers the equilibrium nominal interest rate. When the Bank of Canada decreases the money supply the equilibrium nominal interest rate must rise.

Quick Quiz

1. Vertical money supply theory maintains that the central bank changes interest rates by shifting a vertical money supply curve through
   A. altering money demand.
   B. changing the overnight rate.
   C. changing commercial banks' reserves.
   D. announcing a change in the key policy rate.
   E. persuading the public to deposit more or less in banks.

2. The portfolio allocation decision is related to the demand for money because
   A. money can be used to buy a portfolio.
   B. money is one of the many forms in which wealth can be held and is a part of most asset portfolios.
   C. the portfolio allocation decision determines how much of an individual's money is going to be held in the form of currency and how much in the form of balances in a chequing account.
   D. money is the main form of wealth for most people.
   E. portfolio allocation explains why the amount of money people hold is directly related to interest rates.

3. The "demand for money" relates to
   A. commercial banks' requirement for cash deposits.
   B. people's demand for income.
   C. the Bank of Canada's influence over banks' reserves.
   D. the need for money as a unit of account.
   E. people's desire to hold money in chequing accounts and cash.

4. The cost of holding money instead of using it to purchase interest-earning assets is
   A. bank charges when a chequing account is overdrawn.
   B. the inconvenience of having to withdraw frequently for transactions.
   C. the opportunity to hold a chequing account instead of cash.
   D. the store of value.
   E. interest which otherwise could have been earned.

5. A decrease in aggregate real output or income will
   A. decrease the quantity of goods and services that people and businesses want to buy and sell and, thus, decrease the demand for money.

B. decrease the quantity of goods and services that people and businesses want to buy and sell and, thus, increase the demand for money.

C. increase the quantity of goods and services that people and businesses want to buy and sell and, thus, decrease the demand for money.

D. increase the quantity of goods and services that people and businesses want to buy and sell and, thus, increase the demand for money.

E. decrease the quantity of goods and services that people and businesses want to buy and sell but have no effect on the demand for money.

6. At equilibrium in the market for money, the quantity of money demanded is equal to
   A. the money supply chosen by the central bank.
   B. the total currency in coins and paper bills.
   C. the amount of money deposited in the banking system.
   D. the quantity of money demanded at every interest rate.
   E. the money on reserve with the Bank of Canada.

7. Which of the following shifts the money supply curve?
   A. a change in the amount of money demanded.
   B. a shift in the money demand curve.
   C. a change in real income (output).
   D. a decision by the Bank of Canada to target different interest rates.
   E. a change in the price level.

13.2 Modern Central Banking Theory of Interest Rate Determination

▶ **LO 8.   Define the modern central banking theory.**

In contrast to vertical money supply theory, *modern central banking theory of interest rate determination* views that the money supply is not directly controlled by the Bank of Canada. Although there are thousands of different interest rates determined in the financial markets, economists often use the phrase the *nominal interest rate* to refer to an average measure of these interest rates because they tend to rise and fall together. Of all the market interest rates in Canada, the one that is most closely watched by the public, politicians, and the media, however, is the key policy rate or the official interest rate—the Bank of Canada's target for the overnight rate.

▶ **LO 9.   Define the overnight rate and the bank rate and explain why the Bank of Canada now focuses on the overnight rate.**

The *overnight rate* is the interest rate large financial institutions, mainly commercial banks, charge each other for very short-term (overnight) loans. This key policy rate is closely watched because the Bank of Canada has expressed its policies in terms of a target value for the overnight rate. Because interest rates tend to move together, an action by the Bank of Canada to change its official interest rate generally causes other interest rates to change in the same direction. The tendency of interest rates to move together, however, is not an exact relationship. This means that the actual overnight rate need not be exactly the same as the Bank of Canada's overnight rate target, called the *bank rate*. Nevertheless, the Bank of Canada has managed to keep the actual overnight rate within an operating band of 0.5 percentage points of its target since the mid-1990s.

▶ **LO 10.** **Explain how monetary policy is used to control nominal interest rates.**

If overnight rates differ from the central bank's *target* overnight rate, the central bank can buy or sell government bonds to keep the overnight rates within a target range.

Quick Quiz

8. The difference between "vertical money supply theory" and "modern central banking theory" is that the LATTER
   A. can be both expansionary and contractionary.
   B. relies on changing the central bank's key policy rate.
   C. affects interest rates.
   D. views the money supply curve as vertical.
   E. is not used in Canada.

9. According to modern central banking theory, the Bank of Canada communicates its monetary policy to the public in terms of targets for the overnight rate because it is
   A. the only interest rate that they can control.
   B. the interest rate that most individuals pay when they borrow money to buy a car, a household appliance, or a house.
   C. the interest rate that the Bank of Canada has the greatest control over.
   D. one of the tools of monetary policy.
   E. the most important of all the interest rates that is determined in the various financial markets.

10. According to modern central banking theory, a decrease in the official interest rate
   A. is achieved if the Bank of Canada implements an open-market sale of government bonds.
   B. will decrease the money market equilibrium interest rate.
   C. will increase the money market equilibrium interest rate.
   D. will decrease the price of bonds.
   E. will shift the money supply curve to the right.

13.3 Can the Bank of Canada Control the Real Interest Rate?

▶ **LO 11.** **Discuss the Bank of Canada's ability to control the real interest rate.**

Both theories agree that the Bank of Canada's control over real interest rates is less complete than its control over nominal interest rates. The *real interest rate* equals the nominal interest rate minus the rate of inflation. Because inflation tends to change relatively slowly in response to changes in policy or economic conditions, actions by the Bank of Canada to change nominal interest rates allow it to control real interest rates in the short run. In the long run, however, the inflation rate and other variables will adjust, and the balance of saving and investment will determine the real interest rate.

Quick Quiz

11. The real interest rate
   A. cannot be controlled by the Bank of Canada because monetary policy only affects nominal interest rates.
   B. can be controlled by the Bank of Canada in the short run but not in the long run.
   C. can be controlled by the Bank of Canada in the long run but not in the short run.
   D. equals the nominal interest rate plus the inflation rate.
   E. equals the inflation rate minus the nominal interest rate.

13.4 The Effects of Bank of Canada Actions on the Economy

▶ **LO 12.**   **Explain how interest rates affect consumption and private-sector investment spending, planned aggregate expenditure, and short-run equilibrium output.**

Because the Bank of Canada can control interest rates (at least, in the short run), monetary policy can be used to eliminate output gaps and stabilize the economy. Consumption and planned private-sector investment spending are inversely related to real interest rates, that is, a decrease in real interest rates will cause consumption and planned private-sector investment spending to increase. Because consumption and planned private-sector investment spending are components of planned aggregate expenditure (PAE), changes in real interest rates cause changes in PAE. By adjusting real interest rates, the Bank of Canada can move PAE in the desired direction.

▶ **LO 13.**   **Explain how the Bank of Canada would fight a recession or prevent inflation, by affecting interest rates.**

An *expansionary monetary policy*, or monetary easing, involves a reduction in interest rates by the Bank of Canada, made with the intention of reducing a recessionary gap. If the economy faces a recessionary gap, the Bank of Canada could reduce real interest rates to stimulate consumption and private-sector investment spending. This will increase PAE, and as a result, output will rise and the recessionary gap will be reduced or eliminated. When the economy experiences inflationary pressures, the Bank of Canada may implement a *contractionary monetary policy*, or monetary tightening, by increasing interest rates with the intention of reducing an expansionary gap.

► **LO 14.** **Explain how the simple Keynesian cross model fits with the Bank of Canada's explanation of monetary policy.**

The Keynesian cross model and the Bank of Canada's explanation of the workings of monetary policy have much in common. The Keynesian model used in this text assumes that net exports are fixed, however that assumption could be modified to show the impact of interest rates on the exchange rate and, ultimately, on net exports. Second, the Keynesian cross model assumes that potential output is fixed, and that is a limitation. Third, the Keynesian cross model does not incorporate inflation explicitly.

Quick Quiz

12. Which of the following would NOT decrease as a result of the Bank of Canada raising interest rates?
    A. consumption.
    B. investment.
    C. taxes.
    D. net exports.
    E. planned aggregate expenditure.

13. A contractionary monetary policy is designed to produce a(n)
    A. increase in planned aggregate expenditure and reduce an expansionary gap.
    B. decrease in planned aggregate expenditure and reduce an expansionary gap.
    C. increase in planned aggregate expenditure and reduce a recessionary gap.
    D. decrease in planned aggregate expenditure and reduce a recessionary gap.
    E. increase in planned aggregate expenditure and increase an expansionary gap.

14. Which of these features is NOT part of the Bank of Canada's explanation of monetary policy effects?
    A. interest rate changes.
    B. exchange rate effects.
    C. net export changes.
    D. fixed potential output.
    E. any decrease in equilibrium output.

13.5 Monetary Policymaking and Real-World Uncertainty

► **LO 15.** **Explain the imprecision of monetary policy making in practice.**

In practice, monetary policy making is a complex process because of uncertainties and imperfect knowledge about the real-world economy—such as uncertainties about the timing and impact of interest rate changes on growth. For example, the Bank of Canada cut the overnight rate target nine times in 2001 to avoid a recession without triggering an upsurge in inflation.

Quick Quiz

15. The Bank of Canada has NOT faced uncertainties regarding
    A. the economic well-being of major trade partners.
    B. the size of potential output in Canada.
    C. the time required to recover from a recession.
    D. world political developments.
    E. the overnight rate target.

Self-Test: Key Terms

Use the terms below to complete the following sentences. (Answers are given at the end of the chapter.)

bank rate   money demand curve
contractionary monetary policy   overnight rate
demand for money   overnight rate target
expansionary monetary policy   portfolio allocation decision
modern central banking theory   vertical money supply theory

1. The choice about which forms to hold one's wealth is called the _____ .

2. A reduction in interest rates by the Bank of Canada, made with the intention of reducing a recessionary gap, is achieved through _____ .

3. The Bank of Canada can influence market interest rates by changing its target for the _____ , which is an interest rate that large commercial banks charge each other for short-term loans.

4. An increase in real output or the price level will cause the _____ to shift to the right.

5. The interest rate that the Bank of Canada charges commercial banks for overnight loans is the _____ .

6. If the economy faces an expansionary gap, the Bank of Canada could increase real interest rates by implementing a(n) _____ .

7. The amount of wealth an individual chooses to hold in the form of money is that person's _____ .

8. According to _____ of interest rate determination, the supply of money changes when commercial banks respond to changes in the Bank of Canada's official interest rate.

9. According to _____ of interest rate determination, the Bank of Canada can change interest rates by directly controlling the money supply.

10. The interest rate that the Bank of Canada wants to prevail for borrowing among major financial institutions is the _____.

Self-Test: Multiple-Choice Questions

1. E-Buy, a Web-based auction firm receives an average of $25,000 in payments for its services each day that it deposits in its bank account at the end of each day. E-Commerce Management Systems, Inc. proposed a computerized cash management system to track E-Buy's inflows and outflows of payments and electronically transfer the funds to an interest-bearing bank account. The cost of the system is $500 per year and E-Buy estimates that it would reduce its cash holding by approximately $10,000 per day. E-Buy should
   A. accept the proposal.
   B. reject the proposal.
   C. accept the proposal if the average interest rate they can earn on the funds is at least 10 percent.
   D. reject the proposal if the average interest rate they can earn on the funds is less than 10 percent.
   E. accept the proposal if the average interest rate they can earn on the funds is greater than 5 percent.

2. As the number of ABM machines increases in a country
   A. the supply of money will increase.
   B. the supply of money will decrease.
   C. people will hold more of their wealth in the form of money. (i.e., the demand for money will increase).
   D. people will hold less of their wealth in the form of money (i.e., the demand for money will decrease).
   E. interest rates will increase.

3. When the Bank of Canada buys government bonds, bond prices
   A. increase and interest rates fall.
   B. decrease and interest rates fall.
   C. increase and interest rates rise.
   D. decrease and interest rates rise.
   E. and interest rates fall.

4. If the Bank of Canada implements an open-market sale of government bonds, the
   A. money market equilibrium interest rate will rise.
   B. money market equilibrium interest rate will fall.
   C. price of bonds will rise.
   D. supply of money will increase.
   E. demand for bonds will decrease.

5. If the Bank of Canada implements an open-market purchase of government bonds, this will cause a(n)
    A. decrease in consumption spending, an increase in private-sector investment spending, and an increase in planned aggregate expenditure.
    B. increase in consumption and private-sector investment spending and an increase in planned aggregate expenditure.
    C. decrease in consumption and private-sector investment spending and an increase in planned aggregate expenditure.
    D. decrease in consumption spending, a decrease in private-sector investment spending, and an increase in planned aggregate expenditure.
    E. increase in consumption spending, a decrease in private-sector investment spending, and a decrease in planned aggregate expenditure.

6. According to vertical money supply theory, an expansionary monetary policy will cause a(n)
    A. decrease in interest rates and an increase in planned aggregate expenditure and is designed to reduce an expansionary gap.
    B. increase in interest rates and a decrease in planned aggregate expenditure and is designed to reduce an expansionary gap.
    C. decrease in interest rates and a decrease in planned aggregate expenditure and is designed to reduce a recessionary gap.
    D. decrease in interest rates and an increase in planned aggregate expenditure and is designed to reduce a recessionary gap.
    E. increase in interest rates and increase in planned aggregate expenditure and is designed to reduce a recessionary gap.

7. In practice, Bank of Canada's monetary policy making is based on
    A. scientific, precise statistical modelling of the economy only.
    B. the judgment of the members of the Bank of Canada's Governing Council only.
    C. a mathematical model of the multiplier.
    D. an approximate idea of the effects of its policy on planned aggregate expenditure.
    E. the Bank of Canada's demand for money only.

8. The higher the price of bonds, with no change in the cost of transferring funds between bonds and chequable deposits, the
    A. more likely people are to hold their wealth in the form of bonds than money.
    B. more likely people are to hold their wealth in the form of money than bonds.
    C. greater is the differential between nominal and real interest rates.
    D. smaller is the quantity of money demanded.
    E. greater is the demand for money.

9. The Bank of Canada can control real interest rates in the short run because
    A. the federal government has not given it the legal authority to control interest rates in the long run.
    B. nominal interest rates only adjust slowly to changing economic conditions and policy.
    C. saving and private-sector investment are not relevant to short-run real interest rates.

D. saving and private-sector investment are not relevant to long-run real interest rates.

E. it is able to control the nominal interest rate and the inflation rate only adjusts slowly to changing economic conditions and policy.

10. If the Bank of Canada wants to lower the money market equilibrium interest rate, it could
A. decrease the supply of money.
B. shift the supply of money to the left.
C. sell government bonds with a special purchase and resale agreement.
D. purchase government bonds with a sale and repurchase agreement.
E. decrease the price of bonds.

11. If the Bank of Canada implements a monetary easing, this will cause a(n)
A. increase in planned aggregate expenditure and output and reduce a recessionary gap.
B. increase in planned aggregate expenditure and output and reduce an expansionary gap.
C. decrease in planned aggregate expenditure and output and reduce a recessionary gap.
D. decrease in planned aggregate expenditure and output and reduce an expansionary gap.
E. increase in planned aggregate expenditure, decrease output, and reduce an expansionary gap.

12. The Bank of Canada tends to be cautious with its monetary policy making because
A. of vertical money supply theory.
B. the Bank of Canada does not have precise information about the size of the money supply and the level of interest rates.
C. the Bank of Canada does not have precise information about the level of potential output and the size and speed of the effects of its actions.
D. the Bank of Canada does not have precise information about the level of actual output and the size and speed of the effects of its actions.
E. the Bank of Canada does not have precise information about the level of planned aggregate expenditure and the size and speed of the effects of its actions.

13. To close a recessionary gap, the Bank of Canada should
A. lower interest rates, causing consumption, private-sector investment spending, and planned aggregate expenditure to decrease.
B. lower interest rates, causing consumption, private-sector investment spending, and planned aggregate expenditure to increase.
C. raise interest rates, causing consumption, private-sector investment spending, and planned aggregate expenditure to decrease.
D. raise interest rates, causing consumption, private-sector investment spending, and planned aggregate expenditure to increase.
E. keep interest rates unchanged, causing consumption, private-sector investment spending, and planned aggregate expenditure to remain unchanged.

14. The nominal interest rate affects the demand for money because at higher interest rates
A. people will not want to hold any money in cash.
B. banks will want to make more loans.
C. people will want to hold less money.

D. the Bank of Canada will require more money on reserve.

E. people will want to hold more money.

15. A falling rate of inflation would result in the demand for money

A. increasing because people want to take advantage of good prices.

B. decreasing because people need less money for transactions.

C. remaining the same because people would still have the same money needs.

D. increasing because national incomes would be increasing.

E. decreasing because the economy would most certainly be in a recession.

Self Test: Short Answer Problems

(Answers and solutions are given at the end of the chapter.)

1. Cost and Benefit of Holding Money

The following table shows the estimated annual benefits to Siam of holding different amounts of money.

Average Money Holdings	Total Annual Benefit	Marginal Annual Benefit
$1,000	$ 60	
1,100	72	
1,200	82	
1,300	90	
1,400	96	
1,500	100	
1,600	102	
1,700	102	

A. Complete column 3 by calculating the extra benefit of each additional $100 in money holdings greater than $100.

B. How much money will Siam hold if the nominal interest rate is 10 percent? $_____; if the nominal interest rate is 8 percent? $_____; if the nominal interest rate is 6 percent? $_____; if the nominal interest rate is 4 percent $_____; if the nominal interest rate is 2 percent $_____?

C. On the graph on the next page, plot Siam's money demand curve for nominal interest rates between 2 and 12 percent.

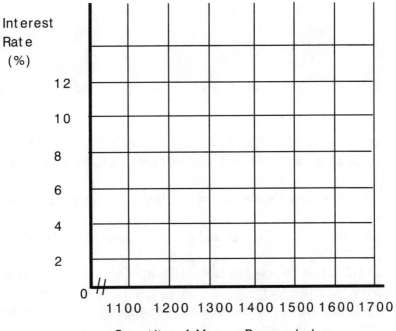

Quantity of Money Demanded

D. If Siam won a million-dollar lottery, his money demand curve shift to the (right/left)
    _____ representing a(n) (increase/decrease) _____ in the demand for money.

2. **Money Market and Equilibrium Interest Rate**
    This problem focuses on vertical money supply theory according to which the Bank of
    Canada controls the money supply to achieve targeted nominal interest rates. Assume the
    planned aggregate expenditure for money (in millions of dollars) is given by the equation M
    = $P(0.33Y - 15,000i)$, the price level (P) equals 1.5, and real output (Y) equals \$9,000 million.

    A. If the Bank of Canada wants to set the nominal equilibrium interest rate at 4 percent, it
        should set the nominal money supply at _____.
    B. If real GDP increases to \$10,000 million, and the Bank of Canada wants to keep the
        nominal equilibrium interest rate at 4 percent, it should (increase/decrease) _____
        the nominal money supply to _____.
    C. If the Bank of Canada now wants to raise the nominal equilibrium interest rate to 5
        percent, it should (increase/decrease) _____ the nominal money supply to

        _____.
    D. If the price level rises to 2 and the Bank of Canada wants to keep the nominal equilibrium
        interest rate at 5 percent, it should (increase/decrease) _____ the nominal money
        supply to _____.

3. **Monetary Policy and Short-Run Equilibrium Output**
    This problem will help you better understand the relationship among interest rates, planned
    aggregate expenditure, output, and monetary policy. The planned aggregate expenditure for
    the economy of Hinderland is given by the following equations:
    $C = 750 + 0.75(Y - T) - 300\,r$
    $I^P = 400 - 600\,r$

$$G = 500$$
$$T = 400$$
$$NX = -55$$

The above equations are measured in millions of dollars. For example, G = 500 means G = $ 500 million.

A. If the Bank of Hinderland sets the nominal interest rate (r) at 0.05 (5%), the planned aggregate expenditure for the Hinderland economy would be represented by the equation PAE = _____ + 0.75Y.

B. Given Hinderland's planned aggregate expenditure, the short-run equilibrium output would equal _____ .

C. If potential output (Y^*) in the Hinderland economy equals $5,050 million, there would be a(n) _____ gap of _____ .

D. If the Bank of Hinderland wanted to close the output gap, it should implement a(n) (expansionary/ contractionary) _____ monetary policy.

E. To close the gap, the Bank of Hinderland would need to (decrease/ increase) _____ nominal interest rates to _____ percent.

SOLUTIONS

Quick Quiz

1. C.
2. B.
3. E.
4. E.
5. A.
6. A.
7. D.
8. B.
9. C.
10. B.
11. B.
12. C.
13. B.
14. D.
15. E.

Self-Test: Key Terms

1. portfolio allocation decision.
2. expansionary monetary policy.

3. overnight rate.
4. money demand curve.
5. bank rate.
6. contractionary monetary policy.
7. demand for money.
8. modern central banking theory.
9. vertical money supply theory.
10. overnight rate target.

Self-Test: Multiple-Choice Questions

1. E. $10,000 × 0.05 = $500. Therefore, an interest rate of greater than 5% would imply that the benefit would be greater than the cost.
2. D.
3. A.
4. A.
5. B.
6. D.
7. D.
8. B.
9. E.
10. D.
11. A.
12. C.
13. B.
14. C.
15. B.

Self-Test: Short-Answer Problems

1. A.

Average Money Holdings	Total Annual Benefit	Marginal Annual Benefit
$1,000	$ 60	—
1,100	72	12
1,200	82	10
1,300	90	8
1,400	96	6
1,500	100	4
1,600	102	2
1,700	102	0

B. $1,200; $1,300; $1,400; $1,500; $1,600.

C.

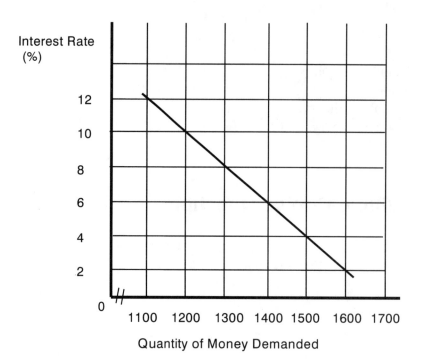

Quantity of Money Demanded

D. right; increase.

2. A. $3,555 million {M= 1.5[(0.33 × 9,000) – (15,000 × 0.04)], or M = 4,455 – 900}.
   B. $4,050 million {M= 1.5[0.33 × 10,000) – (15,000 × 0.04)], or M = 4,950 – 900}.
   C. $3,825 million {M= 1.5[0.33 × 10,000) – (15,000 × 0.05)], or M = 4,950 – 1,125}.
   D. increase; $5,100 million {M= 2.0[0.33 × 10,000) – (15,000 × 0.05)], or M = 6,600 – 1,500}.

3. A. $1,250 million [750 + 0.75(Y – 400) – 300 (0.05) + 400 – 600 (0.05) + 500 + (– 55)].
   B. $5,000 million (Y = 1,250 + 0.75 Y, or 0.25Y = 1,250, thus Y = 1,250 /0.25).
   C. recessionary gap; $50 million (Y* – Y = output gap).
   D. expansionary.
   E. decrease; 3.6 (5,050 = $1,295 + 0.75(5,050) – 900r, or 5,050 = 1,295 + 3,787.5 – 900r. Combining the constant values gives us –32.5 = – 900 × r., or 3.6 = r).

14 The Aggregate Demand–Aggregate Supply Model

OVERVIEW

This chapter presents an economic model where spending, as reflected through aggregate demand (AD), and aggregate supply (AS) interact to determine the equilibrium price and output level. The long-run aggregate supply (LRAS) and short-run aggregate supply (SRAS) reflect the differing behaviour of firms in the two time periods. Aggregate demand is determined by changes in planned aggregate expenditure (PAE) at each price level. The chapter then uses the model to show how output gaps and policy measures affect prices and output. Finally, the chapter explores the relationship between inflation and unemployment as represented by the Phillips curve.

Chapter Review

14.1 Introduction

▶ **LO 1.** **Explain the significance of the aggregate demand–aggregate supply (AS–AD) model.**

The Keynesian cross model developed in Chapters 12 and 13 discussed planned aggregate expenditure, but it assumed that prices were preset. The AD–AS model demonstrates how the general price level changes as a result of changes in AD and/or AS.

NOTE:
As explained in Chapter 6, calculating a change in the consumer price index (CPI) gives a useful idea of the rate of inflation (change in the general price level) between two different years.

Quick Quiz

1. Something which the Keynesian cross model of output determination could not explain, but the AD–AS model could, is
   A. stagflation, where a recession coexists with a rising price level.
   B. the consumer price index.

C. spending by consumers as well as spending by firms.
D. equilibrium output.
E. the effect of changes in spending.

14.2 The Three Components of the Aggregate Demand–Aggregate Supply Model

▶ **LO 2.**   **Discuss the long-run aggregate supply (LRAS) curve and the factors which cause it to shift.**

In the long run, the economy is drawn to its potential output level, regardless of the price level. The LRAS curve represents this level of output and is vertical to signify that this output level will prevail in the long run at any price level. Productivity and the magnitude of real inputs determine the potential output level; a change in one of these factors changes potential output and, therefore, the level of LRAS.

▶ **LO 3.**   **Explain the short-run aggregate supply (SRAS) curve and the factors which cause it to shift.**

As in the Keynesian cross model, prices are assumed to be fixed for the SRAS curve. Therefore, the SRAS is horizontal, with its vertical intercept at that fixed general price level. When operating costs decrease, firms are willing to supply at a lower general price level, and the SRAS correspondingly shifts downward. The reverse is true when operating costs increase.

▶ **LO 4.**   **Discuss the aggregate demand curve, the three reasons why it is downward-sloping, and the factors which cause it to shift.**

The planned aggregate expenditure (PAE) curve presented in Chapters 12 and 13 can be shifted to show the effect of a price change. When prices generally go down, planned aggregate expenditure moves in the opposite direction (increases). Each shift of the PAE results in a new equilibrium level between PAE and actual output. This information about price levels and the corresponding levels of output can be translated into a graph of the aggregate demand (AD) curve. The downward-sloping shape of the AD curve has three traditional explanations: (1) the "real-balances effect" that higher prices cause a diminished-wealth effect whereby people feel less willing to consume; (2) the "interest rate effect" that since higher prices increase money demand and thus the interest rate, spending therefore decreases at higher price levels; and (3) the "foreign trade effect," which assumes that net exports will be inversely related to the overall price level. Right shifts of the AD curve occur because of increases in autonomous spending or expansionary fiscal/monetary policy. Left shifts occur for the opposite reasons.

Quick Quiz

2. Which of the following would NOT cause an increase in Canada's potential output (i.e., a rightward shift of the LRAS)?
   A. a wave of new immigration.
   B. increased investment by businesses in factory machinery.
   C. a sudden increase in consumer spending.
   D. increased participation in the labour force by women.
   E. invention of more efficient computers.

3. If energy costs rose sharply in the economy, the reaction by firms would cause the short-run aggregate supply (SRAS) curve to
   A. become vertical.
   B. become horizontal.
   C. shift downward.
   D. shift upward.
   E. fluctuate up and down.

4. The "real balances effect" is reflected by the
   A. transactions shown on chequing accounts.
   B. the fact that people feel wealthier and spend more when prices decrease.
   C. the tendency for higher prices to push up interest rates.
   D. shift in the aggregate demand (AD) curve when prices change.
   E. decrease in foreign purchases of Canadian exports when prices rise.

14.3 Short-run and Long-run Equilibrium in the AD–AS Model

▶ **LO 5.** **Demonstrate that short-run equilibrium output may occur during a recessionary or expansionary gap, with respect to long-run equilibrium.**

In the short run, the existing equilibrium level of output (at the intersection of the AD and SRAS curves) involves a recessionary gap, when that short-run equilibrium is below long-run equilibrium. On a graph, the short-run equilibrium falls to the left of the vertical LRAS curve. Similarly, when short run equilibrium output is greater than long-run equilibrium, there is an expansionary gap.

▶ **LO 6.** **Explain how prices in the economy eventually change in the long run so that the SRAS curve shifts in the direction of eliminating the output gap.**

The self-correcting adjustment to potential output happens by way of price adjustment. In a recessionary gap, resources are unemployed, and there will be pressure for prices to fall. When these prices, and hence operating costs, decrease, firms are willing to supply at lower prices and the SRAS falls. As seen on the graph, this continues until the intersection of SRAS and AD coincides with the intersection of AD and LRAS. In an expansionary gap, resources are being used beyond their normal rate and there is pressure for resource prices to rise so that firms are now willing to supply only at higher prices. On the graph, the SRAS curve rises upward until it reaches a three-way intersection with the LRAS and AD curves.

Quick Quiz

5. Assuming the economy begins at long-run equilibrium, which of the following could cause short-run equilibrium to occur where there is an expansionary gap? *(Hint: it will help to graph long-run equilibrium and then shift the curve affected.)*
   A. an increase in operating costs, causing firms to sell at higher prices.
   B. the closure of businesses, resulting in decreased output.
   C. an increase in imports by Canadians, resulting in less spending.
   D. a decrease in the cost of energy, prompting firms to sell at lower prices.
   E. a decrease in government spending, leading to less spending.

6. The term "self-correcting" refers to the fact that
   A. government must correct any mistakes it makes in fiscal policy.
   B. private businesses are responsible for their own decisions.
   C. the onus is on the individual consumer and business to correct mistakes.
   D. each sovereign government corrects its economy without foreign input.
   E. prices adjust to automatically cause a shift in the SRAS back to equilibrium.

14.4 The AD–AS Model in Action

▶ **LO 7.**   **Discuss how macroeconomic policy can be used to close output gaps.**

Macroeconomic policy affects spending and, therefore, the aggregate demand (AD) curve. For an economy experiencing a recessionary gap, expansionary monetary policy (interest rate cuts) or fiscal policy (tax cuts and/or increased government spending) will increase aggregate demand. On a graph, the AD curve shifts right until it reaches a three-way intersection with the SRAS and LRAS. For an economy in an expansionary gap, contractionary macroeconomic policy slows down spending; graphically, the AD curve shifts left to the intersection of the SRAS and LRAS.

▶ **LO 8.**   **Define stagflation and explain how an adverse external factor can cause firms to supply at higher prices and, thus, cause a decrease in short-run equilibrium output.**

Stagflation occurs when firms react to an adverse event by supplying at higher prices. Some oil-importing countries experienced such a negative shock during the 1970s when a cutback on oil caused the cost of oil to rise sharply and, consequently, prices of other goods and services related to oil rose. Graphically, this corresponds to an upward shift in the SRAS curve, possibly pushing the economy into a recessionary gap. Unlike a recessionary gap caused by a slowdown in spending and decreased demand, an adverse supply event results in lower equilibrium output but at the same time higher prices. Note that a positive supply event would result in the opposite economic effects; for instance, a decrease in oil prices would enable firms to supply at lower prices, shifting the SRAS downward. Without policy interventions, either a recessionary gap or an expansionary gap would be eliminated through self-correcting price adjustments.

Quick Quiz

7. Which of the following actions would help decrease aggregate demand and close an expansionary output gap?
   A. a decrease in taxes.
   B. a decrease in the interest rate.
   C. an increase in government spending.
   D. a decrease in the money supply leading to higher interest rates.
   E. coordinated fiscal and monetary policies to stimulate spending.

8. In a period of stagflation, prices would _____ and short-run equilibrium output would _____.
   A. rise; rise.
   B. decrease; decrease.
   C. rise; decrease.
   D. decrease; rise.
   E. increase; remain unchanged.

14.5 The Expectations-Augmented Phillips Curve Model as a Supplement to the AD–AS Model

▶ **LO 9.** **Explain the concept of the Phillips curve and why it failed to be consistent with the rates of inflation and unemployment between 1973 and 1982.**

The original Phillips curve suggested a statistical relationship between the rates of inflation and unemployment, involving a tradeoff between the two. A sluggish economy would experience rising unemployment but low inflation, while an expansionary economy would see higher rates of inflation but relatively low unemployment. On a graph with the inflation rate on the vertical axis and the unemployment rate on the horizontal axis, the Phillips curve was downward-sloping to indicate the negative relationship. While that relationship worked well for data of the 1960s, it broke down when both inflation and unemployment were high.

▶ **LO 10.** **Define the expectations-augmented Phillips curve model and its implications for the short run and the long run.**

One explanation for the breakdown of the original Phillips curve is that people adjust their behaviour when they come to expect changing rates of inflation and that the economy gravitates toward natural rate of unemployment in the long run. Graphically, this implies two things: first, in the short run, the Phillips curve shifts upward to accommodate expectations of higher inflation or downward to adjust to expectations of falling inflation rates. Second, the long-run Phillips curve is vertical, indicating that the natural rate of unemployment prevails regardless of the inflation rate.

► **LO 11.   Define adaptive expectations and discuss how they would affect the Phillips curve.**

The idea of adaptive expectations is that people base their future expectations according to their recent experience with inflation. For example, if inflation has been high and the central bank takes measures to reduce it, two things will happen. First, assuming the economy started in equilibrium at the natural rate of unemployment, the contractionary monetary policies would push the unemployment rate higher; graphically, this implies movement down the short-run Phillips curve to the right. Second, people will adapt their expectations to a lower inflation rate; on the graph, this implies that the short-run Phillips curve shifts downward and unemployment self-corrects back to the natural rate in the long run.

Quick Quiz

9. A recessionary economy would experience raised levels of unemployment, and the rate of price rises would
    A. increase because of output shortages.
    B. increase because of higher demand for goods and services.
    C. decrease because of an increased supply of goods and services.
    D. decrease because there would not be enough activity to support higher prices.
    E. remain the same because only unemployment changes during a recession.

10. The long run "expectations-augmented" Phillips curve is vertical because
    A. it coincides with the natural rate of unemployment.
    B. inflation will be infinitely high in the long run.
    C. unemployment will be drawn to a low rate in the long run.
    D. only one rate of unemployment can prevail in a particular year.
    E. the central bank fixes the level of unemployment through monetary policy.

11. "Adaptive expectations" theory suggests that people anticipate future inflation
    A. according to current economic forecasts.
    B. based on the past direction of inflation.
    C. according to current socioeconomic indicators.
    D. because of announcements by the central bank.
    E. based on the direction of the unemployment rate.

Self Test: Key Terms

Use the terms below to complete the following sentences. (Answers are given at the end of the chapter.)

adaptive expectations
aggregate demand–aggregate supply
   model
aggregate demand curve
expectations-augmented Phillips curve
foreign trade effect
interest rate effect

long-run aggregate supply curve
long-run Phillips curve
Phillips curve
real balances effect
self-correcting
short-run aggregate supply curve
stagflation

1. The relationship between potential output and the general price level which prevails over time is reflected by the _____.

2. When prices rise causing people to hold more money and, thus, driving up interest rates, then quantity of spending and aggregate demand both decrease, reflecting the _____.

3. The coexistence of rising inflation and high unemployment is termed _____.

4. An economic model which shows the effects of changes in spending and supply on the general price level is called the _____.

5. The movement of prices to naturally adjust the economy back to long-run equilibrium is known as a(n) _____ effect.

6. The notion that the economy gravitates to the natural rate of unemployment in the long run regardless of the price level is shown by the _____.

7. The model which postulates a statistical relationship between the inflation rate and the unemployment rate is the _____.

8. The idea that aggregate demand and price level are inversely related because higher prices diminish the sense of wealth is referred to as the _____.

9. The relationship between overall spending in the economy and the general price level is depicted by the_____.

10. A model which contains a short-run as well as a long-run graphical representation of the inflation–unemployment relationship is the _____.

11. A method of forming ideas about the future inflation rate that involves looking to past experience is referred to as _____.

12. When Canadian prices rise, foreigners purchase less Canadian exports and Canadians import more foreign goods and services; the relationship of this phenomenon with aggregate demand is termed the _____.

13. The idea that firms supply the output demanded at a fixed price level is illustrated graphically by the _____.

Self Test: Multiple Choice

1. In order to measure the change in prices from year to year, economists can use the following equation based on the consumer price index (CPI)
   A. new CPI – old CPI.
   B. old CPI – new CPI.
   C. (new CPI – old CPI) ÷ old CPI.
   D. (old CPI – new CPI) ÷ new CPI.
   E. (new CPI – old CPI) ÷ new CPI.

2. Something which is missing from the Keynesian cross model, but found in the AD–AS model, is
   A. foreign trade.
   B. business spending.
   C. government policy.
   D. supply decisions.
   E. short-run equilibrium.

3. In the long run, the output level of aggregate supply
   A. is independent of the overall price level.
   B. depends of changes in the overall price level.
   C. creates an expansionary gap.
   D. creates a recessionary gap.
   E. can only be achieved through government policy intervention.

4. The level of potential output this year is higher than it was 10 years ago. That must mean that
   A. the LRAS curve is upward-sloping.
   B. the LRAS curve has shifted right.
   C. the LRAS curve is steeper than it was 10 years ago.
   D. the SRAS curve is steeper than it was 10 years ago.
   E. the SRAS curve is now vertical.

5. If the cost of office computer systems were reduced
   A. the LRAS curve shifts downward.
   B. the LRAS curve shifts right.
   C. the SRAS curve becomes steeper.
   D. the SRAS curve shifts downward.
   E. the SRAS curve shifts left.

6. A lower price level will cause the PAE curve to shift _____ and a _____ the aggregate demand curve.
   A. upward, right shift of.
   B. downward, movement along.
   C. upward, shift left of.

    D. downward, shift right of.

    E. upward, movement along.

7. With respect to the interest rate effect, a drop in the general price level will ultimately cause spending in the economy to

    A. stagnate.

    B. increase.

    C. become more volatile.

    D. cause decreased foreign trade.

    E. decrease.

8. Which of the following would NOT cause a rightward shift of the aggregate demand curve?

    A. a decrease in interest rates engineered by the central bank.

    B. a tax cut.

    C. an increase in export demand.

    D. an increase in business investment spending.

    E. a decrease in the general price level.

9. A good example of "automatic elimination" of an output gap would be when

    A. the federal government increases spending to fight a recession.

    B. the Bank of Canada sells bonds on the open market to contract spending.

    C. sluggish economic activity puts pressure on prices to fall.

    D. government gives tax breaks to businesses, to kick-start a slow economy.

    E. the central bank shifts government deposits to commercial banks to counter a recession.

10. Suppose that the equation for the existing AD curve is given by price = $P = 520 - 0.5*Y$. The horizontal SRAS is at price = 250. The existing level of output is _____, and if the potential output level is 500, then the "constant" number in the AD equation (i.e., 520) needs to be ____, to restore equilibrium at potential output. *(See example 14.3.)*

    A. 520; reduced.

    B. 520; increased.

    C. 540; reduced.

    D. 540; increased.

    E. 500; reduced.

11. On the graph of an economy that is self-sufficient in energy and starts out in long-run equilibrium, the effect of a major increase in the cost of oil as an input would be to

    A. shift the AD curve to the right.

    B. shift the AD curve to the left.

    C. shift the SRAS curve downward.

    D. shift the SRAS curve upward.

    E. shift the LRAS curve to the right.

12. The 1960s data plotted on the Phillips curve showed that the relationship between the unemployment rate and the inflation rate was
  A. positive.
  B. inverse.
  C. unpredictable.
  D. volatile.
  E. uncertain.

13. The reason that the expectations-augmented Phillips curve model has both short-run and long-run curves is that when expectations about the inflation rate change
  A. people learn not to trust their expectations.
  B. the economy is drawn to the natural rate of unemployment, and people adjust to what tradeoff would exist between the unemployment and inflation rates.
  C. some new event will occur to make those expectations invalid.
  D. the Phillips curve has to be vertical if the LRAS curve is vertical.
  E. the Phillips curve is invalid in the long run.

14. One implication of the AD–AS model developed in this chapter is that, in the LONG-RUN self-correcting situation, increases in aggregate demand can
  A. increase both potential output and the price level.
  B. increase potential output but decrease the price level.
  C. increase potential output, but the price level will stay at SRAS.
  D. increase the price level, but potential output will not change.
  E. change neither the price level nor the level of potential GDP.

15. Comparing the self-correcting closure of a recessionary gap, with the use of government policy to do so, one advantage of the self-correcting version is that
  A. there is no upward pressure on prices.
  B. government policy makers cannot do much to counter a recession.
  C. it actually moves the LRAS curve to the right.
  D. it is basically contractionary in nature.
  E. the central bank does it, rather than elected officials.

16. A decrease in taxes will cause a
  A. movement downward along the AD curve.
  B. movement upward along the AD curve.
  C. rightward shift in the AD curve.
  D. leftward shift in the AD curve.
  E. decrease in AD.

17. If an expansionary gap exists at the short-run equilibrium output, the
  A. SRAS line will move upward until actual output equals potential output.
  B. SRAS line will move downward until actual output equals potential output.
  C. LRAS line will move upward until actual output equals potential output.
  D. LRAS line will move downward until actual output equals potential output.
  E. LRAS line and SRAS line will move downward until actual output equals potential output.

18. The tendency for the economy to adjust toward its long-run equilibrium
   A. is highlighted by the AD–AS diagram.
   B. is highlighted by the basic Keynesian model.
   C. is an underlying assumption of all macroeconomic models.
   D. implies that fiscal and monetary policies are not needed to stabilize output.
   E. has been called into question by the analysis of the AD–AS diagram.

19. A short-run equilibrium with a recessionary gap implies that
   A. firms will raise the prices of their goods and services more than needed to fully cover their increases in costs.
   B. firms will raise the prices of their goods and services as much as needed to fully cover their increases in costs.
   C. the economy will experience rising prices.
   D. firms have incentives to lower the relative prices of their goods and services.
   E. firms have incentives to raise the relative prices of their goods and services.

20. If a recessionary gap exists at the short-run equilibrium output, the
   A. SRAS line will move upward until actual output equals potential output.
   B. SRAS line will move downward until actual output equals potential output.
   C. LRAS line will move upward until actual output equals potential output.
   D. LRAS line will move downward until actual output equals potential output.
   E. LRAS line and SRAS line will move upward until actual output equals potential output.

Self-Test: Short-Answer Problems

(Answers and solutions are given at the end of the chapter.)
This problem is designed to help you understand the relationship between the calculation of equilibrium between aggregate demand and aggregate supply and its graphical representation.

   A. The aggregate demand (AD) is represented by price $= 150 - 0.03Y$, short-run aggregate supply (SRAS) is horizontal at a price level of 90, and the long-run aggregate supply (LRAS) is vertical at 900.

   i.   The short-run price level is $\$$_____, and the long-run equilibrium price is $\$$_____.

   ii. The short-run equilibrium output level is _____ and the long-run equilibrium output level is _____.

   B. On the graph on the next page, plot the AD, SRAS, and LRAS curves, using the equations in Part A above. Indicate the short-run price and equilibrium as P* and Y*. Show the long-run equilibrium price and output as P** and Y**.

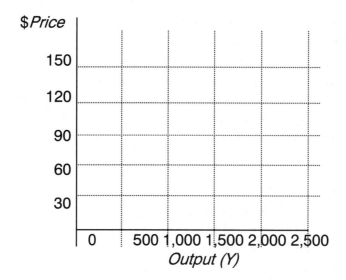

C. At the intersection of SRAS and AD, what kind of output gap exists?_____
How large is the gap?_____

SOLUTIONS

Quick Quiz

1. A.
2. C.
3. D.
4. B.
5. D.
6. E.
7. D.
8. C.
9. E.
10. A.
11. B.

Self-Test: Key Terms

1. long-run aggregate supply curve.
2. interest rate effect.
3. stagflation.
4. aggregate demand–aggregate supply model.
5. self-correcting.
6. long-run Phillips curve.

7. Phillips curve.
8. real balances effect.
9. aggregate demand curve.
10. expectations-augmented Phillips curve.
11. adaptive expectations.
12. foreign trade effect.
13. short-run aggregate supply curve.

Self-Test: Multiple Choice

1. C.
2. D.
3. A.
4. B.
5. D.
6. E.
7. B.
8. E.
9. C.
10. C.
11. D.
12. B.
13. B.
14. D.
15. A.
16. C.
17. A.
18. A.
19. D.
20. B.

Self-Test: Short-Answer Problems

A. i. \$90 (determined by SRAS = \$90); \$123 (P = 150 – 0.03[900])
    ii. 2000 (If P = 90, then P = 150 – 0.03Y becomes 90 = 150 – 0.03Y); 900, determined by LRAS at that output level

B.

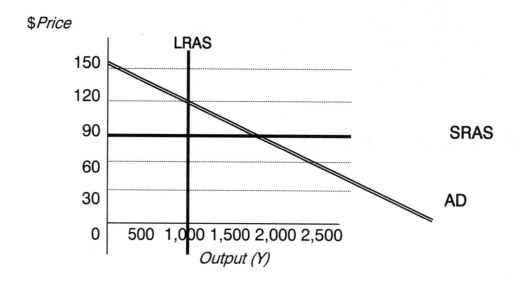

C.   expansionary output gap; 1,100.

15 Inflation and Output

OVERVIEW

This chapter introduces a framework for understanding inflation and the policies used to control it. The basic Keynesian model of Chapters 12 and 13 explained short-run spending under the assumption that prices were preset. Chapter 14 introduced the aggregate demand–aggregate supply model, which showed how changes in spending and supply affected prices and output. This chapter adapts the model to show the causes of ongoing inflation, how macroeconomic policies affect inflation and output, and the difficult tradeoffs policy makers sometimes face.

15.1 Inflation, Spending, and Output: the Aggregate Demand/Inflation (ADI) Curve

▶ **LO 1.**   **Define the ADI curve.**

To incorporate inflation into the model, a new relationship is introduced between aggregate demand and the rate of inflation (π). Graphically, this relationship is called the aggregate demand/inflation (ADI) curve. Because short-run equilibrium output equals aggregate demand, the *aggregate demand/inflation curve* not only shows the relationship between short-run equilibrium output, Y, and inflation.

▶ **LO 2.**   **Explain the policy reaction function and its impact on the downward slope of the ADI curve.**

An increase in the rate of inflation tends to reduce aggregate spending and demand, *assuming* that the Bank of Canada raises real interest rates in response to higher inflation rates. That higher interest rate is what acts to reduce aggregate demand and, consequently, the short-run equilibrium output. The ADI curve is, therefore, downward sloping. The assumption of a given policy change in response to some factor in the economy is called the *policy reaction function*. When policy makers respond mildly to changes in the inflation rate, the policy reaction function graphically exhibits a relatively flat slope; a strong policy reaction reflects a steeper slope.

▶ **LO 3.**   **Discuss factors which cause the ADI curve to shift.**

Two factors will cause the aggregate demand curve to shift. First, for a given level of inflation, any exogenous (autonomous) change in the economy that affects aggregate spending will cause the ADI curve to shift. Such changes might include autonomous consumption, taxes, autonomous private-sector investment spending, government purchases, and net exports. An increase in any of the components will cause the ADI curve to shift to the right, while a decrease in any of these components will cause the ADI curve to shift to the left. Second, a shift in the policy reaction function will shift the ADI. If the Bank of Canada's reaction function shifts upward (i.e., the Bank of Canada chooses a "tighter" monetary policy by setting the real interest rate higher than normal for a given rate of inflation), the ADI curve will shift to the left. An easing of monetary policy (the Bank of Canada's reaction function shifts downward) causes the ADI curve to shift to the right.

Quick Quiz

1. With respect to the ADI curve, increases in inflation lead to _____ in planned spending and _____ in equilibrium output.
    A. increases; increases.
    B. decreases; decreases.
    C. increases; decreases.
    D. decreases; no change.
    E. decreases; no change.

2. The "policy reaction function" assumes that policy makers react in a predictable way to rising inflation by
    A. decreasing government expenditure.
    B. lowering the real interest rate.
    C. increasing the money supply.
    D. lowering tax rates.
    E. raising the real interest rate.

3. When the Bank of Canada responds to higher inflation by raising real interest rates
    A. consumption and private-sector investment spending rise, and, thus, ADI increases.
    B. consumption and private-sector investment spending fall, and, thus, ADI increases.
    C. consumption and private-sector investment spending rise, and, thus, ADI decreases.
    D. consumption and private-sector investment spending fall, and, thus, ADI decreases.
    E. the Bank of Canada changes its policy reaction function.

15.2 Inflation and Aggregate Supply

▶ **LO 4.**   **Explain inflation inertia and its causes.**

Inflation tends to change relatively slowly from year to year (*inflation inertia*). Inflation inertia is due to (1) the public's inflation expectations for the next few years, which are highly influenced by the recent inflation experience, and (2) long-term wage and price contracts, which tend to build the effects of people's inflation expectations into current price level. A low actual rate tends to perpetuate itself, in a *virtuous circle*. A high rate implies high expected inflation, contributing to a *vicious circle* of inflation.

▶ **LO 5.   Identify the causal relationship between output gaps and inflation.**

Although the rate of inflation is inertial, it does change over time. An important factor influencing the rate of inflation is the output gap. If the output gap is zero, the rate of inflation will tend to remain the same. When an expansionary gap exists, the rate of inflation will tend to increase because firms react to excess demand by trying to raise their prices. A recessionary gap tends to cause the rate of inflation to decrease because firms are selling less than their capacity and try to reduce prices in order to sell more.

▶ **LO 6.   Draw the ADI–inflation adjustment (ADI–IA) diagram.**

The ADI–IA diagram illustrates graphically the adjustment of inflation in response to an output gap. The ADI curve already introduced is joined with a horizontal inflation adjustment (IA) line showing the prevailing level of inflation, π. This prevailing level stems from past expectations as well as past pricing decisions. Finally, the magnitude of potential output Y* is signified by the long-run aggregate supply (LRAS) line, which reflects long-run equilibrium. Short-run equilibrium is shown where the ADI curve meets the current level of inflation at IA. When that short run level is not at the same output level as potential output (i.e., at the LRAS), then an output gaps exists.

▶ **LO 7.   Explain the process of adjustment when there is an output gap.**

If an output gap exists, the economy will not remain at that level of output. For example, if a recessionary gap exists at the short-run equilibrium output, it will cause the inflation rate (IA) to fall. As the inflation rate gradually declines (and through policy reaction the Bank of Canada lowers real interest rates), the short-run equilibrium output point moves down the ADI curve to close the recessionary gap. At this point, *long-run equilibrium* occurs and there is no further downward pressure on inflation. Graphically, long-run equilibrium occurs when the ADI curve, the IA line, and the LRAS line all intersect at a single point. An expansionary gap at the short-run equilibrium output would set in motion a similar adjustment process, but in the opposite direction (e.g., inflation adjustment rate would rise). Although this self-correcting adjustment process eventually brings the economy back to long-run equilibrium, policy makers may elect to utilize monetary or fiscal stabilization if the adjustment is regarded as too slow.

Quick Quiz

4. Inflation inertia is attributable to
   A. inflation shocks and shocks to potential output.
   B. output gaps and inflation shocks.
   C. disinflation and inflation shocks.
   D. output gaps and disinflation.
   E. inflation expectations and long-term wage and price contracts.

5. When an expansionary gap exists, the rate of inflation will
   A. tend to rise.
   B. tend to fall.
   C. remain unchanged.
   D. become disinflation.
   E. shift the SRAS line downward.

6. The IA line is horizontal because
   A. there is only ever one rate of inflation in the economy.
   B. the Bank of Canada has declared the target rate of inflation.
   C. people demand a certain rate of inflation.
   D. the inflation rate in Canada is equal to the world inflation rate.
   E. it signifies the current rate of inflation.

7. If, at the short-run equilibrium output, an expansionary gap exists, the
   A. IA line will move upward until actual output equals potential output.
   B. IA line will move downward until actual output equals potential output.
   C. LRAS line will move upward until actual output equals potential output.
   D. LRAS line will move downward until actual output equals potential output.
   E. LRAS line and SRAS line will move downward until actual output equals potential output.

15.3 Sources of Changes in Inflation

▶ **LO 8.   Discuss how excessive aggregate demand can accelerate inflation.**

Increased spending relative to the economy's output potential (Y^*) triggers inflation, since the excess of buyers tends to bid up prices ("too much spending chasing too few goods"). Graphically, this is seen as a rightward shift of ADI. Wars and military buildups have historically been one reason for excessive aggregate demand. The central bank does have the ability to dampen increased inflation; a higher real interest rate (tightening of monetary policy) will rein in spending (graphically, causing the ADI curve to shift back left).

▶ **LO 9.**   **Explain the meaning of inflation shocks and demonstrate the consequences of self-correction from the resulting output gap, compared with the consequences of policy intervention.**

An *inflation shock* is a sudden change in the normal behaviour of inflation, unrelated to the nation's pre-existing output gap. The textbook offers the example of the sharp increase in oil prices plus agricultural shortages of 1973–74, which lead to stagflation (recession and higher inflation). The ADI–IA diagram makes the important general point that the economy tends to be self-correcting in the sense that given enough time, output gaps tend to disappear. Active monetary or fiscal policy can be used to shorten the recession but will also lock in higher inflation since expansionary policy increases spending (shifting the ADI curve right).

▶ **LO 10.**   **Define shocks to potential output and explain why they imply rising inflation.**

A *shock to potential output* is a sharp change in potential output, shifting the LRAS line. Like an inflation shock, an adverse shock to potential output results in stagflation. The adverse shock to potential output, however, implies that productive capacity has fallen and, therefore, output does not recover as it does following an inflation shock. Both adverse inflation shocks and shocks to potential output are *aggregate supply shocks*; both reduce output and increase inflation.

Quick Quiz

8. Excessive aggregate demand can result in
    A. a recessionary gap and a rising inflation rate.
    B. too many goods chasing too little spending.
    C. an expansionary gap and an increasing inflation rate.
    D. an expansionary gap and an increasing unemployment rate.
    E. a recessionary gap and a rising unemployment rate.

9. If the self-correction process of the economy takes place very slowly so that actual output differs from potential output for protracted periods of time, then active
    A. stabilization policies are probably not justified.
    B. stabilization policies may end up doing more harm than good.
    C. use of monetary and fiscal policies can cause actual output to overshoot potential output.
    D. use of monetary and fiscal policies can help stabilize output.
    E. stabilization policy can cause the output gap to become larger.

10. Unlike an adverse inflation shock, an adverse shock to potential output causes
    A. temporarily lower output and higher inflation.
    B. higher output and lower inflation.
    C. no output losses.
    D. only temporarily lower inflation.
    E. permanent output losses.

15.4 Controlling Inflation

▶ **LO 11.** **Explain the difference in short- and long-run effects of anti-inflationary monetary policy.**

In order to achieve a low and stable inflationary environment, policy makers can reduce inflation through tight monetary policies that reduce aggregate demand. In the short run, the main effect of monetary tightening is reduced output and higher unemployment as the economy experiences a recessionary gap. Graphically, this is seen as a left shift of the ADI curve. The recessionary gap eventually will cause disinflation, a substantial reduction in the rate of inflation. As the inflation rate falls output and employment will return to normal levels. On a graph, this is reflected by a downward shift of the IA curve, until the economy is at long-run equilibrium—but at a lower rate of inflation than before the monetary tightening. A tight monetary policy, thus, inflicts short-term pain (lower output, higher unemployment, and higher real interest rates) to achieve a long-term gain (a permanent reduction in inflation).

Quick Quiz

11. If the Bank of Canada decides to tighten monetary policy because the inflation rate has risen to a level inconsistent with its inflation-control target range
    A. in the short run, the SRAS curve will shift downward, and a recessionary gap will be created.
    B. in the long run, the AD curve will shift to the left, and the long-run equilibrium will be restored.
    C. in the short run, the AD curve will shift to the right, and an expansionary gap will be created.
    D. in the short run, the AD curve shifts to the left, and a recessionary gap will be created.
    E. in the short run, the AD curve shifts to the right, and a recessionary gap will be created.

15.5 Limitations of the Aggregate Demand/Inflation–Inflation Adjustment Model

▶ **LO 12.** **Discuss the limitations of the ADI–IA model.**

While the ADI–AS model of this chapter is a major improvement over the simple Keynesian model to analyze the inflation process, it has a number of possible limitations. First, the LRAS might be a thick line or a band, instead of a thin vertical line, because potential output cannot be precisely estimated. Moreover, the traditional vertical LRAS curve might bend upward to the left when inflation either exceeds some high threshold level or falls below some low threshold level. In other words, potential output might be reduced if inflation was too high or too low. Finally, the assumptions of fixed potential GDP and of autonomous net exports are unlikely to hold in the real world.

Quick Quiz

12. It might be more appropriate to express the LRAS line as a band or thick line than a thin line because
    A. potential output is a large number.
    B. potential output fluctuates over time.
    C. potential output cannot be precisely estimated.
    D. actual output cannot be accurately measured.
    E. of business cycles.

Self-Test: Key Terms

Use the terms below to complete the following sentences. (Answers are given at the end of the chapter.)

aggregate demand/inflation (ADI) curve
aggregate supply shock
excessive aggregate demand
inflation adjustment (IA) line
inflation inertia

inflation shock
long-run aggregate supply (LRAS) line
long-run equilibrium
policy reaction function
short-run equilibrium

1. Inflation may arise from excessive aggregate demand or from a(n) _____ .

2. In the ADI–IA diagram, a horizontal line showing the current rate of inflation, as determined by past expectations and pricing decisions, is called the _____ .

3. In the ADI–IA diagram, the relationship between aggregate demand and inflation, as well as the relationship between short-run equilibrium output and inflation, is shown by the

   _____ .

4. When the ADI curve, the IA line, and the LRAS line all intersect at a single point, the economy is at the _____ .

5. A sudden change in the normal behaviour of inflation that is unrelated to the nation's output gap is caused by a(n) _____ .

6. In the ADI–IA diagram, a vertical line is drawn at the economy's potential output (Y*) to represent the _____ .

7. When inflation equals the value determined by past expectations and pricing decisions and output equals the level of short-run equilibrium output that is consistent with that inflation rate, the economy is at its _____ .

8. When the action that a policy maker takes depends on the state of the economy, it is referred to as a _____ .

9. Changes in prices tend to move slowly from year to year in a phenomenon known as

_____.

10. Wars and military buildups push spending and aggregate demand beyond the economy's productive potential, resulting in _____.

Self-Test: Multiple Choice

1. If the Bank of Canada were to shift its policy reaction function downward (i.e., an easing of monetary policy), the
  A. IA line would shift upward causing an increase in the inflation rate.
  B. LRAS line would shift upward causing an increase in the inflation rate.
  C. IA line would shift downward causing a decrease in the inflation rate.
  D. ADI curve would shift to the left.
  E. ADI curve would shift to the right.

2. A current high rate of inflation will tend to promote a
  A. virtuous circle of high expected inflation and a high rate of actual inflation.
  B. virtuous circle of low expected inflation and a low rate of actual inflation.
  C. vicious circle of high expected inflation and a high rate of actual inflation.
  D. vicious circle of low expected inflation and a low rate of actual inflation.
  E. built-in expectation of low inflation in the future.

3. A short-run equilibrium with an output gap of zero implies
  A. zero inflation in the near future.
  B. the rate of inflation will remain the same.
  C. the rate of inflation will rise.
  D. the rate of inflation will fall.
  E. firms have no incentive to raise the prices of their goods and services.

4. Inflation escalated to the double-digit level in the United States during the 1970s because of
  A. excessive aggregate demand due to the military buildup under President Reagan.
  B. an adverse inflation shock caused by the military buildup under President Reagan.
  C. adverse inflation shocks caused by two oil crises that significantly raised world oil prices.
  D. a positive inflation shock that resulted in high inflation and a recessionary gap.
  E. a positive inflation shock that resulted in two periods of stagflation.

5. In the late 1970s and early 1980s, the Bank of Canada followed the U.S. Federal Bank to dramatically tighten monetary policy to fight inflation. The impact of the Bank's policy and the spillover effect of the American economy on the Canadian economy was
  A. disinflation during 1981–85 and a depression during 1981–82.
  B. a recession during 1981–82 and disinflation during 1981–85.
  C. lower nominal and real interest rates during 1980–82 and strong economic growth and disinflation during 1981–85.

D. an expansionary gap during 1980–82, and strong economic growth and disinflation during 1983–85.

E. an expansionary gap during 1980–82, and weak economic growth and disinflation during 1983–85.

6. At high rates of inflation, the productive capacity of an economy is impaired. As a result, the LRAS curve
A. shifts to the right.
B. shifts to the left.
C. bends upward to the left above a certain inflation rate.
D. bends downward to the right below a certain inflation rate.
E. remains unaffected.

7. The development of new cost-saving technology would
A. increase autonomous consumption spending and, thus, shift the ADI curve to the right.
B. increase autonomous consumption spending and, thus, shift the ADI curve to the left.
C. increase autonomous investment spending and, thus, shift the ADI curve to the right.
D. increase autonomous investment spending and, thus, shift the ADI curve to the left.
E. increase net exports and government purchases and, thus, shifts the ADI curve to the right.

8. When a recessionary gap exists and firms are selling less than their capacity, the consequent self-correcting adjustment in prices causes the
A. ADI curve to shift right.
B. ADI curve to shift left.
C. LRAS to shift left.
D. LRAS to shift right.
E. IA curve to shift downward.

9. When the Bank of Canada moves to slow down inflation, the corresponding change seen on a graph is a shift of the
A. IA line up.
B. IA line down.
C. ADI curve right.
D. ADI curve left.
E. LRAS line left.

10. The "policy reaction function" shows that, as _____ increases, _____.
A. inflation, spending increases.
B. inflation, spending decreases.
C. the interest rate, spending decreases.
D. spending, the interest rate increases.
E. inflation, the interest rate increases.

11. A change in variable which would NOT directly shift the ADI curve is
  A. government spending.
  B. business investment.
  C. the inflation rate.
  D. the income tax rate.
  E. Canadian exports.

12. Which of the following would NOT cause the inflation rate to change?
  A. a recessionary gap.
  B. a shock to potential output.
  C. an inflation shock.
  D. a shift of the IA line.
  E. an expansionary gap.

13. The public's expectations about the future will enter a "virtuous circle" when
  A. past inflation rates have been low.
  B. the public expects low inflation rates to continue.
  C. wages and contracts as determined by an expected low rate of inflation.
  D. inflation is inertial.
  E. all of the above.

14. On an ADI graph, SHORT-RUN equilibrium is where
  A. the ADI curve meets the IA line.
  B. the ADI curve meets the LRAS line.
  C. the IA line meets the LRAS line.
  D. the IA line meets the ADI curve after it adjusts for price changes.
  E. the output level is equal to the LRAS line.

15. One disadvantage of allowing a self-correction from an output gap is that
  A. monetary authorities may target the interest rate wrong.
  B. a protracted period of adjustment may be painful.
  C. adjustment may occur in the wrong direction.
  D. government officials may be criticized for unpopular policies.
  E. self-correction always results in higher prices.

Self-Test: Short-Answer Problems
(Answers and solutions are given at the end of the chapter.)

1. Aggregate Demand/Inflation (ADI) Curve
This problem is designed to help you better understand why the ADI curve is downward-sloping and the factors that can cause the ADI curve to shift. Assume the aggregate demand/inflation is given by the equation, $ADI = \$950 + 0.75Y - 900r$.

A. Complete the table below by calculating the level of aggregate demand, AD, for rates of inflation from 0 to 4 percent.

Inflation Rate, π (0.01 = 1%)	Interest Rate, r (0.01 = 1%)	Aggregate Demand, ADI ($ billion)
0.00	0.03	
0.01	0.04	
0.02	0.05	
0.03	0.06	
0.04	0.07	
0.05	0.08	
0.06	0.09	

B. On the graph below, draw the ADI curve that is shown in the above table, and label it ADI.

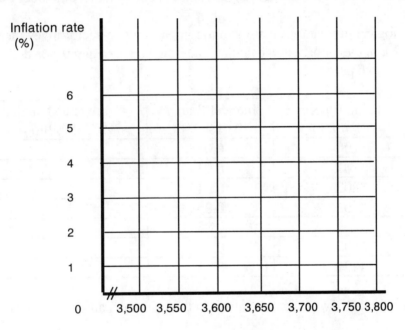

Aggregate Demand/Inflation
ADI ($billion)

C. Assume that the Bank of Canada shifts its policy reaction function downward by reducing the nominal interest rates by one percentage point at each rate of inflation. Complete column 2 of the following table, by indicating the new interest rates for rates of inflation from 0 to 6 percent.

Inflation Rate, π (0.01 = 1%)	Interest Rate, r (0.01 = 1%)	Aggregate Demand, ADI ($ billion)
0.00		
0.01		
0.02		
0.03		
0.04		
0.05		
0.06		

D. Complete column 3 of the above table, by calculating the new levels of aggregate demand (ADI) for rates of inflation from 0 to 6 percent.

E. On the graph, draw the new ADI curve shown in the above table, and label it ADI_1.

F. If new technological innovations caused autonomous private-sector investment spending to increase by $20, in the table below calculate the new levels of aggregate demand for rates of inflation from 0 to 6 percent.

Inflation Rate, π (0.01 = 1%)	Interest Rate, r (0.01 = 1%)	Aggregate Demand, ADI ($ billion)
0.00	0.02	
0.01	0.03	
0.02	0.04	
0.03	0.05	
0.04	0.06	
0.05	0.07	
0.06	0.08	

G. On the graph, plot the new AD curve shown in the last table, and label it AD_2.

2. ADI–IA Diagram

This problem will give you practice drawing the IA and LRAS lines, determining the short-run and long-run equilibrium, analyzing output gaps, and analyzing the economic adjustments to output gaps.

A. Assume the current inflation rate in the economy is 3 percent, and draw the inflation adjustment (IA) line on the graph below.

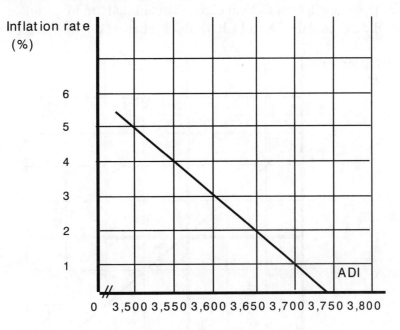

Inflation rate (%)

Aggregate Demand ($billion)

B. Given the ADI curve and IA line on the graph above, the short-run equilibrium output is $_____.

C. Assuming the potential output in the economy is $3,650 billion, draw the long-run aggregate supply (LRAS) line on the graph above.

D. Given the short-run equilibrium output and the potential output, the graph indicates that a(n) _____ gap exists.

E. The output gap will cause the inflation rate to (increase/decrease/ remain unchanged) _____ .

F. As the inflation rate adjusts to the output gap, the (IA/LRAS) _____ line will shift (upward/downward) _____ until the actual output equals the potential output.

G. When the actual output equals potential output, the economy will settle into its _____ equilibrium at $_____ .

3. Sources of Inflation

This problem focuses on the effects of excessive aggregate demand on the economy in the short run and the long run. Assume a hypothetical economy is initially in long-run equilibrium at the point where the ADI curve and the IA and LRAS lines intersect on the graph below.

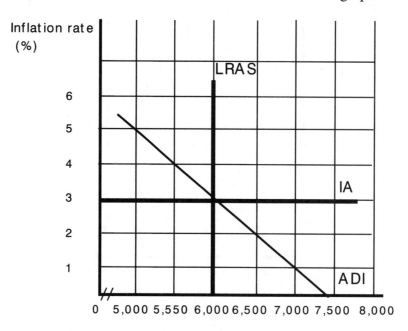

A. Suppose government purchases increase by $500 billion due to a military buildup in anticipation of a war. As a result, the (ADI curve/IA line/LRAS line) _____ will shift _____. Draw the new curve on the graph above.

B. The new short-run equilibrium output will equal $ _____ billion.

C. In the short run, the military buildup has caused the actual output to become (greater than/less than/equal to) _____ the potential output, creating a(n) _____.

D. The output gap eventually will cause the inflation rate to (rise/fall) _____ and the (ADI curve/IA line/LRAS line) _____ will shift _____.

E. Draw the new curve on the above graph, showing its location when the self-correcting process is complete.

F. The economy will achieve its long-run equilibrium output at $ _____ billion, and the inflation rate will equal _____ percent.

G. The long-run equilibrium output after the military buildup is (greater than/less than/equal to) _____ the initial long-run equilibrium output, and the inflation rate is (greater than/less than/equal to) _____ the initial long-run equilibrium inflation rate.

H. If the policy makers decided that the inflation rate had risen to a level incompatible with long-run economic growth, the central bank might implement a(n) (tight/easy) _____ monetary policy that would shift the (ADI curve/IA line/LRAS line) _____ to the _____.

I. In comparison to the case of no change in the central bank's policy reaction function, in the short-run, such a monetary policy would cause a(n) _____, with output (increasing/decreasing/remaining unchanged) _____, and the rate of inflation (increased/decreased/ unchanged) _____.

J. In the long run, such a monetary policy would leave output (greater than/less than/equal to) _____, and the rate of inflation would be (greater than/less than/equal to) _____ they would respectively be without a change in the central bank's policy reaction function.

4. Aggregate Supply Shocks

This problem focuses on the effects of aggregate supply shocks on a hypothetical economy in the short run and the long run. Assume the economy is initially in long-run equilibrium at the point where the ADI curve and the IA and LRAS lines intersect on the graph below.

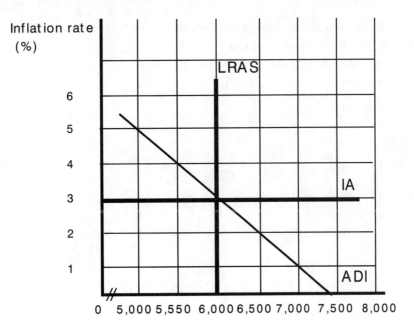

A. Because of a disruption in the worldwide supply of crude oil, the price of energy rises and drives the inflation rate to 4 percent. As a result, the (ADI curve/IA line/LRAS line) _____ will shift _____. Draw the new curve on the graph.

B. The new short-run equilibrium output will equal $ _____ billion.

C. The adverse supply shock has created a(n) _____, combined with a (higher/lower) _____ rate of inflation. This combination is referred to as _____.

D. The output gap eventually will cause the inflation rate to (rise/fall) _____ and the (ADI curve/IA line/LRAS line) _____ will shift _____.

E. When the self-correcting process is complete, the economy will achieve its long-run equilibrium output at $ _____ billion, and the inflation rate will equal _____ percent.

F. The long-run equilibrium output after the adverse supply shock is (greater than/less than/ equal to) _____ the initial long-run equilibrium, and the inflation rate is (greater/less/equal) _____ the initial long-run equilibrium.

G. If the policy makers chose to eliminate the output gap more quickly than the self-correcting process, the central bank might implement a(n) (tight/easy) _____ monetary policy that would shift the (ADI curve/IA line/LRAS line) _____ to the _____.

H. If the policy makers chose to eliminate the output gap more quickly, the long-run equilibrium output would be (greater than/less than/equal to) _____, and the inflation rate would be (greater than/less than/equal to) _____ they would respectively be without a change in the central bank's policy reaction function.

SOLUTIONS

Quick Quiz

1. B.
2. E.
3. D.
4. E.
5. A.
6. E.
7. A.
8. C.
9. D.

10. E.
11. D.
12. C.

Self-Test: Key Terms

1. aggregate supply shock.
2. inflation adjustment (IA) line.
3. aggregate demand/inflation (ADI) curve.
4. long-run equilibrium.
5. inflation shock.
6. long-run aggregate supply (LRAS) line.
7. short-run equilibrium.
8. policy reaction function.
9. inflation inertia.
10. excessive aggregate demand.

Self-Test: Multiple Choice

1. E.
2. C.
3. B.
4. C.
5. B.
6. C.
7. C.
8. E.
9. D.
10. E.
11. C.
12. D.
13. E.
14. A.
15. B.

Self-Test: Short-Answer Problems

1.

A.

Inflation Rate, π (0.01 = 1%)	Interest Rate, r (0.01 = 1%)	Aggregate Demand, ADI ($ billion)
0.00	0.03	$3,692
0.01	0.04	3,656
0.02	0.05	3,620
0.03	0.06	3,584
0.04	0.07	3,548
0.05	0.08	3,512
0.06	0.09	3,476

B.

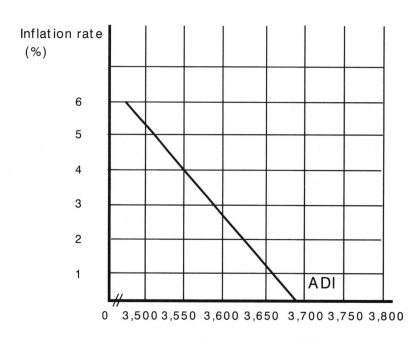

C., D.

Inflation Rate, π (0.01 = 1%)	Interest Rate, r (0.01 = 1%)	Aggregate Demand, ADI ($ billion)
0.00	0.02	$3,728
0.01	0.03	3,692
0.02	0.04	3,656
0.03	0.05	3,620
0.04	0.06	3,584
0.05	0.07	3,548
0.06	0.08	3,512

E.

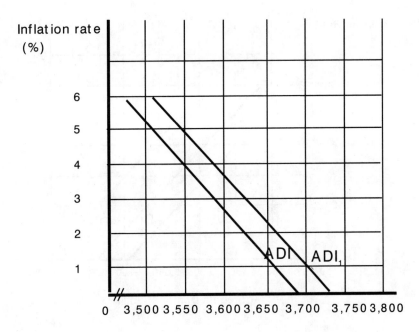

Aggregate Demand ($billion)

F.

Inflation Rate, π (0.01 = 1%)	Interest Rate, r (0.01 = 1%)	Aggregate Demand, ADI ($ billion)
0.00	0.02	$3,808
0.01	0.03	3,772
0.02	0.04	3,736
0.03	0.05	3,700
0.04	0.06	3,664
0.05	0.07	3,628
0.06	0.08	3,592

G.

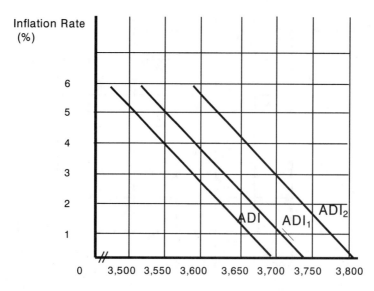

2.

A.

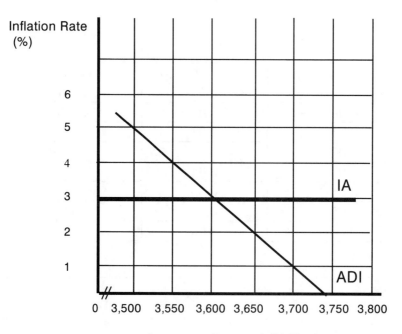

B. $3,600 billion.

C.

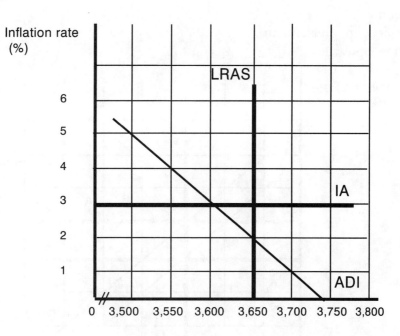

Aggregate Demand ($billion)

D. recessionary.
E. decrease.
F. IA; downward.
G. long-run; $3,650 billion.

3.

A. ADI curve; rightward;

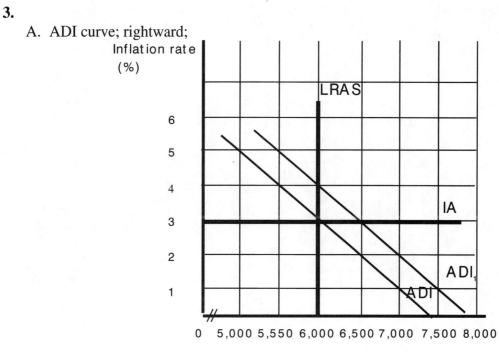

Aggregate Demand ($billion)

B. $6,500 billion.
C. expansionary gap; greater than.
D. rise; IA line; upward.
E.

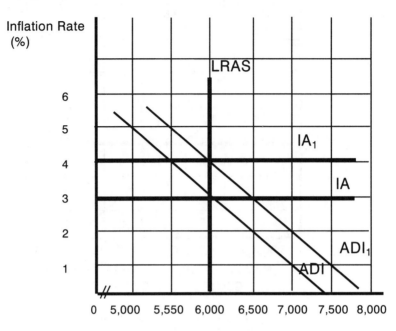

F. $6,000 billion; 4 percent.
G. equal; greater.
H. tight; ADI curve; left.
I. recessionary gap; decreasing; unchanged.
J. equal to; less than.

4.

A. IA line; upward;

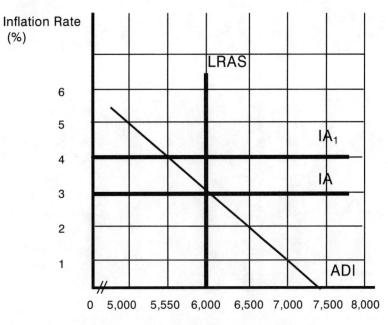

B. $5,500 billion.
C. recessionary gap; higher; stagflation.
D. fall; IA line; downward.
E. $6,000 billion; 3.
F. equal; equal.
G. easy; ADI curve; right.
H. equal to; greater than.

16 International Trade and Trade Policy

OVERVIEW

This chapter addresses the topic of international trade and its effects on the broader economy. It begins with a review of comparative advantage and the benefits of trade and is followed by a discussion of the effects of trade restrictions.

Chapter Review

16.1 Canada in the International Trading System

▶ **LO 1.** **Discuss the importance of international trade in the Canadian economy, relative to other nations.**

Canada has exhibited a relatively high ratio of trade to GDP compared with other similar countries. Whereas the United Kingdom was the most important trading partner, in recent years, more than 80 percent of Canada's exports have been to the United States. The export of industrial products has outweighed natural resource exports.

Quick Quiz

1. Which of the following is NOT one of Canada's four major trade partners?
   A. China.
   B. Germany.
   C. Japan.
   D. United Kingdom.
   E. United States.

16.2 Comparative Advantage as a Basis for Trade

▶ **LO 2.**   **Review the principles of comparative advantage.**

As discussed in Chapter 2, *comparative advantage* relates to the existence of a lower opportunity cost for one party (here, one nation) than for another in the production of a particular good. It implies that one nation can produce relatively more efficiently. Factors such as climate, natural resources, technology, workers' skills and education, and culture provide countries with comparative advantages in the production of various goods and services. The principle of comparative advantage provides support for the argument that we can all enjoy more goods and services when each country produces according to its comparative advantage and then trades with other countries.

Quick Quiz

2. According to the theory of comparative advantage, a country will benefit the most from trade if it
    A. has a closed economy to protect its producers from low-cost, inferior goods produced in low-income countries.
    B. exports to the rest of the world while maintaining protectionist policies on imports into its economy.
    C. has an open economy and subsidizes its less competitive producers.
    D. has an open economy and produces those goods in which it has the lowest opportunity cost and exchanges them for other goods.
    E. has an open economy and produces those goods in which it has the highest opportunity cost and exchanges them for other goods.

16.3 Production and Consumption Possibilities and the Benefits of Trade

▶ **LO 3.**   **Define open economy, closed economy, and autarky**

A *closed economy* is one that does not trade with the rest of the world, while an *open economy* is one that does trade with the rest of the world. A closed economy is an example of *autarchy*, a situation in which a country is self-sufficient producing everything its citizens need to consume.

▶ **LO 4.**   **Construct and explain production possibilities curves.**

A simple production possibilities curve (PPC) reflects all the possible production possibilities of two goods, given the amount of resources available in an economy. The PPC shows that there are tradeoffs, where production of more of one good requires re-allocating some resources away from production of the other good.

▶ **LO 5.** **Apply consumption possibilities to the production possibilities curve and contrast the results for a closed economy and an open economy.**

The term *consumption possibilities* refers to the combinations of goods and services that a country's citizens might feasibly consume. In a closed economy, a society's production possibilities are identical to its consumption possibilities. This contrasts with an open economy where a society's consumption possibilities are typically greater than (and will never be less than) its production possibilities.

▶ **LO 6.** **Explain the benefits of trade.**

With trade, each country specializes in goods it produces most efficiently and then trades away part of that production for goods produced more efficiently in other countries. Because countries take advantage of these efficiencies, more can be produced than if each country tried to produce some of each type of good on its own. When more is produced, more can be consumed.

Quick Quiz

3. Autarky is a situation created by
   A. a trade deficit.
   B. a trade surplus.
   C. protectionist policies.
   D. an open economy.
   E. a closed economy.

4. The slope of a production possibilities curve for a single worker reflects the incremental amount of one product which that worker is able to
   A. consume, by giving up some consumption of the other product.
   B. produce, by giving up some production of the other product.
   C. produce, by adding in the production of a second worker.
   D. consume, once the economy opens to trade.
   E. produce, by giving up some consumption of another product.

5. The most advantageous level for an open economy to produce and consume is where the production possibilities curve (PPC) is just tangent to the consumption possibilities line, because
   A. both products can be produced in the economy.
   B. both consumers and producers are then satisfied.
   C. production is at maximum efficiency, which means more can be gained from trade.
   D. consumers can only consume what is produced.
   E. there will be less unemployment at that point.

6. If a poor country whose workers are paid low wages wishes to trade with Canada
   A. Canada should avoid trade because that country's cheap labour will undermine Canadian opportunities.
   B. there are always more benefits for the poor country than for Canada.
   C. there are always more benefits for Canada than for the poor country.
   D. both countries can benefit so long as each has a comparative advantage.
   E. Canada can only benefit if it insists that the poor country's workers are better paid.

16.4 A Supply-and-Demand Perspective on Trade

▶ **LO 7.**   **Discuss how the world price for a good helps determine how much of that good will be imported or exported.**

The effects of having a difference between prices at home and in other countries are demonstrated using supply-and-demand analysis to compare prices for imported and exported goods and services. The *world price* is the price at which a good or service is traded on international markets. The analysis shows that in a closed economy, if the price of a good or service is greater than the world price and that economy opens itself to trade, the economy will tend to become a net importer of that good or service. Alternatively, if the price of a good or service in a closed economy is lower than the world price and that economy opens itself to trade, the economy will tend to become a net exporter of that good or service.

▶ **LO 8.**   **Identify the winners and losers in international trade.**

Despite the fact that a country can improve its overall consumption possibilities by trading with other countries, not everyone gains from an open economy. Opening an economy to trade with other countries may create groups of winners and losers among producers and consumers. When a country becomes a net importer of a good or service, the domestic consumers benefit from free trade, but domestic producers are hurt by free trade. When, on the other hand, a country is a net exporter of a good or service, the domestic producers benefit from free trade, while the domestic consumers are hurt by free trade.

▶ **LO 9.**   **Define protectionism and compare the economic effects of tariffs and quotas.**

When some groups lose from trade, political pressures may be created to block or restrict trade. The view that free trade is injurious and should be restricted is known as *protectionism*. Supporters of this view believe government should attempt to protect domestic markets through the imposition of tariffs or quotas. A *tariff* is a tax imposed on an imported good. A *quota* is a legal limit on the quantity of a good that may be imported. Supply-and-demand analysis indicates that a tariff raises the price of the imported good or service, harming the domestic consumer but helping the domestic producers and government. Similarly, a quota on a good or service raises the price of the imported good or service by an identical amount as a tariff does, harming the domestic consumer and helping the domestic producer. Government, however, is not helped through quotas because it does not collect additional tax revenues, as it does when a tariff is imposed.

Quick Quiz

7. If the price of commodity X in a hypothetical closed economy is greater than the world price when the economy opens up to trade, the economy will tend to become a
   A. net exporter of that commodity.
   B. neither an exporter nor an importer.
   C. net importer of that commodity.
   D. a major supplier to the world market.
   E. none of the above.

8. When Canada's exports of automobile parts become greater than its imports of these parts, then winners will be _____ and losers will be _____.
   A. producers of exported goods; consumers of exported goods.
   B. consumers of exported goods; producers of exported goods.
   C. consumers of imported goods; producers of exported goods.
   D. consumers of exported goods; producers of imported goods.
   E. producers of imported goods; consumers of imported goods.

9. Compared with a quota, a tariff on shoe imports
   A. avoids an increase in the price of domestic shoes.
   B. does not harm foreign shoe producers, whereas a quota does.
   C. does not harm domestic shoe producers, whereas a quota does.
   D. does not harm foreign shoe consumers, whereas a quota does.
   E. generates revenue for government, whereas a quota does not.

Self-Test: Key Terms

Use the terms below to complete the following sentences. (Answers are given at the end of the chapter.)

autarky   protectionism
closed economy   quota
comparative advantage   tariff
consumption possibilities   world price
open economy

1. The view that free trade is injurious and should be restricted is known as

   _____.

2. A society that does not trade with the rest of the world has a(n) _____

   _____ .

3. The price at which a good or service is traded on international markets is the

_____.

4. The combinations of goods and services a country's citizens might feasibly consume are its

_____.

5. A situation in which a country is self-sufficient is referred to as _____.

6. Legal limits are placed on the quantity of a good that may be imported when a government imposes a(n) _____ .

7. A society that trades with the rest of the world has a(n) _____ .

8. A tax imposed on an imported good is called a(n) _____ .

9. When one country can produce a good at a lower opportunity cost than others, then the country has a(n) _____.

Self-Test: Multiple Choice

1. To maximize its gains from trade, a nation should
   A. maximize net exports (or its trade surplus).
   B. export products in which it has a comparative advantage.
   C. export as many products as possible by subsidizing domestic producers that could not otherwise compete with foreign producers.
   D. create jobs by subsidizing industries that employ the large numbers of workers.
   E. subsidize the purchase of imports in order to achieve the highest level of total consumption.

2. If Sierra Leone has a comparative advantage in the production of coffee and its previously closed economy is opened to trade coffee for imported steel, Sierra Leone's
   A. steel industry will expand at the expense of its steel consumers.
   B. steel industry will expand at the expense of its coffee industry.
   C. steel consumers will not benefit, as will its steel producers.
   D. coffee producers will decrease output.
   E. steel consumers and coffee producers will benefit.

3. If quotas are imposed on French clothing imported into Canada
   A. both French and Canadian consumers are penalized when they buy clothing.
   B. both French and Canadian producers of clothing are penalized.
   C. Canadian producers and consumers of clothing are penalized.
   D. Canadian clothing producers benefit but Canadian consumers of clothing are penalized.
   E. French producers and consumers of clothing benefit.

4. Protectionist policies are implemented by governments because
   A. they benefit the domestic consumers.
   B. they benefit politically powerful groups.

C. they are efficient and, therefore, increase the total economic pie.

D. its unfair for domestic workers and producers to have to compete with the low wages and costs in poor countries.

E. it is the most effective way to protect the global environment.

5. Quotas and tariffs are similar in that both
   A. generate revenues for the government that imposes them.
   B. increase the prices of goods and services in the domestic markets.
   C. increase the revenues of the firms importing the goods and services.
   D. harm domestic and foreign producers.
   E. do not harm domestic and foreign consumers.

6. Canada's most exported type of item is
   A. agricultural products.
   B. forestry products.
   C. energy products.
   D. industrial goods.
   E. machinery and equipment.

7. Two workers can each produce coffee and computers. Worker 1 can produce 100 kg coffee or 2 computers per day, while worker 2 can produce 75 kg coffee or 2 computers per day, then worker 2's opportunity cost of producing ONE computer is
   A. 100 kg coffee.
   B. 75 kg coffee.
   C. 37.5 kg coffee.
   D. 2 computers.
   E. 1 computer.

8. A factor which would NOT give a nation a comparative advantage is
   A. climate.
   B. geographic size.
   C. natural resource endowment.
   D. workers' skills and experience.
   E. available technology.

9. Tariff rates in Canada
   A. dropped below 1 percent by 1996.
   B. have risen considerably in the last 10 year.
   C. have stayed generally the same for the last 50 years.
   D. fluctuated broadly since World War II.
   E. have not existed since the General Agreement on Tariffs and Trade (GATT).

10. The shape of a production possibilities curve (PPC) is increasingly steep as one moves from left to right because of
    A. decreasing opportunity cost.

   B. economies of scale.
   C. diseconomies of scale.
   D. increasing opportunity cost.
   E. decreasing comparative advantage.

11. In a closed economy, a society's consumption possibilities are
   A. unlimited.
   B. limited to the chief products of its trade partners.
   C. limited only by time and its workers' skills.
   D. limited only by the tastes of its consumers.
   E. identical to its production possibilities.

12. If Canada has an absolute advantage in producing both automobiles and clothing, in
    comparison with Fredonia,
   A. there is no point in Canada trading with Fredonia.
   B. Canada will still trade with Fredonia, if each nation as a comparative advantage in
       one of the products.
   C. Canada will trade with Fredonia for political reasons only.
   D. Fredonia will only import both automobiles and clothing from Canada.
   E. Canada will specialize further in exporting both automobiles and clothing.

13. If the world price for a good is BELOW what would have been the equilibrium price in an
    open home economy, a typical buyer at home will
   A. pay the equilibrium price for the home closed economy.
   B. pay no more than the world price for the good.
   C. always pay more than the world price for the good.
   D. always pay less than the world price for the good.
   E. always be prevented from paying the world price because of tariffs.

14. After the imposition of a tariff on a certain imported good, residents of the tariff-imposing
    country will pay a price that is _____ than the world price for that good and will
    import _____ of that good.
   A. higher; less.
   B. higher; more.
   C. lower; the same amount.
   D. lower; less.
   E. lower; more.

15. The revenue generated for government through its imposition of a tariff will be equal to the
    quantity of domestic demand minus the quantity of domestic supply at P_T (world price plus
    tariff), times the
   A. world price.
   B. tariff.
   C. world price plus the tariff (P_T).
   D. home equilibrium price.
   E. home equilibrium price minus the world price.

Self-Test: Short-Answer Problems
(Answers and solutions are given at the end of the chapter.)

1. **Production Possibilities in a Three-Person Economy**
   In this problem, you will draw a production possibilities curve for a three-person economy, reviewing the implications of the principle of comparative advantage for production.

   Assume the country of Islandia has only three workers, Maria, Tom, and Patty, each of whom works 50 weeks per year. Maria can produce 100 shirts or she can catch 10 kg of fish per week. Tom can produce 50 shirts or catch 20 kg of fish per week. Patty can produce 200 shirts or catch 40 kg of fish per week.

   A. Maria's opportunity cost of producing 1 kg of fish per week is _____ shirts, Tom's opportunity cost of producing 1 kg of fish per week is _____ shirts, and Patty's opportunity cost of producing 1 kg of fish per week is _____ shirts.

   B. Maria's opportunity cost of producing 1 shirt per week is _____ kg of fish, Tom's opportunity cost of producing 1 shirt per week is _____ kg of fish, and Patty's opportunity cost of producing 1 shirt per week is _____ kg of fish.

   C. Based on their respective opportunity costs, if Islandia were to allocate resources to the production of shirts, _____ would be the first worker to begin producing shirts, _____ would be the second worker to begin producing shirts, and _____ would be the third worker to begin producing shirts.

   D. On the graph on the next page, construct the annual production possibilities curve for Islandia, identify the location of the "kinks" in the curve (label them A and B), and label each section of the curve to indicate who is producing the shirts.

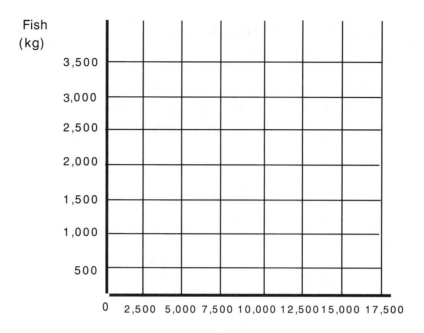

Fish (kg)

Shirts

E. To produce 1 to 5,000 shirts, the opportunity cost of producing shirts in Islandia is _____ kg of fish. To produce 5,001 to 15,000 shirts, the opportunity cost of producing shirts in Islandia is _____ kg of fish. To produce 15,001 to 17,500 shirts, the opportunity cost of producing shirts in Islandia is _____ kg of fish.

F. Thus, as Islandia allocates more resources to the production of shirts, the opportunity cost of producing shirts (increases/decreases/remains constant) _____. This reflects the core principle of _____.

G. As a result of the above core principle, the shape of Islandia's production possibilities curve is _____.

2. **Consumption Possibilities with and without International Trade**
   This problem will help you better understand the gains that a country can achieve by opening its economy to international trade. You will determine the opportunity cost of producing goods, draw a consumption possibilities curve, and calculate the gains from trade.

   Assume the country of Nordica has two workers, Bob and Mary. Bob can produce 1,500 bicycles per year or 1,500 articles of clothing. Mary can produce 1,500 bicycles or 750 articles of clothing per year.

   A. Bob's opportunity cost of producing 1 bicycle is _____ articles of clothing, and Mary's opportunity cost of producing 1 bicycle is _____ articles of clothing.

   B. Mary's opportunity cost of producing 1 article of clothing is _____ bicycles, and Bob's opportunity cost of producing 1 article of clothing is _____ bicycles.

C. If Nordica has a closed economy and Bob only produces articles of clothing and Mary only produces bicycles, identify the point of Nordica's production (label it A) on the graph below.

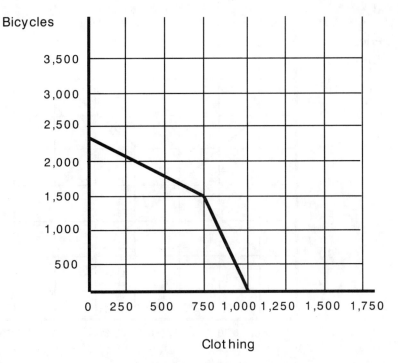

Bicycles

3,500
3,000
2,500
2,000
1,500
1,000
500

0 250 500 750 1,000 1,250 1,500 1,750

Clothing

D. Assume the world prices are such that 2 bicycles can be traded for 1 article of clothing. If Nordica opens its economy to world trade, on the above graph draw its consumption possibilities curve such that it just touches (i.e., is tangent to) Nordica's production possibilities curve at point A.

E. If Nordica chose to trade 250 of the 750 articles of clothing it is producing on the world markets, it could obtain _____ bicycles.

F. On the graph above, locate the point on Nordica's consumption possibilities curve (label it B) that would represent the amount of bicycles and articles of clothing it could consume after it traded 250 articles of its clothing. After the trade, the consumption possibilities curve indicates that Nordica can consume _____ articles of clothing and_____ bicycles.

G. Had Nordica remained a closed economy, it could produce 500 articles of clothing and _____ bicycles.

H. By comparison with a closed economy, opening its economy to world trade resulted in Nordica gaining _____ bicycles.

3. Closed versus Open Economy

In this problem, you will analyze the economic impact of international trade using the supply-and-demand model. The following graph shows the domestic supply and demand for wool in Upland.

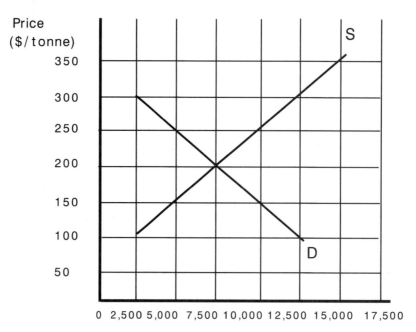

Tonnes of wool

A. If Upland has a closed economy, the equilibrium price of wool would equal $_____ per tonne and Upland would produce _____ tonnes of wool.

B. Assume the world price of wool is $150 per tonne. On the graph above, draw a curve representing the world price of wool (label it P_w).

C. Given the domestic supply and demand for wool and the world price of wool, if Upland opened its economy to trade, it would produce _____ tonnes of wool, consume _____ tonnes of wool, import _____ tonnes of wool, and the domestic price of wool would fall to $ _____ per tonne.

D. As a result of opening the Upland economy to trade, the trade winners would be the (domestic wool producers/foreign wool producers/domestic consumers/foreign consumers) _____ and (domestic wool producers/foreign wool producers/domestic consumers/foreign consumers) _____ , while the trade losers would be the (domestic wool producers/foreign wool producers/domestic consumers/foreign consumers) _____ and (domestic wool producers/foreign wool producers/domestic consumers/foreign consumers) _____ .

E. Assume the domestic wool producers convinced the Upland government to impose a quota of 1,000 tonnes of imported wool. On the graph, draw the curve that would reflect the effect of the quota on the Upland wool market (label it $P_w + Q$).

F. As a result of the quota, the price of wool in Upland would rise to $_____$, domestic consumption would equal _____ tonnes of wool, and domestic production would rise to _____ tonnes of wool. Wool imports would decline to _____ tonnes of wool.

4. Trade Protectionism

In this problem, you will analyze the economic impact of tariffs and quotas using the supply-and-demand model. Assume the demand for cellular phones by the consumers of Sunland is given by $Q_d = 320 - 0.6P$ and the supply by domestic Sunland producers is given by $Q_s = 200 + 0.6P$, where P is the price of cellular phones.

A. Assuming that Sunland is a closed economy, the equilibrium price for cellular phones in the domestic Sunland market would be $_____$, and the equilibrium quantity would equal _____.

B. If the Sunland economy is opened to trade and the world price of cellular phones is $75, the consumption of cellular phones in Sunland would equal _____, domestic production of cellular phones would equal _____, and Sunland would import _____ cellular phones.

C. Assume that at the request of Sunland cellular phone producers, the Sunland government imposes a tariff of $20 per cellular phone. After the imposition of the tariff, Sunland consumption of cellular phones would equal _____, domestic production would equal _____ cellular phones, and Sunland would import _____ cellular phones.

D. The tariff raised the price of cellular phones by $_____$ and reduced imports by _____ . The Sunland government would receive $_____$ from the tariff.

SOLUTIONS

Quick Quiz

1. B.
2. D.
3. E.
4. B.
5. C.
6. D.
7. C.

8. A.
9. E.

Self-Test: Key Terms

1. protectionism.
2. closed economy.
3. world price.
4. consumption possibilities.
5. autarky.
6. quota.
7. open economy.
8. tariff.
9. comparative advantage.

Self-Test: Multiple Choice

1. B.
2. E.
3. D.
4. B.
5. B.
6. E.
7. C.
8. B.
9. A.
10. D.
11. E.
12. B.
13. B.
14. A.
15. B.

Self-Test: Short-Answer Problems

1. A. 10 (=100/10); 2.5; 5.
   B. 0.1 (=10/100); 0.4; 0.2.
   C. Maria, Patty, Tom.

D.

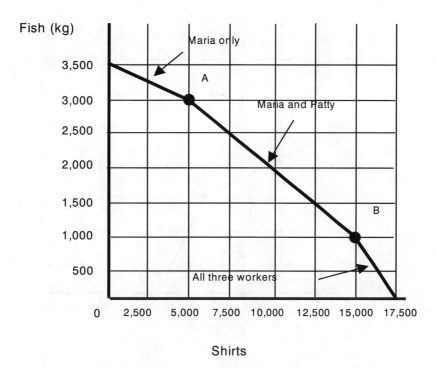

E. 500 kg or [500/5,000 = 0.1] (Maria has a comparative advantage in producing shirts, and she can produce a maximum of 5,000 per year. Because she would be the first worker to produce shirts, Islandia's opportunity cost would equal her opportunity cost); 2,000 kg or 2,000/10,000 = 0.2; 1,000 kg or 1,000/2,500 = 0.4

F. increases; increasing opportunity cost.

G. bowed outward.

2. A. 1 (=1,500/1,500); ½.
   B. 2 (= 1,500/750); 1.

C.

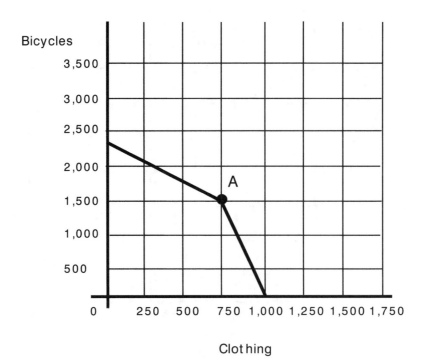

D.

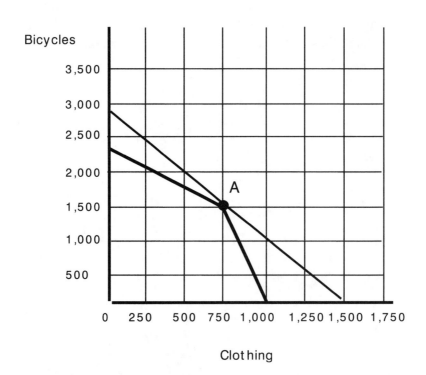

E. 500. (The world price is 2 bicycles = 1 article of clothing. Thus, 250 × 2 = 500).

F.

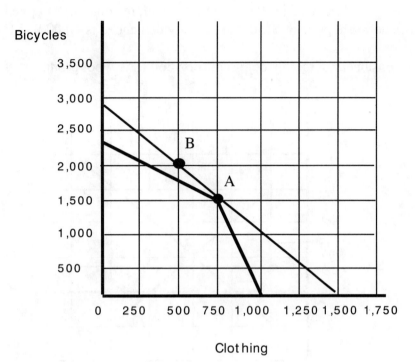

Bicycles

Clothing

F. 500; 2,000.
G. 1,750.
H. 250 (= 2,000 − 1,750).

3. A. $200; 7,500
    B.

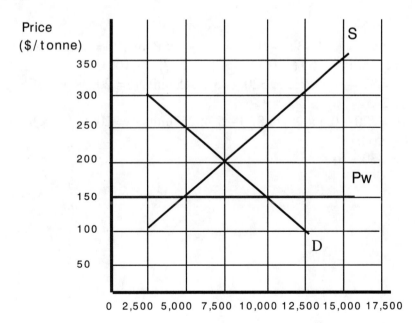

Tonnes of wool

C. 5,000 (at the world price of $150 per tonne of wool, the quantity supplied is 5,000); 10,000 (at the world price of $150, the quantity demanded is 10,000); 5,000 (10,000 – 5,000).

D. domestic consumers; foreign wool producers; domestic wool producers; foreign consumers.

E.

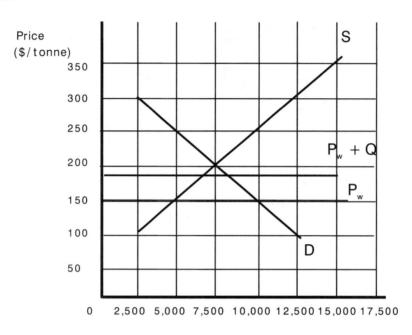

Tonnes of wool

F. $190; 8,000; 7,000; 1,000.

4.

A. equilibrium price = $100 (320 – 0.6P = 200 + 0.6P, or 120 = 1.2P. Thus, 120/1.2 = P); equilibrium quantity = 260 (320 – 0.6 × 100, or 320 – 100).

B. 275 units (D= 320 –0.6 × 75, or 320 – 45); 245 units (S= 200 + 0.6 × 75, or 200 + 45); 30 units (275 – 245).

C. 263 units (D= 320 – 0.6 × 95, or 320 – 57); 257units (S= 200 + 0.6 × 95, or 200 + 57); 6 units (263 – 257).

D. $20; 24 units (30 – 6).

E. $120 (20 × 6).

17 Exchange Rates and the Open Economy

OVERVIEW

This chapter explains the role of exchange rates in open economies. The discussion begins by distinguishing between the nominal exchange rate and the real exchange rate. This is followed by an analysis of how flexible and fixed exchange rates are determined. The chapter concludes with a discussion of the relative merits of fixed and flexible exchange rates and the impact of Canadian monetary policy in the context of flexible exchange rates.

Chapter Review

17.1 Exchange Rates

▶ **LO 1.** **Define the nominal exchange rate, appreciation, and depreciation.**

The economic benefits of trade between nations in goods, services, and assets are similar to the benefits of trade within a nation. There is, however, a difference between the two cases. Trade within a nation normally involves only a single currency, while trade between nations involves different currencies. Because international transactions generally require that one currency be traded for another currency, the relative values of different currencies are an important factor in international economic relations. The rate at which two currencies can be traded for each other is called the *nominal exchange rate*, or simply the exchange rate. Exchange rates can be expressed as the amount of foreign currency needed to purchase one unit of domestic currency, or as the number of units of the domestic currency needed to purchase one unit of the foreign currency. These two ways of expressing the exchange rate are equivalent; each is the reciprocal of the other. Although the exchange rate can be expressed either way, the textbook authors have chosen to define the nominal exchange rate (e) as the number of units of foreign currency that one unit of the domestic currency will buy; (e.g., $0.75 US can be bought with $1 Canadian). Exchange rates change over time. An increase in the value of one currency relative to other currencies is called *appreciation,* and a decrease in the value of that currency relative to other currencies is called *depreciation.*

▶ **LO 2.**   **Calculate the nominal exchange rate between two currencies.**

For a given point in time, data on the nominal exchange rates for one Canadian dollar against various foreign currencies may be used to calculate the exchange rate between two of those currencies. For example, according to the table in the book, one Canadian dollar equals either 0.6144 euros or $0.7544 US. Therefore, 0.6144 euros equal $0.7544 US. To find the exchange rate for $1 US in euros, simply divide both numbers by 0.7544; thus: 0.8144 euros = $1 US.

▶ **LO 3.**   **Define flexible and fixed exchange rates and foreign exchange market.**

Exchange rate regimes can be of two broad types: flexible or fixed exchange rates. A *flexible exchange rate* is not officially fixed but varies according to the supply and demand for the currency in the *foreign exchange market*—the market in which currencies of various nations are traded for one another. A *fixed exchange rate* is an exchange rate whose value is set by official government policy.

▶ **LO 4.**   **Explain the difference between nominal and real exchange rates.**

It is important to distinguish the nominal exchange rate from the real exchange rate. As indicated above, the nominal exchange rate tells us the price of the domestic currency in terms of a foreign currency. The *real exchange rate* tells us the price of the average domestic good or service in terms of the average foreign good or service, when prices are expressed in terms of a common currency. The real exchange rate is equal to the nominal exchange rate times the price of the average domestic good divided by the price of the average foreign good. Consequently, the nominal and real exchange rates tend to move in the same direction.

▶ **LO 5.**   **Calculate the real exchange rate between two currencies.**

Given the prices of a particular good or service in two different currencies, the real exchange rate can be found by converting the foreign currency price into Canadian dollars (or vice versa). The textbook provides the example of equivalent trucks, one priced at $30,000 in Canada, and the other at 1,875,000 Japanese yen from Japan. If the exchange rate is 75 yen per dollar, then dividing the number of Japanese yen by 75 will yield the Canadian dollar price: 1,875,000 *divided by* 75 = $25,000. Thus, the Japanese truck is a better buy, in terms of the Canadian dollar prices.

▶ **LO 6.**   **Discuss the effects of real exchange rates on net exports.**

The real exchange rate has important implications for a nation's trade. A higher real exchange rate implies that domestic producers will have a hard time exporting to other countries, while foreign goods will sell more in the home country. Thus, when the real exchange rate is higher, net exports will tend to be lower. Conversely, if the real exchange rate is relatively lower, domestic producers will find it easier to export and foreign producers will have more difficulty selling in the domestic market. Net exports, therefore, will be higher when the real exchange rate is lower. This cause-and-effect relationship suggests that a strong currency does not necessarily reflect a strong economy.

Quick Quiz

1. A Canadian tourist leaves for the United States when the Canadian dollar is buying $0.80 US. Upon returning to Canada and changing US currency back to Canadian, the tourist gets $1 Canadian for every $0.78 US. Clearly, the Canadian dollar
   A. has depreciated.
   B. has appreciated.
   C. buys more US dollars than before.
   D. has strengthened.
   E. has not really changed in value.

2. During winter 2002, the nominal exchange rate was $1 Canadian to 5.8 Mexican pesos. The dollar per peso equivalent exchange rate equalled
   A. 5.8 dollars per peso.
   B. 0.058 dollars per peso.
   C. 17.2 dollars per peso.
   D. 0.172 dollars per peso.
   E. 172 dollars per peso.

3. Fixed exchange rates
   A. are set in the foreign exchange market.
   B. are set by the International Monetary Fund.
   C. are set by the World Bank.
   D. are set by official government policy.
   E. are tied to the current international price of gold.

4. The nominal exchange rate reflects the money rates at which two currencies can traded for one another, while the real exchange rate reflects the
   A. nominal exchange rate adjusted for inflation.
   B. extent to which the nominal exchange rate has changed over time.
   C. change in a currency in terms of one major currency, such as the euro.
   D. price of the average domestic good or service, in terms of the price of the average foreign good or service.
   E. base year rate at which two currencies traded.

5. A disposable camera cost $12 in Canada and 110 pesos in Mexico during the summer of 2000. The exchange rate at that time was 5.8 pesos per dollar. The real exchange rate of the dollar (for disposable cameras) equalled
   A. 5.8.
   B. 0.63.
   C. 0.84.
   D. 53.2.
   E. 6.3.

6. Since an increase in the real exchange rate means that home prices are higher than foreign prices, the implication for trade is that
   A. net exports will increase.
   B. net exports will decrease.
   C. foreigners will buy more home exports.
   D. residents of the home country will by less imports.
   E. residents of the home country will buy more domestically produced goods.

17.2 Determination of Flexible Exchange Rates

► **LO 7.   Define the law of one price.**

The *law of one price* states that if transportation costs are relatively small, the price of an internationally traded commodity must be the same in all locations.

► **LO 8.   Explain the purchasing power parity (PPP) theory and its implications.**

What determines the value of flexible exchanges rates? The most basic theory of how nominal exchange rates are determined is called *purchasing power parity*, or PPP. This theory stems from the law of one price. If the law of one price were to hold for all goods and services, then the value of the exchange rate between two currencies would be determined by dividing the price of the average good in one country by the price of the average good in the other country. An implication of the PPP theory is that in the long run, the currencies of countries that experience relatively higher inflation will tend to depreciate against the currencies of countries that experience relatively lower inflation rates. The rationale is that because inflation implies that a nation's currency is losing purchasing power in the domestic market, while exchange-rate deprecation implies that the nation's currency is losing purchasing power in international markets.

► **LO 9.   Discuss the shortcomings of PPP theory.**

While many empirical studies have found that PPP theory is useful for predicting some changes in nominal exchange rates over the long run, it still works imperfectly in the long run because not all commodities are traded, nor are all tradable commodities standardized. The theory is even less successful in predicting short-run movements in exchange rates. One reason that PPP works less well in the short run is that the law of one price works best for standardized commodities that are widely traded. Not all goods, however, are standardized commodities, and not all goods are traded internationally. In general, the greater the share of traded and standardized goods and services in a nation's output, the more precisely PPP theory will apply to the country's exchange rate.

▶ **LO 10.** **Use supply-and-demand analysis to determine the equilibrium exchange rate.**

Supply-and-demand analysis is more useful for understanding the short-run movements of exchange rates. Anyone who holds a currency is a potential supplier of that currency, but in practice, the principal suppliers of a currency to the foreign exchange market are that nation's households and firms. The demanders of a foreign currency are, in practice, households and firms that want to purchase foreign assets or goods and services. The supply curve of a currency is upward-sloping and the demand curve is downward-sloping.

▶ **LO 11.** **Define fundamental value of the exchange rate.**

The equilibrium value of a currency, also called the *fundamental value of the exchange rate*, is the exchange rate at which the quantity supplied equals the quantity demanded.

▶ **LO 12.** **Identify the factors that cause changes in the equilibrium exchange rate.**

Factors that cause shifts in the supply and demand for a currency will cause the equilibrium value of the currency to change. Some factors that cause an increase in the supply of the domestic currency are an increased preference for foreign goods, an increase in the domestic real GDP, and an increase in the real interest rate on foreign assets. Factors that will cause an increased demand for the domestic currency are an increased preference for domestic goods, an increase in real GDP abroad, and an increase in the real interest rate on domestic assets.

▶ **LO 13.** **Explain how changes in monetary policy affect the exchange rate.**

Of the many factors affecting a country's exchange rate, among the most important is the monetary policy of a country's central bank. If Canadian monetary policy has resulted in increases in real interest rates in Canada, Canadian financial assets become more attractive to foreign investors, thus raising the demand for the Canadian dollar on foreign exchange markets and causing the Canadian dollar to appreciate. In an open economy with a flexible exchange rate, the exchange rate serves as another channel for monetary policy that reinforces the effects of real interest rates. Higher real interest rates, for example, reduce domestic consumption and private-sector investment. They also cause appreciation of the currency, and as a result, imports rise and exports fall, reducing net exports. The decline in net exports, thus, reinforces the domestic effects of the tightened monetary policy. Monetary policy, therefore, is more effective in an open economy with flexible exchange rates.

Quick Quiz

7. Disregarding transport costs, which one of the following would most likely be a good example to demonstrate the law of one price?
   A. a haircut.
   B. a brand of shampoo.
   C. a tonne of grain.

D. a locally designed dress.

E. a box of chocolate.

8. Between 1990 and 1999, inflation in the United States averaged 2 to3% per year, while Mexico experienced double-digit average annual inflation rates. Since the Mexican government did not try to maintain a fixed exchange rate, PPP theory would suggest that in the long run, the Mexican peso

   A. appreciated against the dollar, and Mexico's net exports to the United States decreased.

   B. appreciated against the dollar, and Mexico's net exports to the United States increased.

   C. depreciated against the dollar, and Mexico's net exports to the United States increased.

   D. depreciated against the dollar, and Mexico's net exports to the United States decreased.

   E. remained stable relative to the dollar, with no change in Mexico's net exports to the United States.

9. PPP theory works less well in the short run than it does in the long run because

   A. the law of one price only pertains to the short run.

   B. not all goods and services are traded internationally, and all goods are heterogeneous commodities.

   C. all goods and services are traded internationally, and not all goods are heterogeneous commodities.

   D. not all goods and services are traded internationally, and not all goods are standardized commodities.

   E. all goods and services are traded internationally, and all goods are standardized commodities.

10. The fundamental value of the exchange rate for a currency is most likely to be achieved through

    A. the help of monetary policy.

    B. intervention by the International Monetary Fund.

    C. a fully flexible exchange rate.

    D. a fixed exchange rate.

    E. a crawling peg system.

11. The fundamental value of a country's exchange rate is

    A. constant over a prolonged period of time.

    B. determined by the supply of the country's currency in the foreign exchange market.

    C. determined by the demand for the country's currency in the foreign exchange market.

    D. determined by the supply of and demand for the country's currency in the domestic financial market.

    E. determined by the supply of and demand for the country's currency in the foreign exchange market.

12. Which of the following would NOT cause a change in the equilibrium exchange rate for the Canadian dollar?

    A. an increased preference for Canadian goods.

    B. an increase in the interest rate by the Bank of Canada.

   C. an increased preference by Canadians for foreign goods.

   D. an increase in American GDP, since the United States is a major trade partner of Canada.

   E. an increase in the quantity of Canadian dollars which would be demanded when less foreign currency is required to purchase $1 Canadian.

13. If the Bank of Canada were to respond to a slowdown in the domestic economy by lowering real interest rates, one would predict in the short run

   A. no change in the Canadian dollar's external value.

   B. a higher value of the Canadian dollar in foreign exchange markets.

   C. a lower value of the Canadian dollar on foreign exchange markets.

   D. higher borrowing costs.

   E. decreased private-sector investment spending.

17.3 Fixed Exchange Rates

▶ **LO 14.**   **Explain how a fixed exchange rate is set.**

Fixed exchange rates are a historically important alternative to flexible exchange rates. Fixed exchange rates also are still used in many countries, especially small and developing nations. The value of a fixed exchange rate is determined by government (in practice, usually the by the finance ministry or treasury department, in cooperation with the country's central bank). For many countries on fixed exchange rates today, the rate is often set in terms of a major currency (e.g., the US dollar or the yen), or relative to a "basket" of currencies, typically those of the country's trading partners. Historically, currency values were fixed in terms of gold or other precious metals.

▶ **LO 15.**   **Define devaluation, revaluation, and overvalued and undervalued exchange rates.**

Once an exchange rate has been fixed, government usually attempts to keep it unchanged for some time. Economic circumstances, however, can force government to change the value of the exchange rate. A reduction in the official value of a currency is called *devaluation*; and increase in the official value is called a *revaluation*. Fixed exchange rates are not always consistent with the fundamental value of a currency (as determined by supply and demand). When the officially fixed value of an exchange rate is greater than its fundamental value, the exchange rate is *overvalued*, and when it is less than its fundamental value, it is *undervalued*.

▶ **LO 16.**   **Discuss the alternative actions a government can take when its currency is overvalued.**

When the officially set value of an exchange rate is overvalued, government has several alternatives for dealing with the inconsistency. It could devalue its currency, restrict international transactions, or become a demander of its currency. The most common approach is for government to become a purchaser (demander) of its currency.

► **LO 17.   Define international reserves and balance-of-payments deficit/surplus.**

To be able to purchase its own currency and maintain an overvalued exchange rate, a government (usually the central bank) must hold foreign-currency assets called *international reserves*, or simply reserves. Because a government must use part of its reserves to maintain an overvalued currency, over time, its reserves will decline. The net decline in a country's stock of international reserves over a year is called its *balance-of-payments deficit*. Conversely, if a country experiences a net increase in its international reserves over a year, it has a *balance-of-payments surplus*.

► **LO 18.   Calculate the balance-of-payments deficit/surplus.**

Given the equations reflecting the demand for a currency and that currency's supply, the first step in judging whether there is a deficit or a surplus is to find the equilibrium exchange rate by setting the demand equation equal to the supply equation. If the existing exchange rate is above equilibrium, then the quantity supplied of that currency exceeds the quantity demanded. In that case, government will have to purchase the excess supply in order to maintain the value above equilibrium. This purchase of currency constitutes a "balance-of-payments deficit." The opposite occurs when the existing exchange rate is below equilibrium, in which case government will have to sell off currency, resulting in a "balance-of-payments surplus."

► **LO 19.   Explain how monetary policy can help eliminate an overvaluation.**

As an alternative to trying to maintain an overvalued currency, a government can take actions to try to increase the fundamental value of its currency and eliminate the overvaluation problem. The most effective way to increase the fundamental value of a currency is through monetary policy. A tightening of monetary policy that raises real interest rates will increase the demand for a currency and, in turn, will raise its fundamental value. Although monetary policy can be used in this manner, it has some drawbacks. In particular, if monetary policy is used to set the fundamental value of the exchange rate equal to the official value, it is no longer available for stabilizing the domestic economy.

► **LO 20.   Define speculative attack.**

The conflict between using monetary policy to set the fundamental value of a currency or using it to stabilize the domestic economy is most severe when the exchange rate is under a *speculative attack*, involving massive selling of domestic-currency assets by financial investors. Although a government can maintain an overvalued exchange rate for some time by purchasing its own currency, there is a limit to this strategy because no government's reserves are unlimited. Eventually, a government will run out of reserves, and the fixed exchange rate will collapse. A speculative attack can quickly end a government's attempt to maintain an overvalued currency. Such an attack is most likely to occur when financial investors fear that an overvalued currency will be devalued. A speculative attack, therefore, can be self-fulfilling.

Quick Quiz

14. Which of the following would NEVER have represented a way of fixing an exchange rate?
    A. allowing the market to set the fundamental value of the exchange rate.
    B. tying the currency value to the value of gold.
    C. setting the value of a currency relative to a basket of different currencies.
    D. pegging a unit of currency to the US dollar.
    E. allowing the finance ministry and central bank to determine the currency's value.

15. If China allows its currency to be devalued, that is analogous to a
    A. revaluation.
    B. depreciation.
    C. appreciation.
    D. crawling peg system.
    E. rise in the fundamental value of the Chinese currency.

16. If a country's currency is overvalued, one possibility is to cause an actual appreciation in the equilibrium value of its currency by
    A. controlling currency transactions by its citizens.
    B. devaluing its currency.
    C. causing the currencies of its trade partners to depreciate.
    D. selling its foreign currency assets.
    E. purchasing foreign currency assets.

17. When a country is continually selling its international reserves in exchange for its own currency, the country is experiencing a
    A. balance-of-payments deficit.
    B. balance-of-payments surplus.
    C. devaluation.
    D. flexible exchange rate.
    E. depreciation.

18. If the demand for and supply of Latinia pesos in the foreign exchange market are: Demand = $20,000 - 30,000e$ and Supply = $15,000 + 20,000e$, then the equilibrium exchange rate in dollars per peso is _____. At a fixed exchange rate of $0.08 per peso, the government must _____ (buy/sell) _____ pesos to maintain the fixed rate.
    A. 0.125; sell; 1,000.
    B. 0.100; sell; 1,000.
    C. 0.125; buy; 1,200.
    D. 0.100; buy; 1,200.
    E. 0.080; sell; 1,000.

19. The reason that an increased interest rate will help increase the value of the home currency is that higher interest rates
   A. prompt local businesses to invest more.
   B. encourage more consumer spending on durables.
   C. signal that the home economy is healthy.
   D. attract foreign financial investors to buy home financial assets.
   E. cause home residents to buy fewer imports.

20. A speculative attack occurs when
   A. a country raises its interest rate sharply.
   B. a country maintains too much control over international capital flows.
   C. the value of a currency is expected to fall and so financial investors sell the currency.
   D. the value of a currency is expected to rise and so financial investors sell the currency.
   E. a currency has recently been devalued.

17.4 Should Exchange Rates Be Fixed or Flexible?

▶ **LO 21.   Summarize the benefits and disadvantages of flexible versus fixed exchange rates.**

There are two important issues in comparing flexible and fixed exchange rates—the effects on monetary policy and the effects on trade and economic integration. A flexible exchange rate strengthens the impact of monetary policy on aggregate demand, when a fixed exchange rate prevents policy makers from using monetary policy to stabilize the domestic economy. Large economies should almost always employ flexible exchange rates because it seldom makes sense for them to give up the power to stabilize the domestic economy via monetary policy. For small economies, however, giving up this power may make sense when their history suggests an inability to use monetary policy to control domestic inflation. On the issue of trade and economic integration, supporters of fixed exchange rates have argued that an officially fixed exchange rate reduces or eliminates uncertainty about future exchange rates and, thus, provides incentives for firms to expand export business. The problem with this argument is that a fixed exchange rate is not guaranteed to remain fixed forever, especially if the currency comes under a speculative attack. Some countries, such as 11 western European nations, have tried to solve the problem of uncertain exchange rates by adopting a common currency.

Quick Quiz

21. Monetary policy makers might be reluctant to use interest rate changes to increase the value of the home currency when that would conflict with other policy goals, such as
   A. attracting foreign financial investment.
   B. stimulating the bond market.
   C. promoting higher imports.

    D. cooling down spending in an overheated economy.

    E. stimulating spending in a sluggish economy.

17.5 The Impact of Monetary Policy with a Flexible Exchange Rate: A Restatement

▶ **LO 22.** **Given an overview of the relationship between monetary policy, resulting exchange rate effects, and the ultimate impact on a country's GDP.**

Changes in the exchange rate have an important effect on the Canadian economy. In the context of monetary policy, changes in the exchange rate that result from monetary policy tend to intensify the impact of that monetary policy. For instance, if the Bank of Canada undertakes expansionary policy by reducing interest rates, two results ensue. First, the lower cost of borrowing prompts more spending on private sector investment and consumer durables. Second, on the international side, lower relative returns on home financial assets cause foreign financial investors to look elsewhere; they, therefore, demand less home currency, resulting in a depreciation of the currency. That depreciation spurs higher interest in home exports, and net exports rise. The opposite is true for contractionary monetary policy.

Quick Quiz

22. If the Bank of Canada raises interest rates, the expected results would be _____ in domestic investment spending and _____ in net exports.

    A. an increase; an increase.

    B. an increase; a decrease.

    C. a decrease; an increase.

    D. a decrease; a decrease.

    E. no change; a decrease.

Self-Test: Key Terms

Use the terms below to complete the following sentences. (Answers are given at the end of the chapter.)

appreciation	international reserves
balance-of-payments deficit	law of one price
balance-of-payments surplus	nominal exchange rate
depreciation	overvalued exchange rate
devaluation	purchasing power parity (PPP)
fixed exchange rate	real exchange rate
flexible exchange rate	revaluation
foreign-exchange market	speculative attack
fundamental value of the exchange rate	undervalued exchange rate

1. The exchange rate at which the quantity supplied equals the quantity demanded is the

   _____ .

2. When the officially set value becomes a(n)_____, government

   must either devalue its currency, restrict international transactions, or become a demander of

   its currency.

3. The nominal exchange rate times the price of the average domestic good divided by the price

   of the average foreign good equals the _____ .

4. A government's attempt to maintain an overvalued currency can quickly end when it

   encounters a(n) _____ of massive selling of domestic-

   currency assets by financial investors .

5. A reduction in the official value of a currency is called a _____ .

6. If transportation costs are relatively small, the price of an internationally traded commodity

   must be the same in all locations, according to the _____ .

7. An exchange rate that varies according to the supply and demand for the currency is a(n)

   _____ .

8. The rate at which two currencies can be traded for each other is called the

   _____ .

9. To be able to purchase its own currency and maintain an overvalued exchange rate, a

   government (usually the central bank) must hold _____ .

10. An exchange rate whose value is set by official government policy is a(n)

    _____ .

11. If a country experiences a net increase in its international reserves over a year, it has a(n)

    _____ .

12. When the officially fixed value of an exchange rate is less than its fundamental value, the

    country has a(n) _____ .

13. An increase in the value of a currency relative to other currencies is called

    _____ .

14. Flexible exchange rates are determined in the _____, where

    currencies from various nations are traded for one another.

15. An increase in the official value of an exchange rate is called _____ .

16. If the law of one price were to hold for all goods and services, then the value of the exchange

    rate between two currencies would be determined in accordance with the theory of

    _____ .

17. The net decline in a country's stock of international reserves over a year is equal to its

    _____ .

18. A decrease in the value of a currency relative to other currencies is called

_____ .

Self-Test: Multiple Choice Questions
(Answers and solutions are given at the end of the chapter.)

1. If the real exchange rate for a country is relatively lower at the end of the year compared with the beginning, we would expect that
   A. net exports will tend to increase.
   B. net exports will tend to decrease.
   C. net exports will not change.
   D. there will be no effect on trade.
   E. the relatively low real exchange rate reflects a weak economy.

2. Between 1973 and 1999, annual inflation in the developing nations that export mainly manufactured goods averaged 23 percent, while inflation averaged 59 percent in countries that mainly export raw materials. Other things being equal, PPP theory would predict that, in the long run, the currencies of the raw materials exporting countries should have
   A. been approximately stable relative to the currencies of countries exporting manufactured goods.
   B. appreciated relative to the currencies of countries exporting manufactured goods.
   C. depreciated relative to the currencies of countries exporting manufactured goods.
   D. had no predictable relationship to the currencies of countries exporting manufactured goods.
   E. been perfectly stable relative to the currencies of countries exporting manufactured goods because they maintained fixed exchange rates.

3. Suppose that interest rates in Canada for Canadian bonds were high. All other things being equal, supply-and-demand analysis of exchange rates would predict that the Canadian dollar would experience _____ relative to other currencies.
   A. depreciation.
   B. appreciation.
   C. devaluation.
   D. revaluation.
   E. purchasing price parity.

4. Suppose that the Bank of Canada raised interest rates in Canada to reduce domestic consumption and private-sector investment spending. In the short-run, one would predict a(n)
   A. depreciation of the dollar and an increase in net exports.
   B. depreciation of the dollar and a decrease in net exports.
   C. devaluation of the dollar and a decrease in net exports.
   D. appreciation of the dollar and an increase in net exports.
   E. appreciation of the dollar and a decrease in net exports.

5. The value of a fixed exchange rate in contemporary economies is
   A. determined by the supply and demand for a currency in the foreign exchange market.
   B. set by government, usually in terms of gold or some other precious metal.
   C. set by government, usually in terms of the currency (or basket of currencies) of the country's major trading partner(s).
   D. set by agreement of the investment banks of the major trading countries of the world.
   E. determined by economic forces.

6. During the 1990s, the government of Thailand fixed the exchange rate of the baht to the dollar. During the summer and fall of 1997, investors perceived that the baht was overvalued and a speculative attack ensued. What alternatives did the Thai government have to deal with this problem?
   A. It could have revalued the baht, limited international transactions, purchased the baht on the foreign exchange market, or tightened domestic monetary policy.
   B. It could have devalued the baht, limited international transactions, purchased the baht on the foreign exchange market, or tightened domestic monetary policy.
   C. It could have devalued the baht, limited international transactions, sold the baht on the foreign exchange market, or tightened domestic monetary policy.
   D. It could have revalued the baht, limited international transactions, sold the baht on the foreign exchange market, or eased domestic monetary policy.
   E. It could have revalued the baht, limited international transactions, sold the baht on the foreign exchange market, or tightened domestic monetary policy.

7. Suppose a monetary policy change by the Bank of Canada has increased real interest rates. The effect will be to
   A. increase borrowing costs and increase returns on Canadian assets.
   B. lower the cost of borrowing .
   C. increase private-sector spending.
   D. increase net exports.
   E. increase GDP.

8. When the real exchange rate of a country's currency is low, the home country will
   A. find it easier to import, while domestic producers will have difficulty exporting.
   B. find it easier to export, while domestic residents will buy more imports.
   C. find it harder to export, while domestic residents will buy fewer imports.
   D. find it easier to export, while domestic residents will buy fewer imports.
   E. find it harder to export, while domestic residents will buy more imports.

9. PPP theory would be most useful in predicting
   A. short-run changes in the exchange rate for a country that mainly produces heavily traded, standardized goods.
   B. long-run changes in the exchange rate for a country that mainly produces heavily traded, standardized goods.
   C. short-run changes in the exchange rate for a country that mainly produces lightly traded, standardized goods.

D. long-run changes in the exchange rate for a country that mainly produces lightly traded, nonstandardized goods.

E. short-run changes in the exchange rate for a country that mainly produces lightly traded, standardized goods.

10. In early 2002, suppose that nominal GDP in Canada was growing faster than in most other industrial countries but the rate of inflation was relatively higher. All other things being equal, supply-and-demand analysis of exchange rates would predict that in the short run, the Canadian dollar would _____ relative to the currencies of the other industrialized countries.

A. remain constant.

B. appreciate.

C. devaluate.

D. revaluate.

E. depreciate.

11. If a country fixes the exchange rate for its currency relative to other currencies and if the official exchange rate is overvalued relative to its fundamental value, then

A. the most likely ultimate outcome is no change in the par value of the currency.

B. the most likely ultimate outcome is a devaluation of its currency.

C. the most likely ultimate outcome is a revaluation of its currency.

D. it will likely be able to indefinitely support its value by using its international reserves to buy its currency on the foreign exchange market.

E. it can ease its monetary policy to increase the fundamental value of its currency and eliminate the overvalued status.

12. If exchange rates are flexible, a surplus in a nation's balance of payments would imply that

A. government will have to devalue the nation's currency.

B. government will not change the par value of the nation's currency.

C. the nation's exchange rate will remain unchanged.

D. the nation's exchange rate will appreciate.

E. the nation's exchange rate will depreciate.

13. Other things being equal, a recession in Canada, combined with a higher inflation rate in Japan relative to Canada's inflation rate, would be expected to cause

A. the dollar to appreciate against the yen.

B. the dollar to depreciate against the yen.

C. the yen to appreciate against the dollar.

D. no predictable change in the dollar–yen exchange rate.

E. Japan's demand curve for dollars to shift to the left.

14. In comparison with a fixed exchange rate system, a flexible exchange rate system
   A. weakens the impact of monetary policy on aggregate demand.
   B. strengthens the impact of monetary policy on aggregate demand.
   C. increases uncertainty about the future exchange rate more than a fixed exchange rate system.
   D. decreases uncertainty about the future exchange rate.
   E. is more likely to suffer from speculative attacks.

15. When the Canadian dollar currency depreciates, Canadian businesses which export are _____, Canadian tourists travelling abroad are _____, and Canadian firms which import goods are _____.
   A. winners; winners; losers.
   B. winners; losers; losers.
   C. winners; losers; winners.
   D. losers; losers; losers.
   E. losers; winners; losers.

Self-Test: Short-Answer Problems
(Answers and solutions are given at the end of the chapter.)

1. Nominal Exchange Rates

In this problem, you can practice calculating the nominal exchange rates of currencies in terms of the amount of foreign currency needed to purchase one Canadian dollar and the number of Canadian dollars needed to purchase one unit of the foreign currency.

Nominal Exchange Rates for the Canadian Dollar (May 26, 2005)

Country	Foreign Currency / Canadian Dollar	Canadian Dollars / Foreign Currency Unit
Britain (pound)		2.3084
Us (dollar)		1.2681
Europe (euro)		1.5873
Switzerland (franc)	0.9750	
Japan (yen)	85.16	
Mexico (peso)	8.6356	

Source: *Globe and Mail*, May 27, 2005.

   A. Based on the number of dollars needed to purchase one unit of the foreign currency, calculate the amount of foreign currency needed to purchase $1 Canadian for the British pound, US dollar, and the European euro in the second column of the above table.
   B. Based on the amount of foreign currency needed to purchase $1 Canadian, calculate the number of dollars needed to purchase one unit of the foreign currency for the Swiss franc, Japanese yen, and Mexican peso in third column of the above table.

C. Suppose the Thunderbird was advertised in Canada at $45,500 Canadian. Suppose the same make of automobile is advertised in a newspaper in a city in the United States at a price of $26,000 US. Based on the above US$/C$ exchange rate and the advertised prices for the automobile, the real exchange rate (for the automobile) equalled _____ (round your answer to the nearest hundredth).

D. The real exchange rate for the automobile implies that the price of the Canadian automobile is (more/ less) _____ expensive than the American automobile, putting the (Canadian/US) _____ product at a disadvantage.

2. **Supply-and-Demand Analysis of the Exchange Rate**

In this problem, supply-and-demand analysis is applied to the determination of the exchange rate between the euro and the Canadian dollar. You will determine the equilibrium exchange rate and analyze the effects of changes in various factors on the supply of or demand for Canadian dollars to determine the impact on the equilibrium exchange rate. Answer the questions below based on the following graph illustrating the supply and demand for Canadian dollars in the euro–Canadian dollar market.

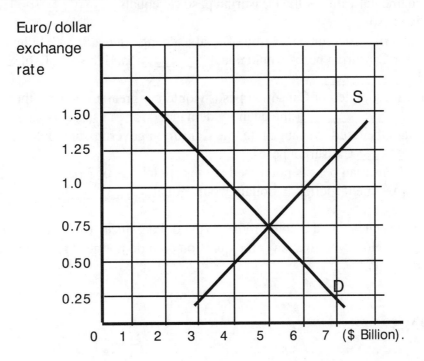

A. The equilibrium exchange rate of the Canadian dollar equals _____ euro(s) per dollar.

B. If European consumers' and businesses' preferences for Canadian goods increases, the (supply/demand) _____ for Canadian dollars in the foreign exchange market will (increase/decrease) _____, and the euro/dollar exchange will (increase/decrease) _____.

C. If the Canadian GDP increases, the (supply/demand) _____ for Canadian dollars in the foreign exchange market will (increase/decrease) _____, and the euro/dollar exchange will (increase/decrease) _____.

D. An increase in the real interest rate on European assets will (increase/decrease) _____ the (supply/demand) _____ of (for) Canadian dollars in the foreign exchange market, and the euro/dollar exchange will (increase/decrease) _____.

E. If the Bank of Canada changes monetary policy so that Canadian real interest rates increase, the (supply/demand) _____ for Canadian dollars in the foreign exchange market will (increase/decrease) _____, and the euro/dollar exchange will (increase/decrease) _____.

3. **Fundamental Value of a Currency and the Balance of Payments Deficit**
   The demand and supply for Cansurian pesos in the foreign exchange market are given by the following equations (*e* is the Cansurian exchange rate measured in dollars per Cansurian peso).
   Demand = 55,000 – 88,000*e*
   Supply = 25,000 + 32,000*e*

   A. The fundamental value of the Cansurian peso (*e*) equals _____ dollars per Cansurian peso.
   B. If the Cansurian government set the official exchange rate at 0.333 dollars per peso, the demand for Cansurian pesos would equal _____, and the supply of Cansurian pesos would be _____ .
   C. The quantity supplied of Cansurian pesos would be (greater than/less than/equal to) _____ the quantity demanded for Cansurian pesos.
   D. To maintain the fixed exchange rate, the Cansurian government would have to purchase _____ Cansurian pesos.
   E. Since the Cansurian peso is purchased at the official rate of 3 pesos to the dollar, the balance of payments deficit in dollars would equal $_____.

   (Note that in this question, the dollar refers to the dollar, since "peso" countries usually peg to the US dollar. However, to answer the question, you do not need to convert the US dollars to Canadian dollars.)

SOLUTIONS

Quick Quiz

1. A.
2. D. (=1/5.8).
3. D.
4. D.
5. B. (=[5.8 × 12] / 110).
6. B.
7. C.
8. C.

9. D.
10. C.
11. E.
12. E. This reflects a movement along the demand curve, not a shift of the demand curve.
13. C.
14. A.
15. B.
16. D.
17. A.
18. B.
19. D.
20. C.
21. E.
22. D.

Self-Test: Key Terms

1. fundamental value of the exchange rate.
2. overvalued exchange rate.
3. real exchange rate.
4. speculative attack.
5. devaluation.
6. law of one price.
7. flexible exchange rate.
8. nominal exchange rate.
9. international reserves.
10. fixed exchange rate.
11. balance-of-payments surplus.
12. undervalued exchange rate.
13. appreciation.
14. foreign-exchange market.
15. revaluation.
16. purchasing power parity (PPP).
17. balance-of-payments deficit.
18. depreciation.

Self-Test: Multiple Choice Questions

1. A.
2. C.
3. B.
4. E.
5. C.
6. B.

7. A.

8. D.

9. B.

10. E.

11. B.

12. D.

13. A.

14. B.

15. B.

Self-Test: Short-Answer Problems

1. A., B.

Country	Foreign Currency /Canadian Dollar	Canadian Dollar / Foreign Currency
Britain (pound)	0.4332(=1÷2.3084)	2.3084
US (dollar)	0.7886	1.2681
Europe (euro)	0.6300	1.5873
Switzerland (franc)	0.9750	1.0256
Japan (yen)	85.16	0.0117
Mexico (peso)	8.6356	0.1158

    C. 1.38 (= [0.7886 × 45,500] / 26,000).

    D. more; Canadian.

2.

    A. 0.75

    B. demand; increase; increase.

    C. supply; increase; decrease.

    D. increase; supply; decrease.

    E. demand; increase; increase.

3.

    A. 0.25 [55,000 − 88,000e = 25,000 + 32,000e] or [30,000 = 120,000e].

    B. Demand: 25,696 pesos (=55,000 − 88,000 × 0.333); Supply: 35,656 (=25,000 + 32,000 × 0.333).

    C. greater than.

    D. 9,960 (= 35,656 − 25,696).

    E. $3,320 (= 9,960 / 3).

Principles of Macroeconomics

Sample Mid-Term Examination
(Based on material in Chapters 4–10)

This examination consists of two parts and carries a total of 50 marks. Follow the instructions carefully.

Part A: Multiple-Choice Questions (20 Marks)

Answer all questions. Select the best responses to the following 20 multiple-choice questions. Each question carries one mark.

1. Which of the following would be included in the calculation of GDP for 2005?
   A. the price of a home built in 1991 and sold in 2005.
   B. the price of a new punch press built and purchased in 2005 to replace a worn-out machine.
   C. the price of a classic 1960 Thunderbird purchased in 2005.
   D. the price of 100 shares of Imperial Oil stock purchased in 2005.
   E. the price of a used bicycle purchased at a garage sale in 2005.

2. The growth of average labour productivity is important to the economy because
   A. without it, real GDP per person must decrease.
   B. without it, real GDP per person cannot increase.
   C. it is a key to improving living standards in the long run.
   D. the fraction of the total population that is employed is constant over time and, thus, real GDP per person is solely dependent on average labour productivity.
   E. it implies more resources are being employed to produce less output.

3. In the monthly Labour Force Survey conducted by Statistics Canada, a person who was not working during the previous week and was not actively seeking work during the last four weeks is classified as
   A. employed.
   B. unemployable.
   C. underemployed.
   D. part-time employed.
   E. not in the labour force.

4. Real GDP is nominal GDP adjusted for
   A. changes in the quality of goods and services.
   B. value added during a previous year.
   C. the percentage rate of change in the price level.
   D. imports.
   E. changes in the cost of intermediate goods and services.

5. International data on the relationship between the amount of capital per worker and average labour productivity indicate that there is
   A. a negative relationship between the two variables.
   B. a positive relationship between the two variables.
   C. no relationship between the two variables.
   D. a positive relationship between the two variables for some countries, but a negative relationship between the two variables for other countries.
   E. a positive relationship between the two variables for some countries, but no relationship between the two variables for other countries.

6. The Consumer Price Index is a measure of the change in prices of
   A. a standard basket of all goods and services measured in GDP.
   B. a standard basket of goods and services determined by the family expenditures surveys, relative to the cost in a base year.
   C. a standard basket of agricultural goods determined by the agricultural expenditure survey.
   D. a standard basket of selected items in wholesale markets.
   E. a standard basket of machinery, tools, and new plant.

7. Microland has a population of 70 people, and 50 of them worked last year, with a total output of $100,000. The average labour productivity of Microland equalled
   A. $100,000.
   B. $100.
   C. $4,000.
   D. $2,000.
   E. $20,000.

8. John can purchase a delivery truck for $20,000, and he estimates it will generate a net income (i.e., after taxes and maintenance and operating costs) of $1,000 per year. He should
   A. not purchase the truck if the real interest rate is less than 2 percent.
   B. not purchase the truck if the real interest rate is greater than 2 percent.
   C. purchase the truck if the real interest rate is less than 5 percent.
   D. purchase the truck if the real interest rate is greater than 5 percent.
   E. none of the above.

9. The unemployment rate is the
   A. number of unemployed people.
   B. number of people who would like to be employed but can find work.
   C. fraction of people who are not working.
   D. number of people who are not working.
   E. the number of unemployed workers divided by the labour force.

10. Government policies that affect the performance of the economy as a whole are called
    A. positive analysis.
    B. normative analysis.
    C. macroeconomic policy.
    D. microeconomic policy.
    E. aggregation.

11. A decrease in the corporate income tax on income generated from investment in new capital will
   A. shift the demand for investment curve to the right.
   B. shift the demand for investment curve to the left.
   C. shift the supply of saving curve to the right.
   D. shift the supply of saving curve to the left.
   E. decrease real interest rates.

12. When the Bank of Canada sells government bonds, the commercial banks'
   A. reserves will decrease and lending will contract, causing a decrease in the money supply.
   B. reserves will increase and lending will expand, causing an increase in the money supply.
   C. reserve requirements will increase and lending will contract, causing a decrease in the money supply.
   D. reserves–deposit ratio will increase and lending will expand, causing an increase in the money supply.
   E. reserves–deposit ratio will decrease and lending will contract, causing an increase in the money supply.

13. Double coincidence of wants is avoided if money is used as a
   A. measure of value.
   B. store of value.
   C. standard of deferred payment.
   D. medium of exchange.
   E. tool of monetary policy.

14. If the Consumer Price Index was 130 at the end of 2001 and at the end of 2002 it was 140, then during 2002, the economy experienced
   A. inflation.
   B. deflation.
   C. hyperinflation.
   D. indexing.
   E. deflating.

15. A financial system is an effective mechanism for channelling funds from savers to borrowers with productive investment opportunities because it
   A. reduces the risk faced by each saver.
   B. shift the risk of investing from borrowers to savers.
   C. diversifies the risk of investing by savers and financial investors.
   D. pools the costs of gathering information about prospective borrowers.
   E. facilitates the direct lending of funds by savers to borrowers.

16. Suppose the National Accounts recorded the nominal GDP for Canada in 2002 as $850 billion. In the same year, the real GDP (1997 base year) was $810 billion. The implicit price index [GDP deflator] is (rounding your answer)
   A. 105.
   B. 100.
   C. 40.
   D. 120.
   E. 95.

17. When an individual deposits currency into a chequing account
   A. bank reserves decrease, which reduces the amount banks can lend thereby reducing the money supply.
   B. bank reserves increase, which allows banks to lend more and, ultimately, increases the money supply.
   C. bank reserves are unchanged.
   D. bank reserves decrease, which increases the amount banks can lend thereby increasing the money supply.
   E. bank reserves increase, which reduces the amount banks can lend thereby reducing the money supply.

18. Suppose that investors feel uncertain about prospects for stocks and thus increase their demand for bonds. Selling prices on the bond market would
   A. go up and effective interest rates would increase.
   B. go up and effective interest rates on bonds would decrease.
   C. go down and interest rates would remain the same.
   D. go down and effective interest rates on bonds would increase.
   E. go down and effective interest rates on bonds would decrease.

19. The investment demand curve indicates that there is a(n)
   A. positive relationship between the real interest rates and the level of investment spending, all other things being equal.
   B. inverse relationship between the real interest rates and the level of investment spending, all other things being equal.
   C. direct relationship between the real interest rates and the level of investment spending, all other things being equal.
   D. inverse relationship between the determinants of investment and the level of investment spending, holding interest rates constant.
   E. positive relationship between the determinants of investment and the level of investment spending, holding interest rates constant.

20. Which of the following is NOT a determinant of average labour productivity?
   A. size of the workforce.
   B. amount of physical capital.
   C. amount of natural resources.
   D. introduction of new technology.
   E. compatibility of legal and political environment.

Part B: Short-Answer Questions (30 Marks)

Answer THREE of the following four questions. Each question carries an equal weight of 10 marks.

1. Suppose we have data on the inflation rate, measured by the GDP deflator index, and nominal interest rates, measured by the interest rate on long-term bonds, as shown in the following table:

Year	Inflation Rate	Interest Rate
1979	8.9	9.5
1983	3.5	10.2
1987	5.0	9.5
1991	3.3	8.0
1995	2.5	6.9

A. What was the real interest rate on long-term bonds in 1991? _____ percent.
B. In what year was the real interest rate on long-term bonds the highest? _____
C. In what year was the real interest rate on long-term bonds the lowest but still positive? _____

D. Assuming that the nominal interest rate remains unchanged, a lower inflation rate would (increase/decrease) _____ the real interest rate.
E. Assuming that the nominal interest rate remains unchanged, the holders of long-term bonds would (gain/lose) _____ from higher inflation.

2. From the following table, answer the questions below. (Assume there is no statistical discrepancy.)

Expenditure Components	Year 2000 ($ Billion)
Business fixed investment	170.1
Durable goods	150.2
Exports	450.7
Government current purchases	300.0
Imports	415.2
Inventory investment	5.7
Semi- and nondurable goods	134.6
Residential investment	60.3
Services	310.0
Government investment purchases	25.3

A. Total consumption spending in the Canadian economy during the year 2000 equalled $_____ billion.
B. Investment spending of the private sector in the Canadian economy during the year 2000 equalled $_____ billion.
C. Net export spending in the Canadian economy during the year 2000 equalled $_____ billion.
D. Total government purchases in the Canadian economy during the year 2000 equalled $_____ billion.
E. The expenditure method of calculating indicates that gross domestic product for the Canadian economy during the year 2000 equalled $_____ billion.

3. Answer the questions below based on the following the supply and demand curves for saving in Macroland, a hypothetical economy.

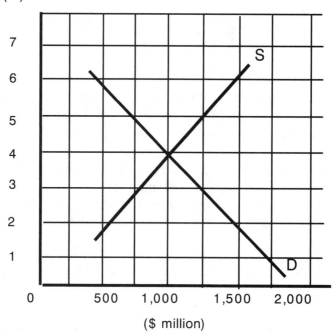

Real Interest Rate (%)

($ million)

A. The equilibrium real interest rate is _____ percent and the equilibrium quantity of saving/ investment is $_____ million.
B. A government budget surplus is the excess of _____ over government spending. The latter consists of government current purchases of goods and services, government _____ (e.g., government fixed capital formation), and government _____ (e.g., government interest payments on the public debt).
C. An increase in the government budget surplus would cause the (supply/demand) _____ curve for saving to (increase/decrease) _____ . On the above graph, draw a new curve that would reflect the change caused by the increased government budget surplus.
D. As a result of the increased government budget surplus, the equilibrium real interest rate _____, and the equilibrium quantity of saving/investment _____ .

4. Consider the following *initial* balance sheet of the banking system of Moneyland, a hypothetical economy, shown below:

Balance Sheet of the Banking System of Moneyland

Assets	*Liabilities*
Currency (= reserves) $10,000	Deposits $10,000

Assuming that the banking system is competitive and that loans are redeposited into the banking system, answer the following questions:

A. If the banking system of Moneyland has a desired reserve–deposit ratio of 5 percent, it can make new loans of $_____ in the form of new _____. After making the new loans, the banking system of Moneyland will have total deposit liabilities of $_____ , and currency (= reserves) of $_____. Its total assets will then equal $_____ .

B. Now, assume the Central Bank of Moneyland buys $5,000 of government securities from Mr. Rich and he deposits the $5,000 in his chequing account at the banking system of Moneyland. Following the deposit and making new loans, the banking system of Moneyland would have currency (= reserves) of $_____, total loans of $_____, and total deposit liabilities of $_____. By doing so, it would (increase/decrease) _____ the money supply by $_____ .

Principles of Macroeconomics

Solutions to
Sample Mid-Term Examination
(Based on material in Chapters 4–10)

<u>Part A:</u>   **Multiple-Choice Questions (20 marks)**

1. B.
2. C.
3. E.
4. C.
5. B.
6. B.
7. D.
8. C.
9. E.
10. C.
11. A.
12. A.
13. D.
14. A.
15. C.
16. A.
17. B.
18. B.
19. B.
20. A.

<u>Part B:</u>   **Short-Answer Questions (30 Marks)**

1.
   A. 4.7 percent, that is, the difference between the interest rate on long-term Government of Canada bonds (8%) and the inflation rate (3.3%).
   B. 1983; the real interest rate is $10.2 - 3.5 = 6.7\%$.
   C. 1979; the real interest rate is $9.5 - 8.9 = 0.6\%$.
   D. increase.
   E. lose.

2.

    A. $595.0 billion. [150.2 + 134.6 + 310.2].

    B. $175.8 billion. [170.1 + 5.7].

    C. $35.5 billion. [450.7 – 415.2] Surplus.

    D. $325.3 billion.

    E. $1131.6 billion. [595 + 175.8 + 35.5 + 325.3].

3.

    A. 4 percent; $1,000 million.

    B. tax revenue or collection; investment; transfers.

    C. supply; increase; draw new supply curve S_1 as shown below.

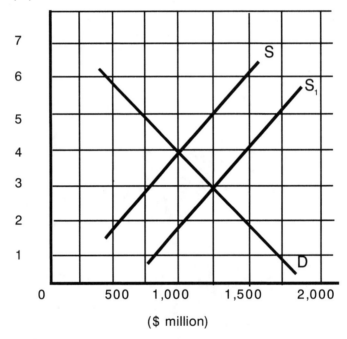

    D. Decreased; increased.

4. A. 190,000; deposits; 200,000; 10,000; 200,000.

    B. 15,000; 285,000; 300,000; increase; 100,000.

Principles of Macroeconomics

Sample Final Examination
(Based on material in Chapters 4–17)

This examination consists of two parts and carries a total of 100 marks. Follow the instructions carefully.

Part A: Multiple-Choice Questions (50 Marks)

Answer all questions. Select the best responses to the following 50 multiple-choice questions. Each question carries one mark.

1. The real interest rate can be written in mathematical terms as
   A. $r = i +$.
   B. $r = i -$.
   C. $r = 1 /$.
   D. $r = - I$.
   E. $r = + 1$.

2. When the Bank of Canada responds to higher inflation by raising real interest rates
   A. consumption and private-sector investment rise, and, thus, planned expenditure increases.
   B. consumption and private-sector investment rise, and, thus, planned expenditure increases.
   C. consumption and private-sector investment fall, and, thus, planned expenditure decreases.
   D. consumption and private-sector investment fall, and, thus, planned expenditure increases.
   E. the Bank of Canada changes its policy approach.

3. The portfolio allocation decision is related to the demand for money because
   A. money can be used to buy a portfolio.
   B. money is the main form of wealth for most people.
   C. money is one of the many forms in which wealth can be held and is a part of most asset portfolios.
   D. the portfolio allocation decision determines how much of an individual's money is going to be held in the form of currency and how much in the form of balances in a chequing account.
   E. portfolio allocation explains why the amount of money people hold is directly related to interest rates.

4. Unemployment typically
   A. is unaffected by recessions and expansions.
   B. rises during recession and falls during expansions.
   C. falls during recessions and rises during expansions, as does inflation.
   D. rises during recessions and falls during expansions, as does inflation.
   E. falls during recessions and rises during expansions.

5. When an expansionary gap exists, the rate of inflation will
   A. tend to fall.
   B. tend to rise.
   C. remain unchanged.
   D. become disinflation.
   E. shift the SRAS line downward.

6. The fact that in an economy operating at capacity, a higher living standard tomorrow must typically be obtained at the cost of current consumption and leisure is an example of the
   A. equilibrium principle.
   B. efficiency principle.
   C. principle of unequal costs.
   D. scarcity principle.
   E. principle of increasing opportunity cost.

7. A decrease in taxes will cause a
   A. movement downward along the AD curve.
   B. movement upward along the AD curve.
   C. left shift in the AD curve.
   D. right shift in the AD curve.
   E. decrease in AD.

8. The self-correcting mechanism of the ADI–IA model eliminates output gaps over time through inflation rate
   A. decreases if actual output exceeds potential output.
   B. increases if actual output is less than potential output.
   C. decreases if a recessionary gap exists.
   D. decreases if an expansionary gap widens.
   E. stability.

9. During short-term economic fluctuations, inflation tends to
   A. fall following an economic peak and rise soon after the trough.
   B. fall following an economic peak and fall soon after the trough.
   C. rise following an economic peak and rise soon after the trough.
   D. rise following an economic peak and fall soon after the trough.
   E. move in the same direction as unemployment.

10. The difference between the total (or official) unemployment rate and the natural rate of unemployment
   A. represents that portion of total unemployment that economists call frictional unemployment.
   B. is negative during a recession.
   C. is positive during an expansion.
   D. is positive during a recession.
   E. represents that portion of total unemployment that economists call structural unemployment.

11. If a recessionary gap exists at the short-run equilibrium output, the
   A. LRAS line will move upward until actual output equals potential output.
   B. LRAS line will move downward until actual output equals potential output.
   C. LRAS line and SRAS line will move upward until actual output equals potential output.
   D. SRAS line will move upward until actual output equals potential output.
   E. SRAS line will move downward until actual output equals potential output.

12. Okun's Law is a quantitative relationship between
   A. cyclical unemployment and output gap.
   B. unemployment and inflation.
   C. natural unemployment and potential output.
   D. inflation and output gap.
   E. actual output and potential output.

13. Unlike an adverse inflation shock, an adverse shock to potential output causes
   A. higher output and higher inflation.
   B. higher output and lower inflation.
   C. no output losses.
   D. only temporary output losses.
   E. permanent output losses.

14. Excessive aggregate demand can result in
   A. a recessionary gap and a rising unemployment rate.
   B. a recessionary gap and a rising inflation rate.
   C. too many goods chasing too little spending.
   D. an expansionary gap and an increasing inflation rate.
   E. an expansionary gap and an increasing unemployment rate.

15. To close a recessionary gap, the Bank of Canada should
   A. lower its overnight rate target, causing market interest rates to decrease and planned expenditure to increase.
   B. increase its overnight rate target, causing market interest rates to increase and planned expenditure to decrease.
   C. lower its overnight rate target, causing market interest rates to increase and planned expenditure to increase.
   D. raise its overnight rate target, causing market interest rates to decrease and planned expenditure to increase.
   E. lower its overnight rate target, causing market interest rates to decrease and planned expenditure to decrease.

16. The cost-benefit principle suggests that higher economic growth
   A. should not be pursued as long as the marginal costs are positive.
   B. should be pursued as long as the marginal benefits are positive.
   C. should be pursued only if the marginal benefits equal the marginal costs.
   D. should be pursued only if the marginal costs outweigh the marginal benefits.
   E. should be pursued only if the marginal benefits outweigh the marginal costs.

17. A contractionary monetary policy is designed to produce a(n)
  A. increase in planned expenditure and reduce an expansionary gap.
  B. increase in planned expenditure and reduce a recessionary gap.
  C. increase in planned expenditure and increase an expansionary gap.
  D. decrease in planned expenditure and reduce an expansionary gap.
  E. decrease in planned expenditure and reduce a recessionary gap.

18. If a firm's actual sales are greater than expected sales
  A. actual inventories will be greater than planned inventories, and actual investment will be greater than planned investment.
  B. actual inventories will be greater than planned inventories, and actual investment will be less than planned investment.
  C. actual inventories will be less than planned inventories, and actual investment will be greater than planned investment.
  D. actual inventories will be less than planned inventories, and actual investment will be less than planned investment.
  E. planned inventories will be less than actual inventories, and planned investment will be greater than actual investment.

19. In the long run, the output level of aggregate supply
  A. is independent of the overall price level.
  B. depends of changes in the overall price level.
  C. creates an expansionary gap.
  D. creates a recessionary gap.
  E. can only be achieved through government policy intervention.

20. If autonomous consumption equals $200 billion, the marginal propensity to consume (MPC) is 0.75, private-sector investment equals $150 billion, government purchases equal $60 billion, net taxes equal $160, and net exports equal minus $30 billion, the planned aggregate expenditure equation equals
  A. $540 billion + 0.75Y.
  B. $550 billion + 0.25Y.
  C. $505 billion + 0.75Y.
  D. $260 billion + 0.75Y.
  E. $600 billion + 0.25Y.

21. Under interest rate targeting, the Bank of Canada _____ government bonds when the overnight rate _____ its target.
  A. buys; is the same as.
  B. sells, is the same as.
  C. sells; is higher than.
  D. buys; is higher than.
  E. buys; is lower than.

22. Suppose the equation for planned aggregate expenditure is given by PAE = $250 billion + 0.5Y. (Assume net taxes and net exports are zero for this economy.) The slope of the PAE function is _____ and the income expenditure multiplier is _____.
   A. 0.2; 5.
   B. 0.5; 2.
   C. 2; 2.
   D. 250; 5.
   E. 0.2; 2.

23. At high rates of inflation, the Bank of Canada tends to
   A. lower the real interest rate, causing the level of aggregate demand to decline.
   B. lower the real interest rate, causing the level of aggregate demand to rise.
   C. raise the real interest rate, causing the level of aggregate demand to decline.
   D. raise the real interest rate, causing the level of aggregate demand to rise.
   E. raise the real interest rate, causing the level of aggregate demand to remain unchanged.

24. John Maynard Keynes believed that the most effective stabilization policy was
   A. the self-correcting process of the market to reduce or eliminate output gaps.
   B. monetary policy to reduce or eliminate expansionary gaps.
   C. changes in government spending to reduce or eliminate recessionary gaps but monetary policy to reduce or eliminate expansionary gaps.
   D. changes in taxes to reduce or eliminate output gaps.
   E. changes in government spending to reduce or eliminate recessionary gaps.

25. The faster the rate of technological change, the
   A. lower is the saving rate.
   B. lower is the rate of economic growth.
   C. lower is the rate of capital accumulation.
   D. higher is the rate of productivity growth.
   E. higher is the rate of unemployment.

26. The short-run equilibrium in the basic AD–AS model occurs where
   A. actual inventories are greater than the level planned by businesses.
   B. actual inventories are less than the level planned by businesses.
   C. aggregate demand equals the potential output.
   D. aggregate demand is greater than aggregate supply.
   E. aggregate demand equals short-run aggregate supply.

27. With respect to the interest rate effect, a drop in the general price level will ultimately cause spending in the economy to
   A. stagnate.
   B. increase.
   C. become more volatile.
   D. cause decreased foreign trade.
   E. decrease.

28. Which of the following contributed to the worldwide slowdown in productivity since 1973?
   A. the decline the quality of public education.
   B. the increase in the price of oil that followed the Arab–Israeli war of 1973.
   C. a dearth of technological innovations during the 1970s.
   D. the improvement in the measurement of productivity growth.
   E. an increase in technological innovations during the 1970s.

29. If a country has real assets of $14 billion, financial assets of $16 billion, and financial liabilities of $17 billion, then the national net worth is
   A. $17 billion.
   B. $16 billion.
   C. $14 billion.
   D. $13 billion.
   E. $30 billion.

30. If autonomous exports are equal to $50 billion, autonomous imports are equal to $10 billion, and the marginal propensity to import is 0.05, the net export function is given by
   A. $50 - 0.05Y$.
   B. $40 - 0.05Y$.
   C. $40 + 0.50Y$.
   D. $50 + 0.05Y$.
   E. $40 + 0.1Y$.

31. In a closed-economy loanable funds model, an increase in the government budget deficit will
   A. decrease real interest rates and increase the equilibrium quantity of saving supplied and demanded.
   B. decrease real interest rates and the equilibrium quantity of saving supplied and demanded.
   C. decrease real interest rates and the equilibrium quantity of saving supplied and demanded will remain unchanged.
   D. increase real interest rates and the equilibrium quantity of saving supplied and demanded.
   E. increase real interest rates and decrease the equilibrium quantity of saving supplied and demanded.

32. Fiscal policy is not always flexible enough to be useful for economic stabilization because
   A. automatic stabilizers counteract the stabilizing features of government spending and taxation.
   B. other objectives of policy makers may conflict with the need to stabilize aggregate demand.
   C. the legislative process requires policy makers to take action quickly leaving them inadequate time to determine the economic needs for stabilizing aggregate demand.
   D. it affects both aggregate demand and potential output.
   E. the only effects of fiscal policy that matter are its effects on potential output.

33. If a bank's desired reserve–deposit ratio is 0.20 and it has deposit liabilities of $200 million and reserves of $50 million, it
    A. has too few reserves and will reduce its lending.
    B. has too many reserves and will increase its lending.
    C. has the correct amount of reserves and outstanding loans.
    D. should increase the amount of its reserves.
    E. should decrease the amount of its reserves.

34. To maximize its gains from trade, a nation should
    A. maximize net exports (or its trade surplus).
    B. export as many products as possible by subsidizing domestic producers that could not otherwise compete with foreign producers.
    C. create jobs by subsidizing industries that employ the large numbers of workers.
    D. subsidize the purchase of imports in order to achieve the highest level of total consumption.
    E. export products in which it has a comparative advantage.

35. A good example of "automatic elimination" of an output gap would be when
    A. the federal government increases spending to fight a recession.
    B. the Bank of Canada sells bonds on the open market to contract spending.
    C. sluggish economic activity puts pressure on prices to fall.
    D. government gives tax breaks to businesses, to kick-start a slow economy.
    E. a central bank shifts government deposits to commercial banks to counter a recession.

36. If quotas are imposed on French clothing imported into Canada
    A. Canadian clothing producers benefit, but Canadian consumers of clothing are penalized.
    B. both French and Canadian producers of clothing are penalized.
    C. Canadian producers and consumers of clothing are penalized.
    D. both French and Canadian consumers are penalized when they buy clothing.
    E. French producers and consumers of clothing benefit.

37. If the Bank of Canada were to shift its policy reaction function downward, the
    A. IA line would shift upward causing an increase in the inflation rate.
    B. LRAS line would shift upward causing an increase in the inflation rate.
    C. IA line would shift downward causing a decrease in the inflation rate.
    D. ADI curve would shift to the right.
    E. ADI curve would shift to the left.

38. When Canadian financial investors pay cash for shares in a French corporation, from the perspective of
    A. Canada, it is a capital inflow.
    B. France, it is a capital outflow.
    C. Canada, it is a trade deficit.
    D. France, it is a trade deficit.
    E. Canada, it is a capital outflow.

39. As the number of ABM machines increases in a country
    A. the supply of money will decrease.
    B. the supply of money will increase.
    C. people will hold less of their wealth in the form of money (i.e., the demand for money will decrease).
    D. people will hold more of their wealth in the form of money. (i.e., the demand for money will increase).
    E. interest rates will increase.

40. A country will benefit the most from trade if it
    A. has a closed economy to protect its producers from low-cost, inferior goods produced in low-income countries.
    B. has an open economy and produces those goods in which it has the lowest opportunity cost and exchanges them for other goods.
    C. has an open economy and subsidizes its less competitive producers.
    D. exports to the rest of the world while maintaining protectionist policies on imports into its economy.
    E. has an open economy and produces those goods in which it has the highest opportunity cost and exchanges them for other goods.

41. When a bank makes a loan by crediting the borrower's chequing account balance with an amount equal to the loan
    A. the bank gains new reserves.
    B. the bank immediately loses reserves.
    C. money is created.
    D. money is destroyed.
    E. the Bank of Canada has made an open-market purchase.

42. An increase in net capital inflows to a country will
    A. increase its real interest rates.
    B. increase its imports.
    C. decrease its exports.
    D. decrease its real interest rates.
    E. decrease its investment in new capital.

43. A country's current account balance and its net capital inflows
    A. must equal domestic investment in new capital goods.
    B. determine the size of the pool of saving available for capital investment.
    C. must always equal the sum of the four components of planned aggregate expenditure.
    D. add up to zero.
    E. are identical in open and closed economies.

44. According to vertical money supply theory, if the Bank of Canada wants to lower the money market equilibrium interest rate, it should
    A. decrease the price of bonds.
    B. decrease the supply of money.
    C. shift the supply of money to the left.
    D. sell government bonds.
    E. purchase government bonds.

45. Suppose the demand for Maldivian pesos is given by Qd = 40,000 − 60,000e and the supply is can be represented by Qs = 20,000 + 20,000e. The equilibrium value of the Maldivian peso in the foreign exchange market is
A 0.75.
B. 0.40.
C. 0.25.
D. 4.00.
E. 1.25.

46. Comparing the self-correcting closure of a recessionary gap, with the use of government policy to do so, one advantage of the self-correcting version is that
A. there is no upward pressure on prices.
B. government policy makers cannot do much to counter a recession.
C. it actually moves the LRAS curve to the right.
D. it is basically contractionary in nature.
E. the central bank does it, rather than elected officials.

47. Suppose that the Bank of Canada raised real interest rates in Canada, which resulted in increased demand by foreigners for Canadian bonds. All other things being equal, supply-and-demand analysis of exchange rates would predict that the Canadian dollar would experience _____ relative to other currencies.
A. depreciation.
B. revaluation.
C. devaluation.
D. appreciation.
E. purchasing price parity.

48. The following variables are related to each other by a stock-flow relationship except
A. personal saving and personal wealth.
B. nonresident saving and net international liabilities.
C. government deficit and government debt.
D. personal saving and personal income.
E. gross saving and national wealth.

49. When the real exchange rate of a country's currency is low, the home country will
A. find it easier to import, while domestic producers will have difficulty exporting.
B. find it easier to export, while domestic residents will buy more imports.
C. find it harder to export, while domestic residents will buy fewer imports.
D. find it harder to export, while domestic residents will buy more imports.
E. find it easier to export, while domestic residents will buy fewer imports.

50. If a country fixes the exchange rate for its currency relative to other currencies under a fixed exchange rate regime, and if the official exchange rate is overvalued relative to its fundamental value, then
A. the most likely ultimate outcome is a depreciation of its currency.
B. the most likely ultimate outcome is a revaluation of its currency.
C. the most likely ultimate outcome is a devaluation of its currency.

D. it will likely be able to indefinitely support its value by using its international reserves to buy its currency on the foreign exchange market.

E. it can ease its monetary policy to increase the fundamental value of its currency and eliminate the overvalued status.

Part B: Short-Answer Problems (50 Marks)

Answer FIVE of the following six questions. Each question carries an equal weight of 10 marks.

1. Use the set of equations below to answer the following questions:

$$C = \$300 \text{ billion} + 0.80(Y - T).$$
$$T = \$150 \text{ billion.}$$
$$I^P = \$150 \text{ billion.}$$
$$G = \$200 \text{ billion.}$$
$$NX = \$40 \text{ billion.}$$

A. Find the equation representing the planned aggregate expenditure curve, that is, PAE = $ _____ billion + _____Y.

B. Solve for the short-run equilibrium output, Y = $ _____ billion.

C. If government purchases decrease by $100 billion, the new short-run equilibrium output will equal $ _____ billion.

D. If instead of decreasing government purchases by $100 billion in question C above, government decreased transfer payments by $100 billion, the new short-run equilibrium output would equal $ _____ billion.

E. In comparing the answers to questions C and D, it is apparent that a change in government purchases has a (greater/lesser/equal) _____ effect on the short-run equilibrium output than does an equal change in transfer payments.

2. You are given the following data for 1998, and the real GDP are measured in 1998 dollars.

Country	Real GDP per Capita (US$)		Ave. Annual Growth (%)	Real GDP per Employed Person (US$)		Ave. Annual Growth (%)	Share of the Population Employed (%)	
	1998	1988	1988–98	1998	1988	1988–98	1998	1988
Canada	25,496	22,429	1.29			1.43	47.5	48.1
Japan	24,170	19,347		47,232	42,171		51.0	45.8
Korea			6.13	33,844	20,033	5.38	43.1	40.1
U.S.A.	32,413	26,649	1.98	65,885	55,727	1.69		

A. Complete the table.

B. In 1998, _____ had the lowest standard of living as measured by
_____.

C. In 1998, _____ had the highest average labour productivity as measured by
_____.

D. The share of the population employed in Canada remained relatively stable over the years 1988–98, but the real GDP per employed person had grown by 1.43 percent a year. What are the possible factors attributable to this growth?

_____

_____

_____

E. Assuming that the growth rates remain constant, would the standard of living of Canada catch up with that of the United States in 2010? Explain.

_____

_____

_____

F. Assuming the growth rates remain constant, would the standard of living of Korea catch up with that of Canada in 2010? Explain.

_____

_____

_____

3. The planned aggregate expenditure for the economy of Newfunland is given by the following equations:

$C = \$750$ billion $+ 0.75(Y - T) - 300r$.
$I^p = \$400$ billion $- 600r$.
$G = \$550$ billion.
$T = \$400$ billion.
$NX = -\$55$ billion.

A. Find the equation for the planned aggregate expenditure (PAE) curve if the central bank sets the real interest rate (r) at 0.05 (5%), i.e., PAE = _____.

B. Solve for the short-run equilibrium output: $Y = \$$_____ billion.

C. If potential output (Y^*) equals $5,050, there would be a(n) _____ gap of
$_____ billion.

D. If the central bank wanted to close the output gap, it should implement a(n) (expansionary/ contractionary) _____ monetary policy.

E. To close the gap, the central bank would need to (decrease/increase) _____ the interest rate *r* to _____ percent.

4. Assume the current inflation rate in a particular hypothetical economy is 4 percent and the potential output in the economy is $3,650 billion.

A. Draw the inflation adjustment (IA) curve and the long-run aggregate supply (LRAS) curve on the graph below.

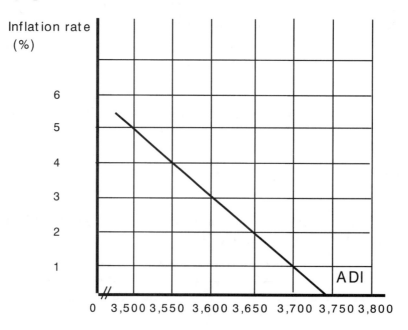

Aggregate Demand ($ billion)

B. The short-run equilibrium output is $_____billion.

C. Given the short-run equilibrium output and the potential output, the graph indicates that a(n) _____ gap exists. The value of the gap is $ _____ billion.

D. The output gap will cause the inflation rate to (increase/decrease/ remain unchanged) _____.

E. As the inflation rate adjusts to the output gap, the (IA/LRAS) _____ line will shift (upward/downward) _____ until the actual output equals the potential output.

F. When the actual output equals potential output, the economy will settle into its _____ equilibrium at $_____billion.

5. You are given the following table of exchange rates:

Nominal Exchange Rates for the Canadian Dollar (June 8, 2005)

Country	Foreign Currency / Canadian Dollar	Canadian Dollars / Foreign Currency
Britain (pound)		2.2849
Us (dollar)		1.2440
Europe (euro)		1.5324
Switzerland (franc)	1.0088	
Japan (yen)	85.92	
Denmark (krone)	5.63	

Source: *Globe and Mail*, June 9, 2005

    A. Define the nominal exchange rate, assuming the Canadian dollar is the domestic currency.

    B. Complete columns 2 and 3 in the above table.

    C. Suppose that a Ford Thunderbird with certain features was advertised in Canada at $48,000 Canadian. Suppose also that a Ford Thunderbird with identical features was advertised in a US newspaper at a price of $26,900 US. Based on the above US dollar/ Canadian dollar exchange rate and the advertised prices for the automobile, the real exchange rate (for the automobile) equalled _____ (round your answer to the nearest hundredth).

    D. The real exchange rate for the automobile implies that the price of the Canadian automobile is (more/less) _____ expensive than the American automobile, putting the (Canadian/American) _____ product at a disadvantage.

6. Assume that the demand for cellular phones by the consumers of Sunland is given by Q = 310 – 0.4 P, and the supply by domestic Sunland producers is given by Q = 150 + 0.4 P, where P and Q are, respectively, the price and quantity of cellular phones.

    A. If the world price of cellular phones is $50, the consumption of cellular phones in Sunland would equal _____, domestic production of cellular phones would equal _____, and Sunland would import _____ cellular phones.

    B. Assume that the Sunland government imposes a tariff of $20 per cellular phone. The tariff would (increase/decrease) _____ the consumption of cellular phones by _____ units, (increase/decrease) _____ domestic production by _____ units, and (increase/decrease) _____ imports by _____.

    C. The Sunland government would receive $_____ from the tariff.

Principles of Macroeconomics

Solutions to
Sample Final Examination
(Based on material in Chapters 4–17)

Part A: **Multiple-Choice Questions (50 marks)**

1. B.
2. C.
3. C.
4. B.
5. B.
6. D.
7. D.
8. C.
9. A.
10. D.
11. E.
12. A.
13. E.
14. D.
15. A.
16. E.
17. D.
18. D.
19. A.
20. D.
21. D.
22. B.
23. C.
24. E.
25. D.
26. E.
27. B.
28. C.
29. D.
30. B.
31. E.
32. B.
33. B.
34. E.
35. C.
36. A.

37. D.
38. E.
39. C.
40. B.
41. C.
42. B.
43. D.
44. E.
45. C.
46. A.
47. D.
48. D.
49. E.
50. C.

Part B: Short-Answer Problems (50 Marks)

1. A. PAE = $570 billion + 0.80Y. Using the given information, substitute into the equation the numerical values for each component of aggregate demand. Y= $300 billion + 0.80 (Y – $150 billion) + $ 150 billion + $200 billion + $ 40 billion. Or after simplifying, that equation yields the equation PAE = $570 billion + 0.80Y.

    B. Y = $2,850 billion. The definition of short-run equilibrium output implies that Y = AD. Replacing PAE with the PAE equation yields Y = $570 billion + 0.80Y. Now, solve for Y in Y – 0.80 Y = $570 billion, or Y = $2,850 billion.

    C. $2,350 billion. If government purchases decrease by $100 billion the new short-run equilibrium output will equal $2,350 billion. Equilibrium Y decreases by 5 × $100 billion = $500 billion decrease.

    D. $2,450 billion. If government decreased transfer payments by $100 billion, the new short-run equilibrium output would equal $2,450 billion. The change in Y is = 5 × [0.8 × ($100 billion)] = 5 × $80 billion = $400 billion.

    E. greater.

2. A. See table below.

Country	Real GDP per Capita (US$)		Ave. Annual Growth (%)	Real GDP per Employed Person (US$)		Ave. Annual Growth (%)	Share of the Population Employed (%)	
	1998	1988	1988–98	1998	1988	1988–98	1998	1988
Canada	25,496	22,429	1.29	53,702	46,605	1.43	47.5	48.1
Japan	24,170	19,347	2.25	47,232	42,171	1.14	51.0	45.8
Korea	14,574	8,040	6.13	33,844	20,033	5.38	43.1	40.1
U.S.A.	32,413	26,649	1.98	65,885	55,727	1.69	49.2	47.8

A. Korea; real GDP per capita.

B. United States; real GDP per employed person.

C. The growth in real GDP per employed person of 1.43 percent a year reflects growth in average labour productivity. As the share of population employed can approximately be treated as constant over the years, the productivity growth can be attributed to technological progress and capital accumulation.

D. No, because Canada's growth rate of 1.29 percent a year is lower than the 1.98 percent of the United States. Based on compounding, Canada's real GDP per capita is approximately $29,735 US in 2010, i.e., $25,496 US × (1+ 0.0129)12 ,whereas that of the United States is about $41,809 US, that is, $32,413 US × (1+ 0.0198)12.

E. Yes, because Korea's growth rate of 6.13 percent a year is higher than the 1.29 percent of Canada. Based on compounding, Korea's real GDP per capita is approximately $29,755 US in 2010, i.e., $14,574 US × $(1+ 0.0613)^{12}$, slightly higher than or about the same as Canada's $29,735 US.

3. A. Substituting r = 0.05 into the components and adding up to get PAE = $750 billion + 0.75(Y − $400 billion) − $300 billion (0.05) + $400 billion − $600 billion (0.05) + $550 billion + −$55 billion. Or PAE =1,300 billion + 0.75Y.

B. The short run equilibrium output is $5,200 billion (i.e., Y = $1,300 billion + 0.75 Y, or 0.25Y = $1,300 billion, thus Y = $1,300 billion/0.25).

C. expansionary or inflationary gap; $150 billion (output gap = Y − Y* = $ (5,200 − 5,050) billion).

D. contractionary.

E. Increase; 9.167 percent. ($5,050 billion = $1,345 billion + 0.75($5,050 billion) – 900r, or
$5,050 billion = $1,345 billion + $3,787.5 billion – 900$r$. Combining the constant values
gives us –$82.5 billion = – 900$r$, or r = 0.09167).

4. A.

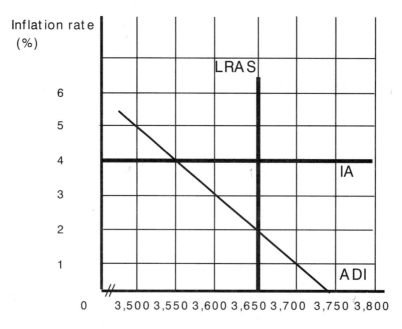

Aggregate Demand ($ billion)

A. 3,550.

B. recessionary; 100.

C. decrease.

D. IA; downward.

E. long-run; 3,650.

5. A. The nominal exchange rate is defined as either the number of Canadian dollars needed to
purchase one unit of the foreign currency or the amount of foreign currency needed to
purchase one Canadian dollar.

B.

Nominal Exchange Rates for the Canadian Dollar (June 8, 2005)

Country	Foreign Currency / Canadian Dollar	Canadian Dollars / Foreign Currency
Britain (pound)	0.4377	2.2849
US (dollar)	0.8039	1.2440
Europe (euro)	0.6526	1.5324
Switzerland (franc)	1.0088	0.9913
Japan (yen)	85.92	0.0116
Denmark (krone)	4.8947	0.2043

C. The real exchange rate (for the automobile) equalled 1.1156 (round your answer to the nearest hundredth). [48000 × 0.6252 / 26,900 = 1.1156].

D. more; Canadian.

6. A. consumption = 290 (i.e., by substituting P = 50 into the demand function); domestic production = 170 (i.e., by substituting P = 50 into the supply function), and Sunland would import 120 cellular phones, i.e., (290-170).

B. decrease consumption by 8; increase domestic production by 8; and decrease imports by 16. After the imposition of the tariff, consumption = 282 (i.e., by substituting P = 70 into the demand function); domestic production = 178 (i.e., by substituting P = 70 into the supply function), and Sunland would import 104 cellular phones, that is, (282 – 178).

C. The Sunland government would receive $2,080 from the tariff. [104 units × $20].